POLITICS AND CULTURE IN MODERN AMERICA
Series Editors: Glenda Gilmore, Michael Kazin, Thomas J. Sugrue

Volumes in the series narrate and analyze political and social change in the broadest dimensions from 1865 to the present, including ideas about the ways people have sought and wielded power in the public sphere and the language and institutions of politics at all levels— national, regional, and local. The series is motivated by a desire to reverse the fragmentation of modern U.S. history and to encourage synthetic perspectives on social movements and the state, on gender, race, and labor, on consumption, and on intellectual history and popular culture.

Before Harlem

The Black Experience in New York City Before World War I

MARCY S. SACKS

PENN

University of Pennsylvania Press

Philadelphia

10 9 8 7 6 5 4 3 2 1

Published by
University of Pennsylvania Press
Philadelphia, Pennsylvania 19104-4112

A Cataloging-in-Publication record is available from the Library of Congress

ISBN-13: 978-0-8122-3961-4
ISBN-10: 0-8122-3961-X

A Rodolfo, para siempre
y
para Alejandro y Daniela, la esperanza del futuro

Contents

Introduction

In 1902, James Weldon Johnson left his Jacksonville, Florida, home and his steady job as a school principal to settle in New York City. Neither his decision to leave the South nor his choice of destinations came unexpectedly. He had already made a number of trips to New York, the first in 1884 when he was still a boy. From his earliest encounter with Manhattan, Johnson loved the city and its "cosmopolitanism." "It would not have taken a psychologist to understand that I was born to be a New Yorker," he admitted in his autobiography. He felt a strong emotional connection to New York and often heard his parents "talk . . . about the city much in the manner that exiles or emigrants talk about the homeland."[1]

On his first visit, Johnson saw New York through the eyes of a child. He loved the ferryboats, was awed by the crowds and noise, and admired the "biggity" boys. He thrilled at the chance to cross the East River from his aunt and uncle's Brooklyn home and spend the day wandering through Lord and Taylor's. One of his sojourns to Manhattan struck him with particular meaning as he recalled his experience nearly a half century later. He reminisced about a time when his uncle took him on an excursion "far up toward Harlem, a region then inhabited largely by squatters and goats." Johnson perhaps exaggerated Harlem's emptiness; in the 1880s it housed a genteel community of upper-class white elites— Manhattan's first residential suburb. Still, the contrast with the Harlem of the 1930s, when Johnson published his autobiography, could hardly have been more dramatic. In the intervening period between Johnson's first visit and the time he wrote his memoirs, Harlem had become a neighborhood transformed, housing 50,000 black residents in 1914 and nearly 165,000 by 1930.[2]

Johnson noted that he had few black playmates during his childhood stay, not especially surprising in 1884, when the black population of Manhattan was just over twenty thousand and scattered throughout the city. Only about ten thousand black people lived in Brooklyn, where Johnson spent most of his time.[3] Despite the shortage of friends, Johnson remembered that T. Thomas Fortune, another Florida native who had recently settled in New York, often spent time at Johnson's aunt's house.[4] As more and more black people migrated to New York City from the South and the Caribbean, many surrounded themselves with acquaintances from home states and islands in order to create a sense of identity in the anonymous and crowded world of the big city.

Along with his brother, Rosamond, Johnson first returned to New York as an adult in 1899 on a summer hiatus from his teaching job in Jacksonville. The city had literally grown up since his childhood days. Scrambling to find space for its burgeoning business district, architects who felt constrained by Manhattan's geographic limitations began looking upward. During the 1880s the city constructed its first elevator buildings, soon to become the workplaces of nearly one-third of the city's black men. New architectural initiatives and revised building codes allowed for still taller buildings and created a new cultural milieu of high-rises and skyscrapers. Visitors to the city at the end of the nineteenth century marveled at the "slender stone shafts incredibly rising out of the sea to pierce the sky." Five massive skyscrapers adorned the southern tip of Manhattan Island by 1898, the tallest boasting twenty-six stories. A half-century later, commemorating the fiftieth anniversary of the consolidation of the City of Greater New York, a commentator declared those five skyscrapers the symbol of "the strength and pride and driving ambition of New York."[5] Throughout the "golden nineties," this captivating image attracted migrants and immigrants from around the country and the world.[6]

During their summer in the city, the Johnson brothers immersed themselves in New York's black bohemia, then flourishing in the old Tenderloin district in lower Manhattan. Though the trip was relatively short, it was a defining moment for James. "These glimpses of life that I caught during our last two or three weeks in New York," he explained, "showed me a new world—an alluring world, a tempting world, a world of greatly lessened restraints, a world of fascinating perils; but, above all, a world of tremendous artistic potentialities." He vowed to return as soon as possible.[7]

James and Rosamond made sojourns during the following two summers before finally settling in New York City permanently in 1902. While in 1899 they felt the exhilaration of newcomers imbibing a world of possibilities, in 1900 they endured one of the city's worst race riots in its history. This experience offered the Johnson brothers a stark lesson in northern race relations, exposing the depth of racial antipathy present in the North. Adding insult to injury, they made so little money in the summer of 1900 that they had to borrow from friends in order to make the return trip to Jacksonville. Despite that humiliation, when he finally made the commitment to give up his teaching job for good and move to New York, James marveled at the change he encountered. "I at once became aware of an expanse of freedom I had not felt before."[8] But by 1902, James confronted a black community that looked markedly different from his earlier recollections. The black population of New York had grown dramatically since his first trip in 1884. More than sixty thousand black people now lived in New York, more than half of whom—like him—had been born outside of the city.[9]

The growing black population of New York sparked an increase in the number of social institutions dedicated to alleviating some of the problems faced by black New Yorkers. White and black reformers alike began focusing on the needs of this expanding group, and by 1915 more than a dozen organizations had been formed for this purpose. These included travelers' aid societies, fraternal and benevolent organizations, day nurseries, orphanages, and industrial improvement associations. In addition, a number of institutions that had long served New York's white citizens began opening their doors to black people. The Charity Organization Society, for example, began providing aid to needy blacks as early as the late 1890s. More and more white organizations followed suit as the plight of destitute black families gained public attention.[10]

Institutional barriers to racial equality began falling in the latter half of the nineteenth century as well. In keeping with the spirit of the post–Civil War era, many northern communities achieved some successes in diminishing institutionalized racism. In 1884, the New York City School Board formally declared that no distinction would be made between white and black schoolchildren in determining which school pupils would attend. In this same period a black man sat on a Manhattan jury for the first time in the borough's history. A state law passed in 1895 prohibited discrimination in public facilities. And in the same year, the school board for the first time appointed a black teacher to a predominantly white school. Numerous prominent blacks commented on the apparent improvement in race relations near the end of the nineteenth century. The city's black weekly newspaper, the *New York Freeman*, noted in an 1887 editorial that "[n]ow in many of the best restaurants, hotels and churches decent colored people receive courteous treatment."[11]

The newspaper's reference to "decent" colored people hinted at some of the tensions that still remained in New York and foreshadowed problems yet to come. The growing population of black southerners in New York City after the 1880s precipitated a decline in the relatively tolerant racial climate of the postwar era. Even as the state enacted laws to guarantee blacks' civil rights, whites demonstrated decreased forbearance toward their black neighbors. New stereotypes of black "coons" emerged in New York City, suggesting that in the urban environment unrestrained black people would become lawless, dangerous, and violent. Churches, restaurants, bars, landlords, and social organizations expressed their increased antipathy toward black people by refusing access to nonwhites.[12]

Joining white critics, many black New Yorkers also opposed the vanguard of black migration, exposing divisions within this increasingly diverse population. As they witnessed the deterioration in racial tolerance, some black elites blamed the newcomers for bringing the South's problems with them. Feeling unwelcome, migrants clung to their regional customs and habits, further emphasizing differences among black people. As the trickle of migrants grew into a flood in the early decades of the twentieth century, however, northern black elites, often themselves transplanted southerners, began to support and encourage the migration. By the eve of the Great Migration, which began with the onset of World War I, black New Yorkers had come to welcome their southern brethren into their midst.[13]

The development of chain migrations had a tremendous impact on the nature of the black community in New York City. No longer complete strangers in an unfamiliar environment, later migrants might arrive in the city with a name and perhaps an address of someone who could possibly help the newcomer find a place to live and maybe even provide a lead on a job opening. In addition, as family connections stabilized with extended kin networks being transplanted to New York City, cultural forms could be replicated as well. Residents of particular villages, regions, or states congregated in New York's tenements, established restaurants that could cater to specific culinary preferences, and prayed together in the profusion of black churches. Forming geographic enclaves in the congestion of New York City, the constant infusion of additional members allowed southerners to begin establishing a degree of cultural continuity in the North. At the same time, while the presence of family members or friends gave new arrivals a certain degree of security, the geographic distinctions being created within New York's black population precluded the formation of a cohesive community able to collectively resist the poverty and racism affecting all black people in the city. The chain migrations thus offered only a mixed blessing, allowing for the preservation of specific identities, but at the same time making racial unity a greater challenge to achieve.

The disparate experiences of the different groups of newcomers helped foster ethnic, class, and geographic distinctions within the burgeoning black population of New York City. The preservation of strong family and island connections among Afro-Caribbeans allowed them to maintain a separate identity from that of other black Americans. Hoping to avoid the mistreatment faced by native-born black people, many specifically chose to distance themselves from their U.S. brethren by refusing to become citizens. Southerners also tended to sustain their particular customs when opportunities allowed them to do so. And northern-born blacks, confronting an aggravation of race relations and a decline in job prospects, often placed the blame at the feet of the newcomers. As their proportion of the population shrank with each passing decade, this group struggled to privilege its heritage as native New Yorkers by staking a claim—without great success—to elite status.

Despite optimistic expectations, few black New Yorkers fared well in the city. At the turn of the twentieth century, most black people labored in unskilled jobs, and many lived in poverty. As a group they paid the highest rents in the city but had the smallest number of organizations to serve their needs. With the exception of the New York Colored Mission, between the Civil War and 1890 no organizations in New York City concerned themselves with the welfare of black citizens. This most impoverished and needy population received the least support from reformers and municipal agencies. Disease ran rampant within congested black neighborhoods, contributing to this population's startlingly high mortality rates—37.5 per thousand in 1890, for example, in contrast to 28.5 for the white population. The statistics for tuberculosis (ironically referred to as the Great White Plague) were especially striking. A study conducted in 1908 found that while 380 whites per 100,000 died in New York from the disease, more than double that number (845) of blacks fell victim to this highly contagious illness. In fact, between 1895 and 1915, the death rate for black New York exceeded the birth rate. The dramatic growth of New York's black population in this period resulted entirely from the arrival of newcomers.[14]

The black community slowly marched uptown during the late nineteenth and early twentieth century. Before the Civil War, the majority of the black people living in the city resided in the lower tip of the island in the infamous Five Points neighborhood, known then as the most depraved of the city's neighborhoods. Junius Browne described a street scene. "A stalwart, cruel-looking negro sits on the dirty door-step, and calls to a white child to get him a dram," he wrote, while a "young mulatto woman . . . leans against the broken door-way with a dirty pipe in her mouth, and leers at you as you go by." From this notorious district, the black population escaped into Greenwich Village.[15]

By midcentury the northward movement pushed into a district bounded by Thompson, MacDougal, Bleeker, Sullivan, and Minetta streets. Italian immigration drove blacks still farther uptown into the Tenderloin district, extending from Twenty-fourth Street to Forty-second Street. The black population in the 1870s and 1880s was centered in the west Twenties and Thirties, though a vanguard headed directly into the Forties and Fifties blocks, just above the northern edge of the Tenderloin. At century's end, the San Juan Hill district, stretching between Sixtieth and Sixty-forth streets and Tenth and Eleventh avenues, claimed the bulk of the city's black population. The district grew with tremendous speed, spurred by the growing migration of black people into the city. The rapid influx of black migrants into this neighborhood made it among the most congested of any in New York City; one block alone housed upward of five thousand residents.[16]

It also became among the most contested areas of the city. Irish immigrants living adjacent to San Juan Hill often clashed with their black neighbors. And within the black population, different classes and ethnicities endured an awkward coexistence within the overcrowded tenements and blocks. Mary White Ovington, a white reformer who dedicated much of her life to improving conditions in New York City and nationwide for black people, spent eight months in 1908 living in this notorious neighborhood. She described conditions as "little better than Hell's Kitchen, the picturesque Irish gangster neighborhood a few blocks south." Ovington vividly described the conflicting mass of humanity that lived there: "There were people who itched for a fight, and people who hated roughness. Lewd women leaned out of windows, and neat, hard-working mothers early each morning made their way to their mistresses' homes. Men lounged on street corners in as dandified dress as their women at the wash tubs could get for them; while hard-working porters and longshoremen, night watchmen and government clerks, went regularly to their jobs."[17]

As this neighborhood expanded, the number of institutions housed there increased as well. Like the hotels and clubs, black churches followed their constituents to midtown. St. Mark's Methodist Episcopal, Mount Olivet Baptist, and St. Benedict the Moor all opened new buildings on West Fifty-third Street during the 1880s and 1890s. The rapid increase in the southern-born black population in this district contributed to the proliferation of storefront churches as well, often catering to the specific needs and customs of city newcomers. The YMCA also opened on West Fifty-third Street at the end of the nineteenth century, providing a "home" to "every young man in the South . . . where he can come and find friends." The decades immediately preceding the twentieth century witnessed the formation of numerous fraternal and benevolent societies, including the Grand United Order of Odd Fellows, the Colored Freemasons, and the Negro Elks, most located in San Juan Hill.[18]

The institutions that the black community developed in the decades leading up to the Great Migration further facilitated the movement of thousands of black southerners into the North. Churches, travelers' aid societies, fraternal societies, and charity organizations all eased the transition for newcomers. Most had their roots in the late nineteenth and early twentieth centuries. Likewise the racial attitudes that participants in the Great Migration encountered upon arrival in Harlem in the 1920s also originated in the initial period of sustained migration to New York City. The movement of members of the South's first freeborn black population into the North contributed to the rise of "coon" stereotypes. The hostility directed at black people led to the creation of New York City's first urban ghetto as whites scrambled to confine this population into a single, restricted neighborhood. Later migrants, part of the movement most frequently studied by historians of the twentieth-century black North, arrived already branded as violent and dangerous. Most headed directly for Harlem, settling into patterns that had been laid by their forebears.[19]

During the thirty-five years between 1880 and 1915 that marked the first sustained migration of black people into New York City, blacks and whites together and in opposition forged the contours of race relations destined to affect the city for decades to come. In 1903, Mary White Ovington, upon hearing a speech given in New York by Booker T. Washington, learned to her "amazement" that "there was a Negro problem in my city."[20] But within contested neighborhoods, whites who had been witnessing the growth of this population for years harbored keen resentment toward their black neighbors. As the black population of New York soared, black people made their presence increasingly felt. Whites responded with an intensification of racial intolerance. Within this complex and often daunting world, black people forged their lives, working, praying, loving, and playing as they made New York City their own.

This study jumps into the fray of the decades-long and often acrimonious debate about life for African Americans in the inner city. Beginning in the mid-1960s, historians have examined the evolution of the inner city in the late nineteenth and twentieth centuries. New York City, Detroit, Cleveland, Chicago, Milwaukee, and Philadelphia are among the cities that have faced historical scrutiny. These studies, coming primarily on the heels of the civil rights movement and urban rioting, focused principally on the creation of explosive, desolate inner-city ghettos.[21] While valuable to an understanding of the evolution of urban demographics, these studies have done less to expose the internal workings of urban black populations.

Furthermore, scholars have long limited their discussions of black urban life to structural conditions in the city, most notably residential and economic ones. This narrow framework discounts the broader challenges facing blacks as they made the initial transition toward urbanization. During the first steady growth of the northern urban black population, whites crafted enduring cultural, social, and economic responses to the mounting presence of black people in their midst. These developments impinged upon every aspect of black life in cities and have had stubbornly lasting consequences.

From Daniel Patrick Moynihan's now-discredited thesis of family instability to the more contemporary defenses of the black family's resiliency, this dichotomy has persistently offered stark and unsatisfying alternatives. Historians have not adequately acknowledged the complexity of the middle ground: tremendous economic and cultural pressures imposed on black men and women by their experiences in New York City impeded the sometimes-Herculean efforts to preserve family ties. Although the black family overwhelmingly remained intact, black people nevertheless confronted obstacles that no other group, immigrant or native, experienced in New York City.

While the story of racial retrenchment has been told numerous times and in many ways from the southern perspective, the northern experience has been largely ignored. Yet this was the moment in which the contours of the northern black experience were being crafted. Because of southern attitudes influencing northern whites, because of fatigue over persistent sectional tensions, and because of the influx of blacks into New York City, Yankees *at that moment* developed new attitudes about black people. Earlier stereotypes and caricatures had been less fixed within white society. The immigrant and working classes facing direct economic and residential competition with black residents expressed much of the overt racial tension in antebellum northern cities. In the latter decades of the nineteenth century, however, elite whites joined the lower classes in fostering negative stereotypes. More importantly, the images themselves changed from benign and buffoonish to sinister and dangerous. And for New York's white population, this view was specifically directed toward *urban* blacks. The urban environment, they argued, caused the degeneration of former slaves and threatened the white city.

This moment was critical for the internal development of the black population as well. Despite—and because of—overwhelming homogenizing pressure from whites who saw them as a monolithic group, black New Yorkers laid the foundations of long-standing geographic and ethnic divisions within the community. They created the infrastructure and support networks that would continue to sustain the population for generations to come, and they forged cultural patterns that helped them adapt to a hostile environment. As policy makers continue to grapple with the legacy of economic blight in inner cities and as academics debate the primacy of structural versus racial barriers to black success, we would all do well to understand the moment at which these conditions converged with explosive, surprising, uplifting, and devastating consequences.

Chapter 1

The Most Fatally Fascinating Thing in America

When James Weldon Johnson relocated to New York City in 1902, he joined a growing wave of southern black men and women moving to northern cities. The fall of Reconstruction and the rise of Jim Crow legislation in the South helped precipitate a sharp increase in the number of southern black people seeking friendlier environs in the North. While the net migration of blacks from the South amounted to fewer than 70,000 in the 1870s, during the 1880s it increased to 88,000, more than doubled in the 1890s, and jumped to 194,000 in the first decade of the twentieth century. In the same thirty-year period, 100,000 fewer whites chose to leave their southern homes than black people. By the early twentieth century, every southern state had experienced a decline in the percentage of its black population. Correspondingly, by 1906, New York, Chicago, and Philadelphia all housed more transplanted than native-born blacks within their city limits.[1]

The coming of age of the freedmen's children helped to spur the initial flow of black people out of the South. As the sons and daughters of former slaves approached adulthood, they demonstrated far less willingness than their parents to accept the imposition of an increasingly repressive social and economic order. While former slaves might counsel forbearance to their children, the freeborn generation exhibited a greater inclination to challenge and defy stringent racial codes.[2] "[W]e are now . . . the equal of whites," asserted a group of frustrated young black men, and "should be treated as such." When their demands failed to elicit changes, some directly confronted their tormenters. In 1881, for example, a band of black youths in Atlanta attempted to free two men who had been arrested by the police. Two years later a similar incident prompted one white newspaper to observe acerbically, "The moment that a negro steals, or robs, or commits some other crime, his person seems to become sacred in the eyes of his race, and he is harbored, protected and deified."[3]

The impatience and defiance exhibited by some young black people elicited the attention and ire of concerned southern whites desperate to reinstate tight controls over the black population. In contrast to "faithful old darkies," southern whites complained, the "new Negro" lacked "habits of diligence, order, [and] faithfulness." Growing up "without steady instruction in lessons of propriety and morality," cautioned white social critic Philip Bruce, black adolescents lived by their "impulses and passions." They shirked responsibilities and avoided steady employment. Bruce blamed inept black parents for excessive lenience and for their failure to train children in restraint and obedience. According to Bruce, the weaknesses of black parents produced their children's incorrigibility. By the time black youths reached adolescence, he claimed, they chafed "even under the lax parental authority; every kind of discipline galls [them] beyond endurance."[4] Bruce's simultaneous condemnation of incompetent black adults and unmanageable black children exposed the strategy being developed to forcibly resubjugate the South's black population: by claiming that black people lacked self-control, southern whites could justify harsh and repressive treatment.

Despite southern whites' claims about defiant and rebellious black youths, however, in reality self-preservation prevented most black people from disregarding the South's strict racial codes. Accordingly, some of those most frustrated by worsening conditions in the last decades of the nineteenth century chose to leave rather than subject themselves to segregation or endanger themselves by fighting back. Young and single members of the freeborn generation, those with the greatest ease of movement and the most intractable resentment about the broken promises of Reconstruction, comprised the overwhelming majority of early black migrants to New York City and other northern destinations. Typically, they made their move between the ages of fifteen and twenty-eight. "Young people is more restless than old people," explained a nineteen-year-old South Carolinian in New York. Another young woman who left for New York at the age of fifteen, concurred. "[T]he old people are used to their fare, and they never leave, but the children won't stand for the situation down there." Of 240 migrant men surveyed in New York in 1907, 72 percent had arrived before they were twenty-six years old.[5] Benjamin Mays explained that while "[m]ost Negroes grinned, cringed, and kowtowed in the presence of white people," the younger folk "who could not take such subservience left for the city as soon as they could—with or without their father's permission."[6] Unable to safely fight back against their oppression, growing numbers simply quit the South in search of freedom and brighter opportunities.

These early migrants spoke repeatedly of the destructive impact of being ensnared within Jim Crow's elaborate web of virtually incontrovertible controls, a system created, according to whites, to protect themselves from blacks' "innate" savagery. Freed from the "civilizing influence" of slave masters, whites cautioned, black people would revert to their natural condition and become a menace to white society. Rendered politically powerless and the victims of vicious racial stereotypes, black people endured brutal conditions. Black women faced the particular danger of sexual abuse and rape, acts frequently committed by male employers of live-in domestic servants. "The sad, but undeniable fact," lamented the editor of *Alexander's Magazine*, a black monthly published in the beginning of the twentieth century, is "that in far too many southern homes the Colored waitress or cook is not morally safe."[7] And less frightening but equally degrading assaults on black womanhood occurred with impunity in the South. Not granted the courtesies generally reserved for white women, black women commonly endured insults, harassment, and mistreatment from white men. Unprotected by the southern justice system or the codes of honor required of gentlemen, black women sought to escape the exploitation of their bodies and their labor. They headed northward to a place they believed would offer greater occupational opportunities and the protection of their persons.

White men's predatory attacks on black women affected black men as well, undermining their sense of masculine prerogative and responsibility. Unable to protect their wives, sisters, mothers, or daughters, black men at times admitted to feeling helpless. "[A]fter thinking of my three little girls who might grow to virtuous womanhood, but whose virtue had no protection in public sentiment," a father from South Carolina explained, "I decided to take my chances in a freer, though harder climate." Richard Wright described the sense of emasculation he felt after witnessing a white night watchman slap a black coworker on her buttocks. "I could not move or speak," he recalled. "My immobility must have seemed a challenge to him, for he pulled his gun. 'Don't you like it, nigger?'" the watchman demanded. "Oh, yes, sir!" Wright managed to stammer, as he walked away with the watchman's gun trained on his back. Catching up to the woman, he confessed that he wanted to retaliate for the white man's audacity. "It don't matter," his companion replied in resignation. "They do it all the time." Black women and men felt imprisoned by the abuse perpetrated by white men; it became an effective strategy for maintaining a submissive, docile black population. Repeated violations of black women undermined the women's sense of self-worth. And the terrorization of black men who might try to stop the assaults stripped them of an important symbol of their manhood—the ability to protect their loved ones.[8]

Southern whites promulgated the stereotype of black female promiscuity that rationalized the sexual exploitation of black women. Likewise, they cultivated an image of black males lusting after white women, justifying hundreds of lynchings during the Jim Crow era. Though the alleged rapes were more imagined than real, black men often paid with their lives for the mere suspicion of impropriety.[9] And as the lynchings became increasingly sadistic with the passing decades, the victims regularly paid with their manhood as well; the summary execution of black men frequently included their castration. Through this act whites symbolically and graphically demonstrated the emasculation of southern black men.[10]

Devastated by the constant assaults on their manhood that they experienced in the South, black men employed a range of escapist strategies. "How could I walk the earth with dignity and pride," asked one man. "How could I aspire to achieve, to accomplish, to 'be somebody' where there were for Negroes no established goals?"[11] Referred to as "boys" in the South, treated at best as children and often as far worse, some black men began looking northward in order to achieve respectability in America. "It all gets back to a question of manhood," explained a black preacher when questioned about the causes of migration. "[T]hey're treated more like men up here." A southern transplant in New York City confirmed this assessment. "[W]hen I ceased to be a boy," he explained, "[my father] advised me to live in the North where my manhood would be respected. He himself cannot continually endure the position in which he is placed, and in the summer he comes North to be a man."[12]

Some black leaders in this period used the emerging proclivity for migration as a tool for fighting against the antiblack violence permeating the South. Highlighting the threat that black migration posed to the agricultural economy, critics of the vigilante justice pointed to the South's lynch law as an impetus for flight. "Mob violence," declared an article in a black magazine, led many to quit the South. W. E. B. DuBois suggested that the 1898 Wilmington, North Carolina, race riot alone sent thousands of emigrants to northern cities. Presaging future events, DuBois cautioned that "as the black masses of the South awaken or as they are disturbed by violence this migration will continue and perhaps increase." The Wilmington *Messenger* corroborated DuBois's claim, declaring that nearly fourteen hundred black residents had left the city since the massacre. The Atlanta riot of 1906 likewise drove away black members of the community, some twenty-five families fleeing one small neighborhood alone.[13] Black newspapers and public figures stressed the correlation between vigilantism and migration, hoping that whites' dependence on black labor would induce a retreat from the violence. Though southern whites did exhibit concern about the stability of their workforce, they nevertheless continued to perpetrate violence against black people, spurring further movement out of the South.

Individual testimony confirmed that the fear of falling victim to lynching propelled black people away from their native homes. The New Orleans agent for the *Colored American Magazine* left the South with her husband after a white mob killed her elderly grandparents. She described the mob "running up and down the street howling and crying, 'Kill a nigger and don't leave one. Kill any one you meet so long as he is a nigger, for they are all just alike.'" Adam Clayton Powell explained that he left West Virginia in 1884 "[t]o keep from being lynched or murdered." In 1892, Ida B. Wells sought refuge in New York City after being run out of Memphis by local whites for publishing an incendiary article in her newspaper. She was warned "on pain of death" not to return. Eight years later, James Weldon Johnson barely escaped Jacksonville, Florida, with his life.[14]

Though the violence that pervaded the South during the Jim Crow era clearly played a critical role in the flight from that region, restricted transportation options significantly impacted migration patterns. Black southerners confronting the harshest conditions at home often faced the greatest difficulty escaping. The Deep South, where segregation was the most oppressive, contributed very small numbers to the early migration. Georgia, Alabama, Mississippi, and Louisiana all experienced only very limited outward movement of blacks between 1870 and 1910. Instead, most black people arriving in the North during those decades originated in the upper South and the border states of Virginia, North Carolina, Tennessee, and Kentucky, where the availability of cheap transportation opened opportunities for migration.[15] Travelers from Virginia, for example, took advantage of inexpensive steamer fares. The Old Dominion Steamship Company ran biweekly service between Richmond and New York City carrying "two to three hundred negroes" on each trip. The ticket from Norfolk or Richmond cost between $5.50 and $6.00, a sum within the reach of even poor southerners.[16]

Black youths with only limited attachment to the soil and who felt little optimism about the restricted economic opportunities available to them at home took advantage of the cheap transportation that could send them away from the rural countryside. Many watched their parents struggle to succeed as freemen and women, only to find that land ownership brought new hardships. They had to be "exceedingly careful" lest they be accused of being "uppity" or of trying to "act like a white man." Ned Cobb, whose father had twice been swindled out of his property, explained the economic situation for black people in the South: "[I]t weren't no use in climbin too fast . . . weren't no use in climbin slow, neither, if they was goin to take everything you worked for when you got too high."[17] And sharecropping offered a bleak future. One migrant in New York City captured the paradox of the southern agricultural system:

"I could look around and see how things was going. During summer while you was working your back off in the cotton field, prices would be tree high. Then when you finally pick your cotton and carry it to the store, prices would be down so low that after you sold it, you wouldn't get enough to run you through the winter. . . . Think people want to live in a place like that?"[18] The near impossibility of realizing economic ambitions contributed to black youths' itinerant tendencies. One "victim of the wanderlust" explained that even strong family ties "could not and did not quiet my restless spirit."[19] Young people, sensitive to their parents' inability to accumulate material wealth, had no desire to be trapped in the same cycle of indebtedness and dependency.

Alternatively, New York City offered captivating attractions that built illusions and enticed hopeful (if unsuspecting) black southerners away from home. Like whites from the nation's rural regions making the gradual but relentless push to metropolitan centers, black youths sought the excitement found only in a big city. "I don't know what it was that held me in New York after I got here," admitted one man. "I didn't have a job for some little time but it was just the lure of the city." New York City's dynamic night life created a powerful draw for people accustomed to the quiet rhythms of rural life. "Down there the only recreation we had was prayer meeting and little parties," complained a migrant. But in New York City, he marveled, dances were held "every Saturday night." One woman insisted, "That's why people move more than anything else."[20]

The stories and material possessions that migrants brought back to those in the countryside induced others to follow suit. "I can remember a girl who lived near us," wrote John Dancy, a former southerner. "[S]he went to New York and got a job working as a domestic." Each year she would return to her home in Wilmington, Delaware, "with fine new clothes—and she would live for the day when she could go to church on a Sunday morning and show off her finery." He recalled "hearing the women talk in awed tones about the beautiful clothes Tam Green wore." The young woman reveled in the admiration of her former companions. "She went to New York every year," Dancy explained, "then she would come back to Wilmington with new finery and flabbergast her old neighbors again. It went on year after year."[21] The contrast with the drudgery and poverty of the South could not have been more stark. A South Carolinian living in New York similarly visited his former home with regularity. He regaled the throngs who came to hear his stories. "[M]y mother's house [couldn't] hold all the people," he recalled. "I have set up all night talking to people down there about the things I've seen up here." By the end of each trip, he invariably had friends and relatives begging to go back North with him.[22] The fine

clothes and exciting stories offered a powerful incentive to young people already beginning to feel the tug of wanderlust. With enticements
like that, it was no wonder that black people viewed the North almost as
a utopia.

Youthful bravado impeded the spread of many truthful accounts
about the North. Migrants remained relatively silent about economic
struggles and loneliness, highlighting instead the headiness of city life.
Consequently, New York became nearly mythic in the southern black
imagination. "Every person, I don't care who he is nor where he is,
wants to see New York some day," claimed a South Carolinian. "They
have all kind of ideas about what it is like and still don't have the right
idea." The hyperbolic tales spreading throughout the South of the
northern "promised land" were regularly exaggerated and at times outright lies. "Don't blame us for leaving," begged one migrant. "We hear
'bout people in the North. Some have automobile. Some have victrola."
No one told the southerners that few black people, overwhelmingly relegated to the worst and least-paying jobs, could afford such luxuries.[23]

Labor agents cultivated and exploited misperceptions in order to
entice cheap southern black labor out of the South, typically to fill positions as either servants or strikebreakers. The general manager of the
Pullman Company testified before a Senate committee that he preferred
to hire southern black men to serve as porters. "The younger colored
man that is found around in the slums," he complained, "[is] not always
altogether of the right caliber." The company believed southern black
men to be better imbued with the subservient qualities required of Pullman porters. To find suitable workers, therefore, the company sent representatives into the South who found "men of a desirable class." Labor
agents also placed advertisements in southern newspapers, like one in
the *Colored American Magazine* calling for "good reliable colored help,
both Male and Female." The notice assured southern readers that
"[t]here is a constant demand *here at the North* for good help from the
South."[24]

Deceptive practices utilized by "slick agents" from employment
bureaus led to the arrival of many penniless, friendless black youths in
New York. Some agents used brass bands to attract attention and convince receptive southern black audiences that "the streets will be paved
with gold, and all will be music and flowers." Upon securing a prospective migrant, the agent then furnished a labor contract that typically
bound the worker to one or two months' work without pay in return for
the expenses incurred by the recruiter. Illiterate migrants often unwit-
tingly relinquished their personal belongings in the exchange as well.
The agency then put the migrants "aboard the boat with but one
address," complained a northern critic. "Many of them are told that

their steamship tickets include meals, and find this is not true, and being without money, endure the entire journey without food."[25]

As the enticements and pressures convinced growing numbers of black people to head north, white southerners became alarmed by the prospect that the "wholesale exodus" would cause labor shortages that would precipitate an economic disaster. Mobile southern blacks weakened the elaborate system of controls created by the system of sharecropping and debt peonage imposed in the post–Civil War south as a mechanism for maintaining a cheap and stable labor force. If black people could leave the plantations in search of better conditions, then competition for workers would drive wages higher and loosen the vise of white supremacy. Not surprisingly, therefore, white southerners quickly sought ways to hinder black mobility, highlighting itinerant black youths as evidence of the race's degeneracy. Envisioning "cotton lands [that] will lie fallow" and "fertile fields" that "cease to yield their valuable staples," southern states implemented emigrant agent laws that impeded labor recruiters' ability to draw workers away from the region's farms. Georgia initiated the trend in 1876 with legislation requiring that individuals engaged in such activities obtain special licenses and pay state taxes. North and South Carolina implemented even more restrictive laws in 1891, as the migration from the South became steadier and more damaging to southern planters. Both states imposed a prohibitive annual tax of $1,000 on agents for each county in which they wished to work.[26]

But the news that reached the South of substantially higher wages to be made in New York City overrode the threats and obstacles inflicted by whites. Poor blacks learned "that a man can earn ten dollars a week instead of the five he earns at him home." Indeed, black men received on average from three to five dollars more per week in New York than their southern counterparts while women made one to three dollars more than in the South. William Jenkins wrote enthusiastically to Booker T. Washington during a trip north: "Hotel waiters earn from twenty five to thirty dollars per month with board and lodgings," he exclaimed. "Our head waiter receives $100.00 per month."[27] Enticed by such possibilities, southern black youths expected to arrive in New York City and find a wealth of lucrative opportunities.

The prospect of high wages precipitated not only permanent migrations but temporary sojourns as well. Many southern black people who never intended to leave home for good nevertheless made brief forays to New York. "Peculiar," noted Mamie Garvin after spending a summer working in a Massachusetts resort town, "the servant in the North earning more than the teacher in the South." She returned to Charleston with her wedding trousseau purchased from her summer earnings. During vacation periods, the higher wages drew southern black college students who needed to earn the next year's tuition. They went back to school each fall with new clothes and stories about their experiences. During peak summer travel, the Pullman Company hired extra workers for its additional train runs. "We have got quite a number of men from these southern schools," testified the Pullman general manager before the Commission on Industrial Relations, "who are very glad to get something to do during the summer months, and they have proved very efficient." Benjamin Mays remembered working as a porter. "Luckily for me, the Pullman Company was coming South each spring to recruit students for summer jobs." Excited by the chance to see and experience new things, Mays "jumped at the opportunity" to make his first trip north. He began the school year "all dressed up" with two suits after one summer of work.[28]

With each person who relocated away from Jim Crow, especially those who regularly returned home, the lines of communication from the North to the South increased and improved. After a southerner moved north, a young migrant in New York City explained, he "writes back about his job, his pay, the city. Another comes up, and another, and another." Martin Washington, who left the South in 1901, explained his decision to migrate. While economic conditions were hard in his hometown, one of his brothers who lived in New York City urged Washington to try his luck there. "[I]ndications were that he was doing well, for he would send five dollars, and sometimes ten dollars to our mother. This, of course, gave me an incentive to visit and find out if the Empire City had anything in store for me."[29]

Washington's experience illuminates the creation of chain migrations from the South. Though the very first migrants often struck out alone, going to a new place with no one to assist them, as the decades progressed and the exodus grew in size more and more black southerners looking northward for a variety of reasons could rely upon relatives for information, encouragement, and assistance. "In 1899," explained Viola Ware, "my cousin in New York wanted me to pay her a visit." Believing a brief sojourn to the city to "make some money" would help her family back home in South Carolina, she accepted the offer. Ware never returned to the South. "Truth, though," she confessed, "I didn't think I was leavin' for good when I left." Samuel J. Battle moved from North Carolina in the same year, when his sister in Connecticut sent for him. "I left with my mother," he told an interviewer some years later. "My mother was coming to visit her people, some relatives, brothers and sisters in Brooklyn." She remained and he went on to Hartford. He later returned to New York City to live and became Manhattan's first black police officer.[30] By the eve of the Great Migration, over 32 percent of

those canvassed in a survey conducted in New York said they had come
to the city with a parent or to join a family member already living there.[31]

Although alluring news of the North began reaching the South in the
late nineteenth century, New York City nevertheless remained foreign—
and even frightening—to the majority of rural southerners. Without an
established social or kin network in the North to guide and support
them, some hesitated before quitting the South altogether. Consequently, the "migratory disposition" exhibited by many young black
men and women first pushed many from the rural countryside to southern cities. Between 1880 and 1910, the black population in sixteen principal southern cities grew from 341,907 to 706,352, more than doubling
in just thirty years. In places like Charleston, Atlanta, Richmond, and
New Orleans, black people savored their first taste of city life. In the
words of one observer, this move often acted as a "first step, first stop,
stepping-stone, and gate-way" to the eventual migration to New York.
According to one study, prior to 1910 over half of the black southerners
heading north came indirectly, having first relocated to a southern city.
It was only during the Great Migration, after family and institutional networks had already been established by these early pioneers, that the proportion of southerners leaving rural areas and migrating directly to
northern industrial centers rose significantly.[32]

The early migrants were consequently more likely to have some experience with city life than those who came during and after World War I.
To some degree, then, the first wave of migrants arrived in New York
better prepared than later generations to confront the conditions of
urban life in New York. Arriving at a time when there was little infrastructure in place to assist them in making the transition to the North,
these early arrivals needed to rely on their previous experiences in
southern cities to help them adjust to the congestion, working conditions, and excitement of the city. On the one hand, by establishing organizations, boardinghouses, churches, and other services catering to
black people, and by acting as the advance guard for family migrations,
they made it easier for subsequent generations of southern blacks to
come directly from rural areas and survive in New York City. On the
other hand, this vanguard had minimal forewarning about the challenges that they would encounter: the high cost of living, housing
restrictions, economic hardships, and—most surprising of all—pervasive
racism. For many who believed that New York City would be their
"promised land," its reality often proved to be a cruel hoax.

Black newcomers from the Caribbean arrived in far smaller numbers
than their southern counterparts prior to 1915, yet their presence
helped to lend a distinctive character to the social and cultural atmo-

sphere of New York City. A total of 51,174 Caribbean immigrants entered the United States between 1900 and 1915. Of this number, the largest group chose to settle in New York City. During the era of Jim Crow and lynch laws in the South, Caribbean immigrants expressed a preference for disembarking in the North rather than closer southern ports with more appealing climates. Stories of southern violence had reached them on the islands.[33]

As a result, while at the turn of the century a mere five thousand foreign-born blacks lived in New York City, by 1910 that number had more than doubled to nearly twelve thousand. The Caribbean newcomers composed just over 10 percent of the total black population of the city, which approached ninety-two thousand in that year. They represented the largest group of Caribbean-born blacks anywhere in the United States. Like southern migrants, this group proved to be the vanguard of a larger migration still to come; in 1930, despite the imposition of immigration restrictions, forty-thousand foreign-born black people lived in Manhattan, most of them in Harlem.[34]

Economic conditions on the Caribbean islands drove the migration in the late nineteenth and early twentieth centuries to the Americas and elsewhere. During the late 1880s, sugar prices throughout the world dropped significantly, not to see a resurgence until World War I. At the same time, changes in British economic policies removed the protections on colonial sugar and permitted the free importation of beet-root sugar into its markets. The lifeblood of Barbados, British Guyana, St. Kitts, Nevis, and Antigua, as well as an important factor in the economies of St. Lucia, Trinidad, and Jamaica, this crop drove the Caribbean economy. On the British islands, the source of the largest cohort of black Caribbean immigrants to New York City, production plummeted to levels reminiscent of those at midcentury and to percentages of world market share not seen at any time during the previous one hundred years. By 1903, the British colonies could claim only a meager 2 percent of the world market as compared with 15 percent immediately subsequent to emancipation in 1838. In societies profoundly dependent upon a single crop, a drop in prices and production had a devastating effect on job prospects. Unemployment was rife among the islands' black populations during these decades. Anticipating little improvement at home, many islanders began considering other options.[35]

The widespread poverty among blacks on the islands and despondency about future opportunities were by far the greatest influences driving people out of the Caribbean. The caste system, which relegated blacks to the bottom of economic and social hierarchies, was virtually unbreachable. "You were never able to come out of the class in which you were born down there," recalled Caribbean immigrant Harold Ellis.

"In America, you could go in any damn place. There was prejudice here, but it was better than having no hope down in the West Indies." Ellis prevailed on his mother to allow him to leave for New York. Richard Moore earned ten dollars a month working in Barbados after leaving school in 1905. "No prospect appeared of any further increase in pay and the proceeds of two small properties, one formerly owned by [my] mother and the other inherited by [my] step-mother, had almost been spent to defray the family's living expenses." Seeing a bleak future, he too headed to New York.[36]

Even lighter-skinned black islanders who belonged to the middle tier of the Caribbean's caste hierarchy could aspire to little better than clerk-ships. James Watson explained that he resigned from steady positions "as bookkeeper and as chief clerk, respectively, at the Myrtle Bank and Constant Spring Hotels (two of the largest hotels in that island) . . . only because of my desire to travel and to acquire a profession." Knowing he could not do so in his native Jamaica, he relocated to New York City and became a lawyer. Another ambitious immigrant explained his motives to an interviewer. "With all the comforts of my home life and all the joys of my island I longed to go abroad. My one hope, the aim of my life, was being stifled. At home I saw nothing ahead for me but either to be a clerk in some mercantile house with a small salary and a large head, or to become a tailor badly paid." He emigrated at age fifteen. After years of poverty and struggle he brought his mother and sister to join him and eventually became the pastor of a black church.[37]

The serious problem of overcrowding that plagued many of the islands further encouraged emigration from the Caribbean. This was particularly true in Barbados. The island colony had more than 122,000 inhabitants by the middle of the nineteenth century, making it among the most densely populated places in the world. In 1897, to combat this persistent problem, the colonial government established the Victoria Emigration Society to provide monetary assistance for "the emigration of poor women who are compelled to earn their living but are unable to do so in Barbados." Though most of those receiving aid came from the island's white population, some black Barbadians managed to enter the program. And even without the government's assistance or encour-agement, residents fled Barbados and other Caribbean islands experi-encing similar difficulties throughout the nineteenth and into the twentieth centuries.[38]

The emergence of the banana industry brought new opportunities to island residents. The United Fruit Company, developing this crop, also helped to establish the tourist industry in the Caribbean. The banana boats brought visitors to the islands and transported emigrants away from their homelands. This marked the beginning of regular steamship service between the Caribbean and the Atlantic ports of the United States, in particular New York City. Initially, travel between the United States and the Caribbean was relatively inexpensive, making it accessible to many. In the early years of the twentieth century, second-class passage could be purchased for approximately twenty-five dollars. By 1914 the price had jumped to forty-five dollars. In addition, workers on the ships had easy access to U.S. ports. "My father left the West Indies when he was twelve," recounted Rosanna Weston. "At that time, they used to take the young boys aboard ships, and my father went on a ship when he was twelve years old, and he never returned." Census records document the correlation between the establishment of steamship lines that ran from the United States to the islands and the onset of steady Caribbean immigration.[39]

A sizable contingent of the immigrants came to New York indirectly, having gone first to work on the canal in Panama, on banana plantations and the railroad in Costa Rica, and on islands such as the Dominican Republic, Trinidad, and British Guyana, which had nascent sugar industries at the end of the nineteenth century. One typical immigrant in New York explained how he landed in the city. "I was born in the West Indies," he told an interviewer, "and I traveled ten years at sea. And then . . . I helped to dig the Panama Canal." Like thousands of other unskilled laborers, he found himself evicted from the isthmus upon the canal's completion. Considering his limited options, this man chose to adopt New York City as his new home.[40]

Though many of the impulses pushing islanders to the United States were similar to those impelling southern blacks from their homes, the Caribbean migration to New York City differed from the southern movement north in some important respects. Immigration laws required that a relative or guardian meet each new arrival to the United States and claim financial responsibility for the newcomer. Furthermore, prospective emigrants were required to deposit a thirty-dollar bond to demonstrate their financial solvency. Those unable to meet this condition or to pass physical and literacy exams could find themselves deported to their homeland.[41] Ben Croft, a native of St. Kitts who immigrated to New York in 1915, recalled being forced to wait on Ellis Island for days while he was checked for disease and parasites. He was eventually allowed to enter the United States.[42] Others were not so fortunate. Fred Challenor wrote to his wife about a friend, Mr. Jones, who had arrived in the United States from Barbados in 1910, "but is having some trouble with the authorities as they think he is too old and upwards of today he hasn't been allowed to leave Ellis Island." The government ultimately denied Jones entry and forced his return to Barbados.[43]

Because newcomers needed to be met at the docks, Caribbean New

Yorkers tended to arrive in a series of chain migrations that helped them maintain ties with friends and families. Richard Moore and his step-mother decided to leave Barbados for New York City in July 1908. The choice of destination came logically, having been preceded by her two sisters and then his two sisters. Not long after Barbadian Aletha Dowridge settled in New York, she received an imploring letter from family members back home. A distant cousin, Ada, hoped to make a similar move to the United States but could not afford the steerage ticket. Assuming (incorrectly) that Aletha had achieved financial stability in her new home, the family pressured her to make a contribution to her relative's travel funds. For Aletha and others already in a tight financial bind, these requests could produce family tensions. Nevertheless, the chain migrations helped to replicate original community and familial bonds. Much more than southern migrants, Caribbean immigrants during this early period of transplantation arrived in the city already connected to at least one resident.[44]

The immigrants differed from southern migrants in more than the process of relocation. Islanders arrived in New York with at least some financial stability and typically boasted a better education than black newcomers from the South. The cost of steamship travel, though relatively inexpensive in the early decades of the twentieth century, combined with the financial requirements upon entry into the United States, precluded the most impoverished residents of the Caribbean islands from making the journey. A disproportionate number of light-skinned, middle-class artisans, tradesmen, and shopkeepers formed the group heading to the United States. While the lower classes made temporary sojourns to other Caribbean islands to harvest sugar cane and to Central America to help build the Panama Canal or work on banana plantations, the middle-class young men and women who desired a change more often chose a permanent move to the United States, where they expected to avoid manual labor. As a result, between 1901 and 1915, over 39 percent of Caribbean immigrants had work experience in industry, commerce and finance, or the professions. These island transplants to New York used their skilled backgrounds to position themselves relatively quickly as members of the economic, professional, and political elite of the city's black population.[45]

The final decades of the nineteenth century heralded a period of tremendous insecurity in New York City, as "a surge of immigra[nts] so vast and alien" as to seemingly threaten the Anglo-Saxon republic took residence in Manhattan, bringing with them a babble of sounds, foreign customs, and abject poverty. Longtime Yankees witnessed their arrival with trepidation, drawing links between the newcomers' presence and the increase in crime, vice, and corruption sweeping New York.[46] Seeking to reclaim their city, white New Yorkers organized reform efforts targeting the perceived immorality pervading immigrant communities. Significantly, however, despite white New Yorkers' disparagement of European newcomers for their transgressive, un-American conduct, the very existence of myriad reform organizations offered evidence of the reformers' conviction that the immigrants had the capacity for rehabilitation. Though immigrants needed training in normative behaviors, reformers essentially believed that the newcomers could, in fact, be redeemed. For black migrants in New York City, arriving simultaneously with the new wave of European immigrants, the reception proved elementally less welcoming. Black people, not the recipients of white reformers' attention prior to World War I, instead bore the brunt of the blame for the city's ills. Virtually alone among the newcomers, blacks came to be viewed as incapable of reformation, and white New Yorkers treated them accordingly.

As a result of these racialized perceptions, white New Yorkers observed the influx of black people with particular anxiety. "One who looks Southward can almost see the army of Negroes gathering from out of the cities, villages, and farms," wrote Ray Stannard Baker ominously in 1908, "bringing nothing with them but a buoyant hope in a distant freedom, but tramping always Northward." The trend was equally disturbing among Caribbean-born blacks, Baker affirmed, who "look . . . wistfully toward the heralded opportunities of America," arriving on New York's shores in unprecedented numbers. The *New York Times* cautioned its readers in 1892 that the "great exodus" would have a profound impact on race relations. "The result will be that the South will have solved what the Yankees call its negro problem in a very simple though unexpected way . . . by sending enough of its negroes to the North so that both halves of the country will be in the same boat."[47] The newspapers' exaggeration of the extent of blacks' movement reflected the depth of northern whites' apprehension.

Northerners who worried about the moral condition of their cities expressed particular anxiety about "unscrupulous agents" who lured "green helpless negro wom[e]n" out of the South and into New York's red-light districts. They "drive through the country in a buggy," complained one observer, enticing girls with stories "of the fine positions awaiting them." The agents charged their recruits up to twenty-two dollars for travel fare to New York City, commanding a profit of nearly 300 percent. The victims arrived in the city deeply in debt and friendless, and found themselves thrown into "dirty ill-smelling apartments" where "moral and immoral, temperate and intemperate, are indiscriminately mixed," railed white reformer Frances Kellor. Susceptible black women lapsed into "immoral habits, vice and laziness." Under such circumstances, Kellor cautioned, "[I]s there any escape from the disorderly house?"[48]

Concerned about the effects of prostitution in the city—though not especially worried about the girls themselves—Kellor began to focus in earnest on the problem of employment agencies that sent "unscrupulous runners and procurers" into the South to ensnare hapless, "friendless girls" into New York's "disorderly houses." At least half of these agencies, she claimed, violated the law by operating within the tenements and by failing to furnish women with the names and addresses of their prospective employers. Shutting these agencies would immediately diminish the number of blacks entering the city, an ideal she preached to all who would listen. For those women who still chose to leave their southern homes, the "cry of the [white] housewife for maids and cooks and laundresses," offered a solution. Kellor sought to place missionaries at the docks to "reach the negro girl before she has gone astray or has become incompetent, immoral, intemperate, and imbued with the idea that in this great city she need not work."[49]

Kellor's opposition to the growth of New York's black population informed the tone of her call for action. But even sympathetic observers were struck by the disproportionate growth of New York's black female population. Mary White Ovington reported on "the boats from Charleston and Norfolk and the British West Indies bringing scores and hundreds of Negro women from country districts, from cities. . . , all seeking better wages in a new land." Many who arrived were ill prepared for the harsh environment of New York City, struggling with everything from the right clothes to wear in winter to finding jobs and a place to live.[50] A group of reform-minded black women in New York, hoping to offer a "friendly helping hand" to black newcomers to the city, translated their concerns into the creation of the Association for the Protection of Colored Women (APCW) in 1905. Addressing the alarming rise in the demographic imbalance within New York's black population (in 1900 the city housed 124 females to every 100 males), the association went into the South to create an information network through southern churches, schools, and newspapers. They hoped to educate young black women "of the dangers" in New York City "and how to guard against them, emphasizing the economic and social struggle which they must face, and asking co-operation in either keeping them at home or equipping them for the journey." A cadre of workers met incoming boats from the South and the Caribbean offering guidance to travelers "deprived of necessary guards to [their] honesty and morality." The association established a consortium of reputable black employment

Figure 1. Guadeloupean immigrants at Ellis Island, circa 1911. Photo by Augustus Francis Sherman. Manuscripts, Archives and Rare Books Division, Schomburg Center for Research in Black Culture, The New York Public Library, Astor, Lenox and Tilden Foundations.

agencies. Over time, the APCW also developed courses for women on etiquette and sexual hygiene.[51]

As migration and immigration increased early in the twentieth century, additional organizations emerged that addressed the social and economic dislocations black newcomers faced in the North. The National League on Urban Conditions, founded in New York City in 1911 by the merger of the National League for the Protection of Colored Women, the Committee on Urban Conditions of Negroes, and the Committee for Improving the Industrial Condition of the Negro in New York, made the direct link between migration patterns and blacks' work experience in the northern city. Continuing the varied philanthropic efforts of its parent organizations, the Urban League (as the National League on Urban Conditions was commonly known) offered travelers' aid along with job training and placement programs for New York's black population. In its earliest years, it also purported to "help counteract" urban migration. But it soon turned its attention instead to assisting those who chose to come, paying particular heed to the greatest challenge facing its constituency—finding work. Recognizing the futility of trying to staunch the flow of black people into New York, organizations like the Urban League had, by the early twentieth century, shifted their focus to easing migrants' transition once they arrived.

But not all black New Yorkers treated black newcomers with sympathy or support. Blaming the "stream of young negro life" for the "spread of race antipathy in the North," some members of the "old time [black] aristocracy bearing Knickerbocker names" pleaded with southerners to remain at home. New York's "Old Settlers" publicly blamed the "epidemic of negrophobia" on the migrants, joining whites in stressing that they hailed from the lowest elements of society. This group denounced the migrants as vehemently as whites did, characterizing the newcomers as "scum," "illiterate," "criminals," "loafers," "thoughtless," "lazy," "overdemonstrative," "undesirable," and "riff-raff." When a black man shot "promiscuously" into a crowd of people disembarking from a ferryboat at New York's dock, the *New York Age* pointedly observed that the man had only recently hailed from South Carolina.[52] Southern migrants "make it hard for us wherever they light," complained a black northerner. "The well-meaning, industrious, progressive Negroes, as a rule, remain in the South to fight out the question there. The lazy, shiftless, worthless class come [*sic*] to northern cities to reduce our opportunities and privileges to a minimum."[53]

The early denunciation of the migration by some black Knickerbockers contributed to mounting tensions within New York City's black population. Many black newcomers felt unwelcomed by both whites and blacks while longtime black residents felt besieged by the influx of people into their community. Northern blacks, including some former migrants themselves, encouraged southern youths to "consider whether it will not be better to bear some of the ills they now do, than fly to others they know not of." The southern states, they insisted, "are the natural habitat of the Afro-American people." Despite the hardships prevalent in the South, contended the opponents of migration, "fresh air at least is plentiful and cheap." Conversely, northern cities offered only squalor and "huge dilapidated tenements." They stressed the merits of agricultural labor. "Surely," remarked an editorial in the *Southern Workman* somewhat disingenuously, "a free, independent, clean and wholesome life on a bit of land of one's own . . . which is possible anywhere in the South, should be far more attractive to the great masses of the Negroes than any fancied advantage to be had in our large Northern cities, where they are sure to be pushed to the wall."[54] The city's black weekly, the *New York Age*, made a special appeal to Caribbean blacks seeking better opportunities in the United States. It is "a sad mistake," wrote T. Thomas Fortune—ironically himself a southern migrant—in 1891, to think of New York as "simply a paradise where employment of all kinds can be had for the asking." He assured the dubious that only menial jobs could be acquired, and not easily at that. Many immigrants discovered that decent work remained the purview of white laborers and found themselves living in poverty. "New York is a good place to shun," cautioned the editor, "unless you have plenty of money or a position secured before coming here."[55]

The warnings against migration had little effect, however, and old-time black New Yorkers found themselves deluged by newcomers. Indeed, by 1906 southerners comprised the majority of New York City's black population.[56] The migration caused substantially increased residential congestion and undermined the geographic demarcation of class distinctions. Elite black people, like ethnic whites who had risen out of poverty, sought to dissociate from the lower classes by escaping residential proximity and asserting a privileged social position. For a time, Brooklyn provided a haven for wealthy blacks who hoped to purchase a home, elude some of the worst racial prejudice, and differentiate themselves from the multitudes in Manhattan. However, by the late nineteenth century the growing population had become increasingly limited in its residential options.[57] The elite suddenly found themselves living within spitting distance of the lower class.

Residential intermingling increased the tendency for white observers to view black people monolithically. The black well-to-do, who regarded the criminal and indigent of the black population with the same contempt and pity that white elites showed toward the lowest classes of their race, worked vigorously to challenge this perception. "There are various grades of colored people," avowed a black woman to the *New York Times*. "No respectable negro would want to associate with [the worst]." She hoped to convince the newspaper's readership that the black population housed the same variety of classes that comprised the city's white population, including many educated and wealthy individuals. The morally righteous, she insisted, "are not to be judged by the street loungers and drunkards of our race." Samuel Scottron, a longtime black Brooklynite and member of the board of education, sought to highlight the difference between black newcomers and the Knickerbockers who boasted of a lengthy history in New York. Echoing the most strident social Darwinist rhetoric of the day, he denounced southern black migrants for their lack of sophistication and crass behavior. The city would either civilize them, Scottron proclaimed, or they would die out.[58]

Nevertheless, whites' growing antagonism toward their black neighbors pushed all black people into increasingly limited residential spaces. Unable to escape their confinement, distinct groups of black people instead clustered in enclaves within black neighborhoods. Though outsiders might perceive an undifferentiated mass within a residential area, in fact, "consciousness of kind" encouraged discrete segregation. "There is a tendency for the better classes to live on the east side of the streets," a sociologist observed, while "the lower classes . . . live on the west end."[59] Both old-time Knickerbockers and newcomers to the city felt the urgency of associating with their own ilk. Often without friends or kin, migrants sought out people who might understand them and could offer a sense of the home and culture left behind. When West Indian-born sociologist Robert Johnstone attempted to conduct a study of the social activities of black New Yorkers, he found himself "thr[own] off [his] mission" by his Caribbean subjects, who wanted to share "a word or two of home." The desperate desire for camaraderie, Johnstone concluded, "is enough to shew that bond which binds me as a West Indian to other W. Indians, which binds like with like."[60]

Compounding the natural tendency to seek out the familiar, the scorn foisted upon American-born blacks encouraged Caribbean immigrants to distinguish themselves as a separate group. "The loyal Britisher," Johnstone noted, "sings the praises of the freedom of British Soil." Former British colonial Harold Ellis, arriving at work on Lincoln's birthday, was startled to find his place of employment closed for the day. When his boss explained that "Lincoln freed the slaves" and suggested that Ellis should be grateful for Lincoln's largesse, the Caribbean migrant insisted, "Lincoln didn't free me. My people were freed by royal decree of Queen Victoria." Like others from the islands, Ellis deliberately set himself apart from the mass of American-born Negroes disparaged by white Americans.[61]

These attitudes resulted in far lower naturalization rates for black immigrants than for their white counterparts—25 percent in 1930, compared with 60 percent among whites.[62] In fact, even native-born blacks could find their condition improved by being mistaken for foreigners. James Weldon Johnson, traveling by train in Florida in 1903 with a black Cuban acquaintance, was asked by the conductor to move to the Jim Crow car. But when the conductor heard them speaking in Spanish, "his attitude changed; he punched our tickets and gave them back, and treated us just as he did the other passengers in the car." When Walter Cook, a white sports promoter, became a financial supporter of a Negro baseball team from Brooklyn, he renamed the club the Cuban Giants. The implication that the athletes hailed from abroad mitigated the widespread prejudice against Negro players. In the 1920s, an editorial in a black newspaper encouraged American-born blacks to learn the Spanish language in order to find better jobs.[63]

The relatively better treatment enjoyed by black immigrants over their native-born counterparts created an immigration experience for blacks that fundamentally differed from that of Europeans. Whereas white immigrants struggled to obscure their foreignness in order to gain acceptance in their adoptive home, West Indians realized that as immigrants they held a privileged status over black Americans. Jamaican immigrant Claude McKay discovered to his amazement that his island accent conferred important advantages and mitigated some of the impediments of racism. Working for the Pennsylvania Railroad during World War I, he was arrested in a police sting to catch "draft dodgers, slackers and vagrants." While other innocent black men received five- and ten-day jail sentences, the judge, upon hearing McKay's accent, "asked me if I were born in Jamaica. I said, 'Yes, Sir' and he commented: 'Nice place. I was there a couple of seasons ago.'" Reviewing McKay's case, the judge "declared that I was doing indispensable work on the railroad and he reprimanded the black detective who had pressed the charge and said the police should be more discriminate in making arrests and endeavor to ascertain the facts about their victims." The case was dismissed. Reflecting on the implications of this experience, McKay resolved "to cultivate more my native accent." For people of African descent living in the United States, acceptance came only in the absence of citizenship. Ironically, as black people put down roots and became Americanized, whites viewed them with increasingly greater contempt.[64]

Tensions developed between Caribbean and native-born blacks as a result of these circumstances. Black Americans bitter over the better treatment of those who had shed no blood or sweat for the United States referred to islanders as "monkey chasers" and taunted the immigrants for their strange clothes and accents. A popular refrain held that natives from the Caribbean came to New York "to teach, open a church, or start trouble." A ditty jeered, "When a monkey-chaser dies / Don't need no undertaker / Just throw him in de Harlem River / He'll float back to Jamaica." On the other side, immigrants insisted that "the West Indian is more forceful and austere in character" than American-born blacks. Consequently, claimed a black sociologist, he "appears to prove on the whole more trustworthy in business." Paule Marshall, a first-generation black American, noted that "the West Indian woman considered herself both different and somehow superior [to black American women]. From the talk which circulated around our kitchen it was clear, for example, that my mother and her friends perceived of themselves as being more ambitious than black Americans, more hard working."[65]

Color played a role in the prejudices. With the high incidence of mixed-race people in the Caribbean, some West Indian immigrants denied even racial identification with American-born blacks. "The bright or fair coloured look down on the dark skin," admitted a man from the British West Indies. Mary White Ovington's dressmaker, a woman born in the Caribbean, insisted "positively that she was not a Negro," despite her "dark" face. A native of the Danish West Indies rebuked the editor of the *Brooklyn Eagle* for referring to "persons of mixed blood" as Negroes. "A mulatto is not a negro," the man counseled, as "he is as much a white man as a black." He stressed the fact that nearly all inhabitants of the Caribbean ("excluding the sprinkling of whites") were not, in fact, Negro. "In the West Indian Islands," he explained, "one would be laughed at for calling a mulatto a *negro*."[66]

The "bitter resentment" grew on both sides, and hostility at times became palpable. Each group accused the other of being "aggressive" and "clannish." While the "northerner dislikes the southerner," commented an immigrant, "[e]ach of these is antagonistic to the West Indian." A study of Caribbean migrants in New York confirmed that they tended to associate only with one another "because of the longer acquaintance, and the prejudice existing between them and the American Negroes." African Americans claimed that the immigrants in their midst did not understand native-born blacks' struggles. The "life of the American colored people," wrote Mary Randolph to West Indian James Watson, "I daresay you don't quite understand as well as I do because the experiences are not a part of your foreparents' lives." The burgeoning friendship between the two permitted her to ask a tentative question: "I have been wondering why you are not like us," she wrote, though she hastened to add, "But the difference is to your credit."[67]

Literary clubs, mutual aid societies, athletic associations, and residential enclaves reinforced the ethnic separation between American and Caribbean blacks. Yet by the turn of the century, the majority of New

York's black population shared the common characteristic of having been born elsewhere, either in the South or outside the country. The transformation was perhaps best reflected in the changing views of the *New York Age*. Twenty years after T. Thomas Fortune had urged black people not to consider New York City as a friendly destination, under the leadership of Fred Moore, also a southern migrant, the newspaper made explicit overtures to discontented black people both in the South and in the islands. The city, he declared, offered black migrants and immigrants alike the opportunity to escape oppression in the South and economic stagnation in the Caribbean. The total reversal on the migration question came as little surprise; by the turn of the century, New York housed more southern- than northern-born black people within its borders. The floodgates had opened.[68] To white Americans, this trend came as an unwelcome reality. "We were all strangers," declared Panamanian Maida Springer Kemp. "The black American, the black foreigner, and we did not like one another, and the white foreigner liked us less and the white American hated all of us."[69]

The enormity and bustle of New York City invariably impressed and often overwhelmed newcomers from other regions of the country and from the Caribbean alike. "What a big, busy place I found New York to be!" exclaimed Henry Proctor, passing through the city on his way from the South to a new job in Connecticut. "What high buildings, what throngs on Broadway, what a crush at Brooklyn Bridge, where everybody seemed to get up and rush for the entrance at the same time." Like many recent arrivals, Proctor experienced the treachery of a seasoned con artist who swindled the minister out of a dollar during a carriage ride to his lodgings. Proctor learned quickly. "That was the most useful dollar I ever spent," he later claimed. "It taught me the habit never to let a person do anything for me without first finding out the cost." Though exciting, his visit left him exhausted. "After a few days spent in the metropolis I was tired and confused," he admitted, "and I rejoiced in the rest and quiet of the boat on the Sound as it bore me from New York to New Haven."[70]

The very excitements that had overwhelmed Proctor affirmed others' decision to remain in New York. "I . . . visited this Metropolitan City in the spring of 1884," recounted Alexander Walters. "I was amazed at its inhabitants, astonished at the enterprise and aggressiveness of its business men and delighted at its beautiful and immense park. I saw for the first time an elevated railroad, transporting to and fro a half million people a day." He settled in New York a few years later.[71] James Weldon Johnson admitted that his thoughts often strayed from his mundane school responsibilities in Jacksonville, Florida, to New York's exciting night scene. He described the addictiveness of New York. "To some natures this stimulant of life in a great city becomes a thing as binding and necessary as opium is to one addicted to the habit. It becomes their breath of life," he continued, perhaps alluding to his own compulsion to eventually relocate. "[T]hey cannot exist outside of it; rather than be deprived of it they are content to suffer hunger, want, pain, and misery; they would not exchange even a ragged and wretched condition among the great crowd for any degree of comfort away from it." Although countless migrants suffered as they experienced firsthand the elusiveness of the city's promise, the diverse array of New York's attractions beguiled many young people willing to endure nearly any hardship in order to escape the mind-numbing boredom of rural life.[72]

Whether drawn by economic aspirations or social enticements, the nature of the post-Reconstruction migration of black people into New York contributed to a high degree of fluidity and instability within the black population. Though the number of black New Yorkers inexorably increased, the population constantly shifted as black people came and went, not well anchored to a city that offered limited social connections and boasted few institutions to serve black residents. Because of the apocryphal stories many heard while still at home, migrants often arrived with misconceptions about life in the city. For many, the reality came as an abrupt surprise as they struggled to adjust to poverty, limited occupational opportunities, and increasingly intractable race relations. Those coming with the address of a friend or relative, as was the case with many arrivals from the Caribbean, fared better than those who had simply chosen to leave the South with no clear sense of where they were going. Alone in the big city, unaccustomed to the ways of city life, some found the city to be a frightening and unfriendly place. Like Henry Proctor, who found himself less a dollar when he trusted the wrong man, an experienced con artist spotting a newcomer might cheat migrants out of their meager worldly possessions. Jobless, friendless, and virtually homeless, many newcomers felt bereft.[73]

They also quickly felt betrayed, having envisioned in the North a society free of racial conflicts and prejudice. Southern blacks were especially anxious to leave the "daily irritations" at home. Haywood Butt, a native of North Carolina, explained that his family moved to New York from North Carolina "because they had segregation down there. They were supposed to be separate but equal, but there's no such animal."[74] Much to their surprise, newcomers frequently discovered that race relations in the North could be as acrimonious as in the South, and even more baffling. The racism in New York often proved subtler than in the South, making behavioral expectations more difficult to identify. While granted the right to vote and assured access to the judicial system, in New York conflicts and violence habitually erupted between blacks and whites. Furthermore, blacks found themselves excluded from skilled jobs, many restaurants, and other public venues and relegated to segregated sections of public transportation and entertainment. Without extensive support systems, these affronts could make life unbearable.

Some who failed to adapt to city life made the reluctant decision to return home. Between 1908 and 1915, 10,240 black immigrants to the United States—over 20 percent of all legal black aliens arriving during those years—departed the country. In 1910, Ben Croft's mother and father emigrated from St. Kitts. Upon landing in New York, Croft's father took an immediate dislike to the city and left soon after. His mother stayed. Thomas Peyton's grandfather struggled to adjust to city life in Brooklyn after selling his farm in North Carolina. But a hard first winter, poverty, betrayal by a "smooth-tongued 'cousin'" who skipped town with most of the family's belongings, and the death of one son to pneumonia convinced the elder Peyton that urban life held no future for him. "Destitute and heartbroken," he decided to go back with his wife and daughter to "the village where his entire life had been spent" and begin again as a farmer. His remaining son chose to pursue his fate in the city. The old man returned once more to Brooklyn some years later after the death of his spouse. Despite his painful first encounter with the city, Peyton finished out his life in the North.[75]

However, the combination of Jim Crow and youthful pride prevented the majority of newcomers from admitting defeat. "Go back!" exclaimed a horrified migrant. "Never! I could not face the folks; I'd rather die." W. C. Handy's early hardships led him to thoughts of returning to Alabama. But every temptation to return was followed by a stronger conviction not to publicize his failures. "What will you be returning to but a chorus of 'I told you so's'?" he asked himself. "You will be advancing under a flag of truce and that flag will not be a white one, it will be yellow." So he, like so many others, perpetuated the myths circulating throughout the South by writing fantastical letters, sending money, and going to visit "with two or three different styles of clothes and two or three rings and shake them people up something wonderful."[76]

Armed with visions of a city replete with economic opportunities, some black people planned brief money-making forays to New York City, expecting to return home with a stockpile of riches. Others came on short visits, hoping for a momentary taste of the city's attractions. These brief sojourns exacerbated the instability of a population whose members seemed to be unceasingly on the move. Mary Rock encouraged family members to "run down to see me on some of the cheap excursions that will soon begin." She promised to give her cousin "a good visit" between her working hours. Rock's aunt Eveline made repeated and extended trips to the city between 1894 and 1903. Others arrived with plans of permanency, only to discover that life in New York could be as cruel as elsewhere. The close ties they preserved with those back home allowed many to return for periods of respite from the city. In a relentless struggle to find work and avoid destitution, others, especially black men, moved in and out of the city as they followed white people's money onto cruise ships and summer resorts.[77]

The temporary migrants, those who came and went as their fortunes changed and those returning home after finding city life unbearable, contributed to the flux of New York's black population during this period. Already reeling from demographic imbalances, extremely rapid growth, and increasing diversity, the black community suffered the constant shifting of its members as individuals moved in and out of the city, ever in search of better circumstances. The weak connections that many maintained to New York challenged family relationships, as spouses had to sustain ties across time and space. Women like Mary Rock found themselves alone in the city while their husbands sought work on ships or summer resorts. Others, like Ben Croft's mother, faced permanent separations due to abandonment or family breakups. Aletha Dowridge spent substantial periods of time back in Barbados while her husband remained in Brooklyn to continue the struggle for economic solvency.[78]

Even for the majority of black people who came to New York with the intention of remaining permanently, forging lasting social connections proved difficult. Upon arrival in their adoptive home, migrants and immigrants alike struggled to adapt to life in an often friendless city. In the early decades of black migration, the absence of extensive kin networks combined with prohibitively high rents forced many newcomers to seek housing with strangers. Despite deplorable living conditions in many of the tenements available to black tenants, black people consistently paid the highest rents of all of New York City's apartment dwellers. Critics charged white landlords with extracting "exaggerated," "usurious," and "exorbitant" rents from black tenants. "We can[']t get one cent ahead here and both of us work," complained Mary Rock. "[W]e pay $12 where we live now just think $6 dollars every other Saturday night and you better have it or out on the Side walk go your things[.]"[79]

White journalist and social reformer Jacob Riis denounced the landlord who "deliberately exploits the prejudice against the black man to make it pan out a profit for him." Riis's observation was repeatedly proven true. Tenement owners, though only reluctantly opening their buildings to black residents, found that they could charge far higher rents to their new tenants, with the percentages growing dramatically over time. On average, black tenants during the 1880s paid from $11 to

$16 for a three-room apartment, and $20 for a four-room dwelling. Whites during this period spent between $7 and $11 for three rooms and $14 for four. A white landlord in 1889 charged $127 a month to the white tenants in his building; when he began leasing to blacks, the ensuing raise in rates earned him an additional $17 in profit. Once blacks made the move to Harlem, landlords' incomes rose dramatically. One landlord, for example, who found his all-white building semivacant, even when he offered relatively low rents between $14 and $17 per month, soon reported earnings of between $20 and $24 per unit each month renting to blacks, with a long waiting list of interested tenants.[80]

High rents and limited available housing obligated a substantial proportion of New York's black residents to sublet their apartments. The "lodging evil," as it came to be known in reforming circles by the end of the nineteenth century, hit the black population very hard. An 1897 survey conducted by the Federation of Churches found that 40 percent of Manhattan's black residents housed boarders, second only to the percentage of the city's Austrian population doing the same. A mere half of the black lodgers claimed a blood relation to their host families. The proportion of black families with lodgers continued to increase in the ensuing decades. In 1905, 42 percent of New York's black families housed non-kin boarders. That percentage grew to 46 in 1912, with some juggling as many as nine boarders at any given time. About one-fifth of Italians and Irish in New York during the same period shared their quarters with non-kin lodgers while Germans virtually never permitted boarders to live in their homes. Only Russian Jews in the overcrowded Lower East Side outpaced blacks, with over half in 1911 sharing their apartments with others. And by 1915, with the shift to Harlem's more expensive housing well underway, as much as one-third of the black population lived as boarders in others' homes.[81]

Lodgers made an important contribution to offsetting the high rents demanded of black tenants. A study conducted in 1916 found that lodgers typically paid between $2.00 and $2.50 per week for their rooms. A single boarder therefore might contribute up to one-third of the monthly rent for the apartment. But even a single room rental often proved too costly for black workers with very low salaries. Two dollars a week represented up to one-third of many workers' wages. Lodgers thus frequently shared their small quarters with roommates. In a practice they called "batching it," several men rented a single room, reserving the right to bring home a woman for the night.[82]

But boarding severely hampered community formation, exacerbating the instability of the black population. Lodgers rarely stayed put for long; the general dissatisfaction on both sides of the agreement conspired to make lodging an ever-changing relationship. Lodgers therefore often had even weaker social ties in the city than other black residents, as they moved with tremendous frequency, not putting down roots and inhibiting the establishment of lasting ties with other members of the city's black population. The loneliness many experienced upon moving to New York consequently encouraged migrants to preserve a strong identification with the home they had left behind. "I am awful homesick and lonesome sometimes to see you all," a migrant wrote to her family. Though she couldn't spare the ten dollars "just yet" to visit her parents and sister, others managed periodic trips home. Annie Randolph left New York for nearly a month to spend time with her mother in Boston. Aletha Dowridge traveled back and forth between New York and St. Michael Parish, Barbados, before finally returning to the island for an extended stay when she and her husband faced destitution in the city. Her mother unabashedly expressed her delight. "Dearest lea," she wrote, "if you ar[e] coming home let me know in time . . . you know I will have to put your bedroom in order for you now." She regularly implored her daughter to visit the folks in St. Michael Parish, explaining that "I like the inocent lookin little lea at home the bess." Her husband, Fred, was not so fortunate. Though desperately trying to save enough to pay his passage to Barbados, all such hope had to be "abandoned" when money was tight.[83] Though they had made a new life for themselves in New York, many black newcomers to the city often still thought of other places as "home."

Family, however distant, continued to play a central role in the lives of many migrants. Sena Etter Williams, from Jacksonville, North Carolina, moved with her husband, Furney Williams, to New York City. She wrote an agitated letter to her mother, Joanna Dixon, about Furney's abusive behavior, begging her mother "for God sake to help her." Joanna, who described herself as "a poor colored woman and a widow" in her later plea to New York municipal authorities for assistance, agreed to send Sena the money to "come home." When her daughter disappeared, Joanna frantically wrote to the New York City police department, pleading for help in finding Sena. Despite the physical separation between mother and daughter, the emotional bond remained vital for both women.[84]

As friends and family members followed each other to New York, they were able to help preserve and strengthen emotional and cultural ties by transporting letters, food, and other items back and forth across the Atlantic. Many emigrants supported family members back home with portions of their earnings made in New York. "I did not want to write you," a woman admitted to her cousin in Barbados, "till I had some money to send." Financial obligations could add to the economic pressures already weighing heavily on black immigrants in New York even as the dollars sent home helped reinforce family connections.[85]

Distance often belied the pressure family could exert on relatives in the city. Aletha Dowridge corresponded regularly with her mother in Barbados, often sending and receiving letters through a network of visitors coming to New York from St. Michael. After meeting her future husband, Fred Challenor, Aletha wrote home to seek permission to marry. Not hearing back quickly enough, she proceeded with the ceremony despite her family's silence. Later, Aletha received a chastising missive, criticizing her for going ahead with the wedding before the family could weigh in on the decision. Some years later Aletha felt compelled by requests from home to help finance the trip of a relative who hoped to come to New York in 1907 to assist another cousin, Wilhelmina, through a difficult pregnancy. When the woman died in childbirth, Aletha took the infant home to its grandparents and kin in the Caribbean.[86] For many families, distance did not diminish familial obligations, it only made them more challenging to fulfill.

Money helped to tie recent arrivals in New York to their families far away by offering one method through which family members could continue to fulfill filial responsibilities, even from a distance. Frederick Challenor nearly always included a few dollars in his letters to his family in Barbados. Aletha Dowridge's father boasted "over my daughter greenback" after she sent him two dollars. In return, family left behind kept the homesick and lonely apprised of gossip and happenings. "[T]ell me all the home news," Mary Rock begged her sister Lizzie. "I will send you the money to have the courier sent me as soon as I can spare it."[87] When Drucilla Green married and moved with her husband to New York City, she kept in close contact with her family back in Connecticut. They visited each other as often as time and money would permit and wrote letters even more regularly. Even after twenty years apart, "Druci" and her sister, Josie, maintained a deep emotional bond. After receiving a Christmas card with money tucked inside, Josie sent a beholden letter back. "Words fail me to attempt to express my pleasure and gratitude," she wrote, "for it came in a very acceptable time." She had just paid for coal and a new stove, leaving her without money for rent or food. "O. what a card it was it seemed to be a gift stright from god an ansing two to my prayer," Josie continued. "[T]he deed of New Years morning 1900 God has written it on his good book and on my heart it is a ever lasting seal of our core friendship."[88] By sending money to those left behind and keeping up with marriages, births, and events within the family and community, migrants adrift in the city with few family connections or ties could enhance the feeling of stability and belonging.

Most participants in the vanguard of black migration and immigration to New York City were moved by personal dreams to relocate. They hoped to find, in the words of one migrant, a "new land, [a] young land," one that would be free of racial restrictions and segregation, one that offered greater economic opportunities than in the South, and one that promised the excitement found only in a big city.[89] For many, New York represented a place "vague and far away, a city that, like Heaven, to them had existed by faith alone."[90] These early migrations set the tenor of the black community for generations to come. As thousands of newcomers arrived from diverse points of origin, including every southern state and many Caribbean colonies—English, Dutch, French, and Spanish—they helped create a diverse community boasting a myriad of languages, habits, and heritages. Although fraught with tensions and divisions, the rich blending of ideas, talents, and traditions helped establish the foundation for making New York City, and especially Harlem, the cultural center of black America. By the time war labor demands inspired hundreds of thousands of black southerners to relocate to the North, tens of thousands of earlier migrants had already established community organizations to assist newcomers and communication lines informing those still living with Jim Crow about the North's possibilities. The additional pull caused by World War I's industrial needs simply expedited a trend already in motion.

But as many black people quickly discovered, New York City often failed to fulfill its promise to newcomers. In 1912, a decade after making the city his permanent home, James Weldon Johnson described New York as "the most fatally fascinating thing in America." He likened the city to "a great witch at the gate of the country, showing her alluring white face and hiding her crooked hands and feet under the folds of her wide garments." Black migrants and immigrants experienced the worst of the city's caprice. Some, Johnson explained, "she at once crushes beneath her cruel feet; others she condemns to a fate like that of galley-slaves; a few she favours and fondles, riding them high on the bubbles of fortune; then with a sudden breath she blows the bubbles out and laughs mockingly as she watches them fall." The hardening of racial prejudices, increasingly rigid residential and occupational restrictions, and tremendous economic challenges tarnished New York City's allure for black newcomers. Nevertheless, migrants put down roots in New York, creating a vanguard for larger influxes of black southerners and islanders still to come in future generations. Their presence in New York established the patterns of community and race relations that would persist into the twentieth century and beyond.[91]

Chapter 2

Purged of the Vicious Classes

On the evening of August 12, 1900, Arthur J. Harris left the room he rented from Annie Johnson at 241 West Forty-first Street to buy cigars and pass some time at McBride's Saloon, located on the corner of Forty-first Street and Eighth Avenue. New York City was in the midst of an excruciating heat wave, and temperatures that day reached higher than ninety degrees. Tenement dwellers poured into the streets and local bars seeking respite from the warmest August on record. Harris, twenty-two years old and a relative newcomer to the city, was among the thousands of young black people who had moved to New York around this time. Born in Richmond, Virginia, he had left his mother's home at age fourteen and had lived in Washington, D.C., for several years. Police later confirmed that he had no criminal record in the nation's capital. In 1899 he moved to Jersey City to visit his father and find work, making money at various odd jobs. A few months later, he and his twenty-year-old common-law wife, May Enoch, relocated to a boardinghouse in New York City's Tenderloin district.[1]

Escaping the sweltering heat of his small rented room, Harris went out for a drink. Enoch followed sometime after midnight, telling him to "come on up home." While she waited outside for Harris to leave McBride's, a plainclothes white policeman, Robert J. Thorpe, approached. To Thorpe, a black woman standing on a street corner late at night could be nothing other than a prostitute; he charged her with soliciting. To Harris, who walked out at just that moment, Thorpe looked like a white man who was harassing his woman: "The policeman grabbed my girl," he said later at his trial. "I didn't know who he was and thought he was a citizen like myself." The officer clubbed him in the ensuing struggle. Harris recalled that Thorpe pummeled him viciously and shouted, "Get up you black son of a bitch." "I thought the man was trying to kill me, and I believed that he would kill me if I didn't protect myself." Harris pulled out a knife and "cut [Thorpe] twice." Enoch ran home during the scuffle. The police arrested her soon after and placed her in a detention center pending further investigation. Harris took a train to his mother's home in Washington, where he was caught within a matter of days and brought back to New York to await trial. Thorpe died in Roosevelt Hospital the next day.[2]

Racial tensions that had been growing with the size of the black population threatened to explode in the aftermath of Thorpe's death. A black man, a recent southern migrant, had killed a well-liked white police officer. His comrades made plans to "punish the Negroes" for Harris's crime. Rumors of violence spread throughout the city. Large crowds, including sixty members of the Thirty-seventh Street police station house, gathered at the home of the Thorpe family on August 15 to pay their last respects. The funeral was scheduled for the next day. Restless and angry, they soon found a target for their frustrations.[3]

That night, New York City erupted in one of the most violent race riots in the city's history. The immediate cause for the outbreak of fighting, three days after the incident between Harris and Thorpe, was an altercation between a twenty-four-year-old black man, Spencer Walters, and a forty-year-old white man, Thomas J. Healy, outside the Thorpe home. Newspaper accounts claimed that Healy was drunk. The Police Board, in its official report, held that Walters had a loaded gun in his possession and attempted to shoot Healy on the street. Black witnesses maintained that Walters had been randomly attacked by a group of whites outraged by the death of the policeman. Regardless of the specific details, a riot ensued.[4]

The neighborhood went wild with rage, finally releasing its pent-up anger. A white mob immediately surged through city streets in pursuit of any black person it could find. "If there had been a carefully arranged plot and this had been the agreed signal, the outbreak could not have been more spontaneous," a journalist reported. "[N]egroes were beaten, jumped upon, and then sent flying" as they tried to flee the violence. The word spread that a "nigger chase" was on. "Up and down the streets, through hotels and saloons, in cellars and streetcars, black people were attacked and beaten." Within minutes the rioting had spread along Eighth Avenue from Forty-first to Thirtieth streets, abetted in large part by the city's police force, most of whom either ignored or directly contributed to the attacks on the city's black residents. A black man, blocked by a mob from entering his apartment, escaped into a saloon. From outside came shouts of "bring him out, we'll lynch him!" Three police officers promptly dragged him to the street, "clubbing him unmercifully." They shoved him into the crowd. Managing to flee, the man was heard to scream for mercy, pleading, "For God's sake don't kill me, I have a wife and children." Two of the officers followed and beat the man senseless. Dozens of black men and women fell victim to similar acts of violence during the rioting.[5]

In the predawn hours of August 17 a providential summer storm drenched the city, cooling temperatures and tempers and ending the rioting. The area hospitals were overflowing with people—mostly black—needing treatment of cracked heads and other injuries, and the city's police stations and local courts were all filled to capacity, also with black people. A local magistrate publicly chastened the police as he arraigned dozens of black defendants. "If accounts are true," he declared in court, "I don't see why you have no white men here." He demanded to see "some of the white persons who participated in this riot." The police moved quickly to comply. A teenager, Frank Minogue, was brought in and charged with trying to trip a policeman who was dispersing a crowd of rioters.[6]

Eighty black men and women later submitted sworn affidavits attesting to mob violence and police brutality. They outlined in vivid detail the inflammatory activities of the city's police force and demanded that the offenders be held accountable and punished. William J. Elliott, a black waiter who fell victim to a particularly vicious attack, took his claims to court in a lawsuit against the city and its hired protectors. He had been arrested during the fighting on the spurious charge of "acting suspiciously." Various reporters declared at the trial that they witnessed him entering the Thirty-seventh Street station house uninjured. When he left the next morning, he was beaten and bloody. Elliott told investigators that as he passed through the muster room someone switched off the lights and he was kicked, punched, and clubbed into insensibility. Three newspaper journalists corroborated his story. The acting police captain, John Cooney, admitted to having been present during the incident, though he claimed to recognize none of the assailants. Cooney suggested that they were all reserves brought in from other precincts and unknown to him. As neither he nor Elliott could identify any specific attacker of the sixty or seventy officers in the station house, the members of the commission charged with investigating the incident found the evidence "contradictory" and ruled that "no conviction or a violation of the rules of the department could be sustained [on it]." Just three months later, in the official report on the inquiry into police conduct during the rioting, Cooney swore contradictorily "that no assault was committed in his presence or to his knowledge." The commission fully exonerated the city's police force. In its annual report published at the end of the year, the police department commended its officers for their "prompt and vigorous action . . . in arresting depredators and dispersing rioters [that] kept the situation under control."[7]

The Tenderloin district gradually returned to a state of uneasy peace. Police Inspector Thompson declared confidently to a worried public that the fighting had been quelled, barring the possibility of some "isolated attacks by negroes on white men." With that claim, he dispatched additional officers to patrol the neighborhood. In fact, isolated clashes continued to plague the area, as whites repeatedly assaulted black people on the streets and in the tenements. In the final tally of the riot, two people were confirmed dead from the fighting and scores of others had sustained serious injuries. Hundreds of black people had been arrested, mostly for carrying concealed weapons. Arthur J. Harris, found guilty of second-degree murder, was sentenced to hard labor in Sing Sing state prison "for the term of his natural life." He died there on December 20, 1908.[8]

New York's black citizens struggled to find redress as city authorities treated black people as the aggressors rather than the victims of violence and demonstrated their unwillingness to punish either the white assailants or the police accomplices. Many armed themselves in preparation for further attacks. Ministers denounced the police and the white mobs from their pulpits. The community held mass meetings in protest. Two hundred British subjects from various Caribbean islands appealed to their consul for assistance, demanding that he take all necessary measures to ensure their protection. A group of concerned black New Yorkers formed the Citizens' Protective League and hired two prominent white lawyers, Frank Moss and Israel Ludlow, to bring lawsuits against the city for damages inflicted on black people by the mob. Despite their rigorous efforts, no black person obtained restitution for personal injuries or property damage. And though the city's official investigators received overwhelming evidence of police brutality, no police officer faced prosecution for any crime—or even an official reprimand for personal conduct—related to activities during the rioting. President York of the Police Board had refused to allow the cross-examination of any police witness.[9]

The violent outburst in the summer of 1900 made very clear to black New Yorkers that race relations in the city had reached a nadir. Though the city had experienced other episodes of racial violence targeting the black population, most recently during the draft riots in 1863, since the Civil War era whites and blacks had lived together in relative peace. In the decades following the Civil War, black men in the city had gained the right to vote, public schools had been integrated, and by the end of the century black men had begun to sit on juries. In 1895, the state passed the Malby Law, extending to all citizens "full and equal accommodations, advantages, facilities, and privileges of inns, restaurants, hotels, eating houses, bathhouses, barber shops, theatres, music halls, public conveyances on land and water, and all other places of public accommodation or amusement" without regard to color, race, or creed. On paper, at least, blacks in New York State had gained the protection of the law.[10]

Yet even as legal barriers to equality were breaking down, racial antipathy was mounting. By the final years of the nineteenth century, white
New Yorkers had begun publicly denouncing the growth of the city's
black population. On Broadway and Tin Pan Alley, in the workplace,
saloons, and tenements, and in the city's police stations and courtrooms,
white New Yorkers followed the lead of their southern compatriots in
disparaging the viability of black freedom and equality. And in the Progressive Era, with reformers focusing public attention on social problems plaguing burgeoning urban centers because of industrialization,
especially perceived threats to moral purity, blacks became easy scape-
goats for the city's social ills.

Progressives' belief that blacks alone could not be redeemed from
their transgressive behavior and the violent upheaval of the 1900 race
riot reflected deep and growing racial prejudices both within the city
and nationwide. In the decades after the Civil War, white northerners
wearied of the continued struggle with the South over the "Negro problem." The flurry of civil rights legislation passed in the late 1860s and
1870s soon gave way to efforts at rapprochement with white southerners.
As memories of the Civil War dimmed into the ever-distant past, and
particularly since 1883 when the Supreme Court repealed the 1875 Civil
Rights Act, the nation's black citizens found their needs repeatedly sacrificed on the alter of sectional reconciliation.[11]

Eager to reunite with their former enemies, Yankees began imbibing—and indeed fostering—a nascent popular culture that elevated the
Old South to mythical status. New Yorkers who not long since had
scorned plantation life as languid, violent, and incompatible with the
industrializing economy emerging in the North now began to lament its
passing. The reconstruction of American collective memory both of the
Civil War and of southern antebellum culture allowed white Americans
to assert a new, coherent national identity. Laying to rest the strife that
had briefly and violently rent the United States into two vying nations,
Civil War nostalgia—though not the war itself—helped forge "the" (sin-
gular) United States from "these" (plural) United States and eased the
country into the "era of great harmony."[12]

Theatrical productions romanticizing the recent conflict became an
early cultural manifestation of the revisionist Civil War history. By the
1880s, this dramatic genre had become the rage in New York's theaters,
helping to soften sectional divisions by evoking sympathy and admiration for the Confederacy and those who had fought and sacrificed to
preserve it. The plays invariably presented an idyllic image of the Old
South that romanticized the genteel manners, chivalry, and charm of
white planters in the antebellum slave society. And the turmoil and
calamity of war were compounded by the often-doomed romance

between a dashing Union officer and a beautiful southern belle, unable to consummate their true love while their societies violently collided around them. Northern white audiences were gently persuaded that the war had been a mistake after all, a tragedy that created an artificial rift between people who had no reason to be divided. Productions such as Bronson Howard's *Shenandoah* and David Belasco's *The Heart of Maryland*, both performed on Broadway and taken on tour after long and successful runs in New York City, helped erase northerners' already dim recollection of the insidious slave power and fiendish slaveholders like Simon Legree. Yankees embraced the glorious memories of a fictive Old South. As one theater critic observed, at the close of each show "there was as much love, and more tears, for the Gray as for the Blue."[13]

In 1890, General William Tecumseh Sherman attended Broadway's 250th performance of *Shenandoah*. The story dramatized the events in Charleston, South Carolina, on the eve of the firing on Fort Sumter and included an ill-fated romance between a lovely Federal woman attracted to a gallant Confederate officer. Sherman, then living in retirement at the Fifth Avenue Hotel in Manhattan, praised the production for its "historical and technical accuracy." Evidently the grizzled old veteran of the March through Georgia had himself begun to look back nostalgically to those happy days before the war, when he had served as the first president of the new Southern military college that was to become Louisiana State University and could bask in the warm glow of southern romantic adulation of military officers. By the final decades of the nineteenth century, the "myth of the lost cause" had gained wholesale credence in the Yankee heart.[14]

As white northerners warmed to the plantation images of the Old South, their opinions of the fabled "old darkey" grew more sympathetic as well. At the turn of the twentieth century, minstrel shows of antebellum origins continued to portray subordinate slaves on large southern plantations. Blacks were represented in rural scenes as tattered but simple and untroubled, often playing the banjo and eating watermelon. They were vulnerable to mistreatment and needed protection from their natural indolence. The plantation legend reflected many whites' sentimental desire that blacks behave as the good-natured, humble creatures that they supposedly had been during slavery days. But minstrel shows also adapted to the events of the post–Civil War era. With characteristic hyperbole, they portrayed hapless black people devastated by the responsibilities foisted upon them with the procurement of freedom. Aged ex-slaves, searching desperately for their former masters, returned home only to find that the plantation had been destroyed during the war. The faithful "darkey" yearned for a return to the carefree, secure, and contented days of slavery.[15]

White New Yorkers projected their longing for the plantation legend onto the servant (and slave) of old who embodied "southern" characteristics. The "old-fashioned, faithful colored servants" are "rapidly passing away," warned the *New York Times* in 1881, as it marked the death of "an aged negress" with a eulogy celebrating her "long and uninterrupted devotion" to a prominent (white) New York family. Mary Jordan Johnson represented an idealized version of black domestic workers from an earlier era. The newspaper dedicated a full column to a detailed account of Mary's special qualities, prominently noting her loyalty and deference to the Talbot family. "In a few years," the article predicted, "there will be none [like Mary] left." Even as white New Yorkers viewed young black newcomers to their city with contempt, the "real genuine southern darkies," remembered as faithful, good-natured, and as fond of their white "families" as of their own, became part of New York's turn-of-the-century lore.[16]

Though slavery had existed in New York City into the first quarter of the nineteenth century, the "passing breed" of ideal servants came to be explicitly associated with the southern slave institution, contributing to the growing nostalgia for the Old South. "All this genuine old time southern atmosphere seems to have disappeared from the colored race as we now know it in New York," a student of New York's social scene noted regretfully at the turn of the century. The tendency to associate the South with the cultivation of "proper" black behavior contributed to the increased popularity of plantation melodies among white northern audiences. Traveling troupes of singers from the Hampton Institute, entertaining Yankees with spirituals and nostalgic visits to antebellum America, found themselves in heightened demand with the passing years. In 1901, the *Southern Workman* reported that a company of Hampton graduates, visiting New York City and Philadelphia at the behest of northern white elites, received tremendous acclaim for their depiction of "certain phases of life among the Negroes of the South." The enthusiastic audience particularly appreciated the singers' musical adaptation of "Christmas on the Old Plantation." A reporter noted that the inclusion of "many folk-lore songs" created "even more enthusiasm than that of last year." Troupes like those from Hampton helped solidify Yankees' nostalgia for the Old South and confirmed the audience's perceptions that southern black people were more docile, tractable, and safe than their urban brethren.[17]

White New Yorkers' empathy for the old Confederacy could be correlated to the growth in the black urban migration. As the number of blacks swelled, Yankees expressed a "prevailing dread of an overwhelming influx from the South" and responded with a hardening of racial lines between white and black. By the turn of the twentieth century, white churches that had previously welcomed black members had begun urging the growing constituency to seek religious ministrations elsewhere. Hotels, restaurants, theaters, and bars refused to serve black patrons. Service organizations such as the YMCA organized segregated branches for the black population rather than permit whites and blacks to share facilities. Hoping to prevent other humiliating defeats like the one that occurred when the boxer Jack Johnson became heavyweight champion in 1908, the New York State Boxing Association prohibited matches between whites and blacks. And though unsuccessful, in 1910 the New York legislature attempted to reinstate a law banning intermarriage.[18]

On the streets, white New Yorkers translated their antipathy into a campaign of harassment against black people in their city. The burgeoning black population led to the increased visibility of black people in the city and a growing incidence of contact between the races. The discomfiture caused by this trend propelled whites to complain to municipal authorities about the behavior of black people and the threats they posed to "respectable" whites. In the language juxtaposing "decent" white "citizens" with "hideous" and "foul" "niggers" and "coons," whites defined civic suitability along racial lines. In an explicit example of this demarcation, a "citizen of New York" (who felt no need to identify his race) begged the police to "do something with those Negroes" on Ninety-ninth Street who made it "almost impossible for a white person to pass through on Sunday or any other day." He asserted his civic right to live unmolested by blacks, having resided and run a business in the neighborhood since long "before the negroes moved in." The problem had reached such grave proportions, the man cautioned the mayor in 1909, that "Respectabel Familys [*sic*] have and are moving" and the street was being overrun by dark invaders. "Does a Citizen have to move on account of such inferior peopel [*sic*]?" he wondered rhetorically. Using similar language, a "taxpayer" (race not specified) and "six (6) other Mothers" bemoaned the changes taking place in their city. "We have lived here a lifetime and are decent citizens," they protested to Mayor Gaynor. "It seems hard that we should give up our homes to make room for negro houses." The letter demanded protection for the "decent white folks that work for their living to support their families" from "the negro street-walkers [who] make night hideous with their shouting at the top of their voices and their foul language."[19] In the fading shadow of the Civil War, white Yankees clearly considered black Americans to belong outside the realm of acceptable compatriots, much less neighbors.

Confident in their own privileged status as citizens, white New Yorkers fully expected municipal authorities to protect them from the black "infestation" that threatened the city. Some expressed genuine surprise when they discovered that the police could not legally halt the encroachment upon their neighborhoods. One white resident lamented the liberties that black people apparently enjoyed. "It seems a shame," he commented, "that a nigger can get such protection [to live in the Tenderloin] against the wishes of respectable white people." Frank Appleman warned ominously in 1904 that the "Negro race . . . are becoming a menace to the city. Something should be done immediately to abate this nuisance."[20] As long as black people had been relatively invisible to white New Yorkers, race relations remained calm. But as blacks' presence became more noticeable, whites rebelled.

Members of New York's wealthiest white community, safely ensconced in their elite residential enclaves, had little direct contact with the growing black population who struggled daily to live and work in the city. Consequently, their perceptions of black people relied heavily on the apocryphal stereotypes increasingly pervading the city. Their comments reveal a certain envy of the libertine lifestyle that they believed black people—who could not or would not conform to the normative expectations of civilized society—enjoyed. "Coontown," an area in contemporary Greenwich Village bounded by Bleeker, Thompson, and Sullivan streets, "had some of the 'attractions' of [1920s Harlem,] that delectable *faubourg*," recalled Henry Collins Brown, marveling at the diverse array of titillating opportunities to be found there. He highlighted the "'Burnt Rag' and the 'Black and Tan' on Bleeker Street, which were a contemporary 'police problem.'" Brown underscored the obvious: "Nobody ever went to these places to hear spirituals." Frank Moss, the renowned New York City attorney who would serve just three years later as the lead counsel on behalf of the aggrieved black population in the case against city police after the 1900 race riot, wove mythical tales about legendary members of the black underworld in his comprehensive, three-volume history of New York City published in 1897. "Minetta Lane," he wrote, "for many years has been the home of a depraved, quarrelsome and criminal colony of negroes." He offered a vivid description. "The time was when the bloodthirsty character of the Minetta negroes was so well established that the street was practically closed to travel. Such men as 'No-Toe Charley,' 'Bloodthirsty,' 'Black Cat,' and 'Jube Tyler,' made national reputations—at least among the colored people—for their dexterity in the sanguinary use of the razor." Moss knew so little about black people's lived experience in New York City that nearly his entire account of the city's black population focused on a brief, stereotypical description of passionate and violent behavior.[21] But the elites' perceptions, though grossly ill informed, influenced wider policies and responses to the growing black presence in New York.

Ironically, although New York's black population became increasingly diverse as it expanded during the final decades of the nineteenth century, whites insisted on viewing their black neighbors monolithically. Charles Morris, minister of the Abyssinian Baptist Church, complained about the unfairness of pigeonholing all black people within the same category. Referring to the arrest of a woman ("branded" a "negress" by the *New York Times* though according to the minister "an octoroon—seven-eighths white"), Morris questioned the media attention devoted to the black community. "There are 40,000 negroes in New York City," he argued, with "large churches, old folks' homes, kindergartens, trained nurses, Young Men's Christian Associations, doctors, lawyers, newspapers, business enterprises, yet all of them together have not awakened one-tenth the interest nor received one-tenth the attention given to one poor guilty woman." This treatment by whites had devastating consequences for black people, forcing all to encounter the overwhelming prejudice resulting from their skin color. "If you could turn black for a few hours," Morris challenged the editor of the *New York Times*, "and meet the frowns and sneers, the high rents and low wages, the barred doors of labor, business, and clerical life; see where and how we are compelled to live . . . how un-Christlike the relentless caste of color that begins at the cradle and pursues us to the grave. . . . I think instead of denouncing a whole race for the shortcomings of the comparatively few who have succumbed to the terrific undertow of discouragement you would wonder that so many have been able to resist it."[22]

Morris's complaints were well founded. The increasingly negative opinions about urban blacks became widely visible in cultural venues that exposed the transformation of white New Yorkers' perceptions. For the first time, whites broadly characterized black people—particularly urban blacks—as dangerous, violent, and menacing. This marked a dramatic shift from earlier views. Though Yankees had long been convinced of black inferiority to whites, they had never formulated a coherent portrait of violent and menacing black people. To the contrary, antebellum images of blacks, popularized by minstrel shows, presented urban blacks as lazy, pretentious buffoons. But by the turn of the twentieth century, both working class and elite white New Yorkers had come to vilify the black people in their midst as a physical and moral threat to the (white) city. This view permitted white northerners to support southern racial policies of terrorism, brutality, and subjugation and to commit their own acts of violence against their black neighbors. The fear of black people provided the common ground on which the white nation became reunited.[23]

The "coon song," created in New York City in the 1890s, emerged as the premier cultural representation of the new urban black stereotype, presenting images of dangerous and libidinous urban black men and women to white audiences nationwide. Black performer Ernest Hogan, known in artistic circles as "The Unbleached American," claimed the dubious honor of giving the coon song its unusual nickname. Hogan composed a syncopated ditty entitled "All Coons Look Alike to Me" in 1890, and it succeeded beyond his wildest dreams. Although the tune actually tells a love story of a "dusky maiden" forced to choose between two handsome young men, the public ignored the lyric and remembered only the title. It soon became a catchphrase, and the latest ragtime numbers came to be known as coon songs. Both black and white composers outdid themselves with tales of the "gastronomical delights of chicken, pork chops, and watermelon, . . . with jamborees of various sorts and the play of razors . . . and with the experiences of red-hot 'mammas' and their never too faithful 'papas.'" James Weldon Johnson described coon songs as crude, raucous, bawdy, and often obscene, and they took the nation by storm.[24]

From the working class immigrant to the blue-blooded elite, white New Yorkers clamored to hear coon songs. The toe-tapping tunes brought an adapted minstrel stereotype onto the Broadway stage, marking the first time that minstrel productions reached "high-brow" audiences. Many among these upper-class New Yorkers had once been at the forefront of the fight for abolition and legislative reforms on behalf of southern blacks. But by the 1890s, they demanded to hear "coon" music alongside their white, working class neighbors, reflecting both a transformation in cultural patterns and the expansion of an audience interested in the consumption of racist material for pleasure. "Men worn out with business cares," wrote a New York social critic, "go [to the minstrel theater on Twenty-third Street] to laugh, and they do laugh most heartily. . . . Families come by the score to laugh at the vagaries of the sable minstrels, and the mirth of the little folks is one of the heartiest and healthiest sounds to be heard in the great city."[25] In a time of dramatic social, economic, and demographic transformation in the city and the country, coon songs helped to homogenize normative values about race, gender, culture, and behavior. Above all, the songs legitimized latent (and explicit) denunciations of the black urban migration, affecting black New Yorkers' everyday struggles to meet the challenges of city life.

Coon songs dealt specifically with urban black men and women, marking an important shift from antebellum minstrel shows that emphasized images of blacks in rural, agricultural settings. Whereas pre–Civil War productions, popular with northern, working class, white audiences, had portrayed black people as "lazy, pretentious, frivolous, improvident, irresponsible, and immature," coon songs suggested something far more brutish. The turn-of-the-century "impudent coon," having left the South in favor of northern city life, succumbed to a life of crime and violence. In the liberal urban environment where blacks lived relatively free of restraint or discipline, the songs suggested, blacks' savage nature became more pronounced and threatened to wreak havoc on the city at large.[26]

With the advent of social Darwinism in the latter decades of the nineteenth century, this image had calamitous consequences. In the industrial era, philosophers began to apply Darwinian evolutionary theories to social experiences, arguing that the trials of urban life exposed the natural hierarchy of the world's races. The relentless competition found in the urban environment allowed the strongest to rise to the top of civilized society while forcing those who could not adapt to slowly weaken and die out. Any effort to tamper with the laws of nature served only to enfeeble humanity and inhibit evolutionary progress by permitting the weak to artificially survive. The city, then, offered a laboratory for racial fitness, and failure to succeed in the urban setting presented prima facie evidence of racial inferiority. Frank Mason North, a white New York missionary, echoed social Darwinist philosophy when he cautioned that "the negro will not be a successful factor in our modern civilization unless he can survive the test of the city." According to the images presented in coon songs, in every way, black people failed. The portrayal of black "coons" confirmed what white southerners had long insisted— that black people belonged in the fields, working under the benevolent and protective care of Christian white masters rather than attempting— and failing—to survive as free men and women.[27]

Coon songs explained blacks' inadequacies within an industrial economy. The lyrics depicted shiftless black men repudiating all legal forms of work and opting instead for underworld endeavors. In "Honey You've Done Me Wrong," a "race-horse dinge" who "throws the con a plenty" steals another man's "gal" even as he cleans out the man's apartment, leaving the "flat dead empty." The song concludes with the injured party vowing to gun down "dat sporty dinge," at once retrieving both the woman and his belongings.[28] Songs like this branded black men as pathological thieves and gamblers, foisting suspicion on any black person with money. Furthermore, the images rationalized white employers' rejection of black workers because "coons" could not—or would not— perform the tasks required of them. Laborers in industrializing America needed to adhere to rigid work routines and maintain discipline and efficiency. Indolent and unreliable black men failed to meet the rigorous standards of industrial workers, thereby legitimating their inability to gain entry into any but the most menial components of the labor force.[29]

Alone among the nation's growing populace, "coons" lacked the aspiration to achieve the "American dream." During the second half of the nineteenth century, the myth of upward mobility—the belief that through hard work and good character anyone might aspire to wealth and success—gained widespread acceptance. Popular novelist Horatio Alger wrote hundreds of stories in the decade following the Civil War that held out the promise of the American dream to white boys. Through the proper combination of "pluck and luck," enterprising rural youth might move to the city and achieve middle class respectability as loyal, efficient, and hard-working employees. Coon songs inverted Alger's success stories, cautioning against the migration of black people to the cities. Immoral, passionate, selfish, and untrustworthy, black "coons" had no place in American industry, or indeed, in civilized society.

With notions of masculinity deeply tied to independence and work, black "coons" also failed miserably as men. According to song lyrics, black husbands disdained their patriarchal role as breadwinners, lacked the "manly" traits of reliability and self-discipline, rejected honest forms of labor, and—most reprehensibly—depended on women's wages for their own material comfort. The song "There Ain't No Use to Keep on Hanging Around," tells the story of a "coal-black coon" who faces rejection by his "saffron-colored wife" because, she complains, "Money home, you never bring." Proving that the relationship had little emotional foundation, the woman warns him that "a score of other darkies are now seeking for my comp'ny." Unwilling to forgo his source of financial security, he issues an ominous warning: "Gal, if I must leave / Your own mother won't recognize you . . . I am goin' to change your face / You'll belong to a different race!"[30] This song accentuates numerous black transgressions, including the unabashed use of violence against women.

Notwithstanding the threatening undertones of those lyrics, in the majority of coon songs the black "gal" controls the love relationship, while a spineless man helplessly follows his "honey" and does her bidding. She constantly threatens to leave her partner; his concern about losing her income produces his simpering and groveling behavior. In this way, black women, like their male counterparts in coon songs, invert gender conventions. Predatory mercenaries on the hunt for a substantial bankroll, female "coons" failed to meet the tests of purity and domesticity essential to the "true woman." "I knowed when you was dressin' fine, but it's been a long time!" announces the female protagonist in "I'se a Picking My Company Now." Tired of her partner's penury, she insists that he "leave ma door and don't come back no more." But a year later, when this "coon" strikes it rich and purchases a "big, white mansion," his wealth lures her back to him. In the greatest violation of true womanhood, she pursues money rather than love. In this song, her cold machinations come to naught; when she tries to curry his favor, he slams the door curtly in her face. The female coon's subversion of traditional gender roles is subtly sinister; even as white audiences ridiculed her absurd conduct, they feared the implications of a woman gaining too much power. By projecting these images onto black people, whites widened the distinctions between the two races and dispelled the possibility that such behavior could prevail among white women.[31]

Through the many lyrics focusing on tension between black men and women, coon songs established a damning assessment of the black family. Notably, "coons" almost never have children, and their marriages are almost universally forged on the basis of greed rather than affection. When "Tildy" abandoned her husband for a "low down nigger," the affronted party expressed little concern about his newfound bachelorhood. "She kin go whar she's a mind to, fer I don't care whar she guine ter," he insisted. Rather, his desolation results from the now-empty apartment. "I squandered all my money," he admits, "On de furniture but Honey / Now I want dem presents back!" When he sees her with her new beau "in a bran new suit of clothes," his despair deepens as he realizes that his own money paid for the man's finery. "She pawned de stove to buy dat ring and dat aint all my woes / Hocked de carpet to buy him shoes, clean shirt for his back." The perception that black relationships held no lasting emotional bonds offered a convenient rationale for the expectation that black women, alone among the city's female population, leave their homes even after marriage and motherhood in order to serve as live-in domestics for white people. No other female cohort in the city, regardless of how destitute, faced remotely similar pressures to abandon their husbands and children in order to find paid employment.[32]

Perhaps most pernicious in an era of exaggerated concern with sexual mores, "coons" were portrayed as sexually promiscuous and thereby a menace to the city's moral integrity. Much of the condemnation fell upon the shoulders of black women, who faced scorn and contempt for embodying everything that a proper lady was not. Coon songs represented black women as libidinous "babies, honeys, and mercenary wenches" who approached relationships with calculation and avarice. They were emotionally fickle and domineering, threatening to emasculate the men in their lives. These images held particular appeal for white men concerned about their own weakening patriarchal control. The "new woman" emerged at the end of the nineteenth century, manifesting her independent spirit, eagerness to hold a career, and new sexuality. By exaggerating black women's repudiation of femininity, white men offered a cautionary against exercising such dangerous levels of liberation.[33]

Black women's ability to wield their sexuality as a weapon with which to dominate men became especially threatening when whites fell victim to their tactics. The suggestion in coon songs that black women had a natural penchant for prostitution emerged during the heyday of reformers' efforts to eliminate the sex trade from the city; the ease with which black women turned to sex for profit suggested that black women were the cause of much of New York's moral decay. It was this prevailing belief about black women's whorish natures that led the white police officer, Robert Thorpe, to automatically charge May Enoch with soliciting, thereby setting in motion the events that culminated in New York City's 1900 race riot.[34]

Most alarming of all, the sinister undertones pervading coon song lyrics suggested that blacks' proclivity for violence could easily threaten innocent white bystanders. The flashing steel straight razor became the dominant symbol of black men in coon songs, fostering an overwhelming image of dangerous and frightening black savages.[35] "Leave Your Razors at the Door," published in the *New York World* in 1900, offered typical imagery of razor-toting, violence-prone black men:

Oh a big burly nigger by de name of Brown
Gave a rag-time reception in des yere town . . .
When they reached the hall an awful sight they saw
'Twas a sign a hangin' on de big front door . . .
Ev'ry coon thought he'd drop dead
For this is what he plainly read

Leave your razors at the door
Don't yer start no rag-time war . . .
If you want some black man's gore
Don't carve him to the core
But take a good sized brick and do the job up quick
Leave your razors at the door
Ev'ry coon in the party anted up his steel
Took his gal up the stairs to have a rag-time reel . . .
[A] fight was started right away
Then down the stairs a lot of coons did swoop . . .
Found that Brown and razors too had flown the coop . . .
There'll be crepe on Brown's front door
He'll never flash this sign no more.[36]

This song, like so many others, implied that in episodes of intraracial violence, no black person escaped blame. The depiction of black men gleefully inflicting harm on one another underscored the perception that innocent victims did not exist within the black population, helping to rationalize police neglect within black neighborhoods. More ominously, vindictive, short-tempered, and belligerent black "coons" had the potential to terrorize the city at large; their penchant and enthusiasm for violence could be easily turned on whites.

While coon songs depicted urban black men and women in exclusively negative terms, the few portraits of southern characters received sympathetic treatment. Elderly "Mammies" with their unbounded capacity for maternal love and understanding rarely appeared without regional connotation. And images of simple southern black folk regretting their misguided choice to move north confirmed whites' denunciation of the urban migration. Miss Jackson, in "I'se Sorry Dat I Left Ma Happy Home," laments her decision to follow a "sporting coon" who promised her wealth and fame in a traveling show. She soon discovers his prevarication when the show proves to be nothing more than a "troupe of old trained monks." She vows,

> If I get home, I'll get my old cook job back;
> Amongst the frying pans and pots is the place for me to act,
> I thought I'd like to tread the boards to see how strange it feels,
> But now I'm awfully satisfied to cook the white folks meals
> Coz, not once since I left my home, No chicken have I had;
> And when a girl is almost starv'd, You is bound to feel dis glad.[37]

This song spoke to one of the principle concerns about black urbanization. Moving to cities, many black women shunned the servant's life in favor of alternatives that might grant them greater autonomy. The prospect of black women's assertions of independence and their refusal to fulfill the demands of elite white households raised the specter of tremendous upheaval in race relations. Relations between blacks and whites remained peaceful only as long as black people accepted their subordinate position in society. Songs like this one confirmed for whites that black people were happier in their servile roles, that their independence had proven a failure, and that they could not adapt effectively to the urban setting. White people delighted at this form of validation for their treatment of blacks and helped make the "coon" stereotype perniciously enduring.

Coon songs remained an integral part of popular culture at least until the 1920s. The nation's newspapers, engaging in circulation wars, began offering coon songs as part of their special features. Printed as sheet music in the Sunday supplements to the *New York American and Journal,* the *New York World,* and William Randolph Hearst's *New York Journal* (along with his newspapers in San Francisco and Chicago), by 1902 coon songs were being seen and possibly played in more than one million homes.[38] The publication of coon songs for a popular audience allowed newspapers to disseminate physical caricatures of black people as well. Ludicrous portrayals of "coons" with animal-like characteristics frequently accompanied the sheet music in Sunday circulars. The birth of America's national consumer culture fostered the spread of these stereotypes as advertisers quickly adopted them for marketing purposes. Between 1880 and 1920, thousands of visual images of blacks were produced for white audiences. They could be found on postcards and trade cards (in the style of contemporary baseball cards), tourist souvenirs, household collectibles, magazine and newspaper advertisements, and countless products for everyday use.[39]

As a harbinger of this trend, renowned lithographers Currier and Ives, remembered today for their romanticized depictions of rural, bucolic America, published a collection of prints during the last two decades of the nineteenth century titled the "Darktown Comics." Boasting nearly two hundred lithographs, this series depicted a fictive community in which blacks, free from all white influence, grappled farcically with the challenges of everyday life. "Characteristic scenes" of "our colored friends" included images of their ludicrous attempts to engage in fashionable activities such as fox hunts and horse racing, only to blunder at every turn. Hapless jockeys fell from scrawny horses (or even mules!), or the ever-present liquor undermined their pretension to sobriety. The comics sold in pairs with the second image providing the punch line. Drawn in the minstrel tradition, the prints portrayed "indescribably funny" black people unsuccessfully attempting to accomplish even the most mundane of tasks.[40]

The lithographs were among the firm's most profitable series and achieved wild popularity among contemporary white audiences. The absurdity of the "coons'" actions and appearance drew humorous praise from observers. In a close billiards match, the "darkey in the picture was shown as intensely absorbed in his own effort to win the game," noted one observer. "His huge eyes almost popped out of their sockets." In the companion picture, "the cue had slipped and hit about a dozen onlookers." The ever-threatening brawl "was in the offing. It was very funny." But the most popular subset of the "Darktown Comics" drew on themes long celebrated by Currier and Ives. "To my mind," recalled a longtime New York socialite, "the series entitled 'The Darktown Fire Brigade' were [sic] the most laughable things I had ever seen. The coons were everlastingly turning the hose accidentally on each other, or a great big wench weighing about five hundred pounds would jump out of a window and be in the act of landing upon the most diminutive member of the brigade. Then other household impedimenta would be descending upon various other gallant fire eaters till the whole scene was side splitting in its effect." These lithographs, a barbed counterpoint to the heroic images of white fire laddies that Currier and Ives produced earlier in the century, reached a wide and appreciative audience. "I used to laugh my head off," wrote one fan. An observer recalled the "gaping crowd" of messenger boys, business men, and "country visitors" in front of 150 Nassau Street in New York City where they could often be found on display and appreciated by a diverse group of spectators.[41]

The glorification of the Old South, the mythology of the contented slave and harmonious master-slave relations, combined with the coon songs and depictions of pathological urban blacks, represented the desire of whites to maintain the subordination of black people in America. Even more insidious, these images justified the subjugation of black people by "proving" their inferiority. Feeling merged into thought, as the combination of the plantation legend and coon song themes of urban degeneracy achieved respectability in northern intellectual circles. Nathanial S. Shaler, renowned Harvard biologist, observed that "coons will get wild when there was [sic] a racket going on, but all they will need is the firm hand of the master race." To the great dismay of worried white people in New York, this was much harder to achieve in northern cities than on southern plantations.[42]

The cultural phenomenon of the late nineteenth century that specifically portrayed urban blacks as physically aggressive and dangerous represented a devastating unification of white racial attitudes. The elite and politically powerful northern whites at last had joined their southern and working class northern brethren in their views of black Americans. The coherence of black stereotypes, embodied in the literature, art, music, and theater of the time, encompassed a range of racist perceptions that laid both the intellectual and emotional foundation for the conviction by northern white people that blacks were biologically inferior, disorderly, emotional rather than rational, and most importantly, unassimilable. The evolution of the attitudes of New York Presbyterian minister and antivice crusader Charles H. Parkhurst was representative of the transformation occurring throughout white New York. Though he had once supported antilynching campaigns, by the early twentieth century Parkhurst expressed a change of heart. "[N]iggers . . . (because that is what they call themselves)," were unqualified for citizenship, he declared, and "they never, never, never will contribute, in any part, toward forming the national type of the Americans of the future." Physical and biological differences proved that blacks could not be integrated into American society. Worse, the racial distinctions suggested something sinister and dangerous. "They grow blacker and

Figures 2, 3, 4, and 5. Popular Currier & Ives "Darktown Comics," often on display on Nassau Street in Manhattan, circa 1880s–90s. Albion College.

blacker every day," Parkhurst avowed. "Their color forms a physical barrier, which even time, the great leveler, cannot sweep away."[43]

Collectively, the coon songs and physical paraphernalia implied that black people might not, in fact, be a part of the human race. From early in the nineteenth century, minstrel images had lampooned blacks' physical features. But the turn-of-the-century portrayals began to imply that blacks had more in common with animals than with humans. Ugly, coarse features, not at all reflecting black people's actual appearance, became standard imagery by the 1890s. Exaggerated lips, bulging eyes, distorted bodies, sloping foreheads (suggesting limited intelligence), all contributed to the association of "coons" with apes. Researchers soon found "proof" for the connection, concluding after supposedly dispassionate studies that blacks were indeed biologically inferior to Anglo-Saxons. In an era of growing violence against black people, the suggestion of their inhumanity helped to justify their exploitation and discredit the urban migration. The city itself, many white New Yorkers asserted, had substantially contributed to blacks' devolution towards savagery.[44]

A cohort of Columbia University social scientists began conducting a series of studies on New York's black population at the turn of the twentieth century. Their findings overwhelmingly depicted black people as incapable of making the transition to an industrialized, urban environment.[45] One sociologist, John Clyde, noted in 1898 that "the Negro may be lazy and in more he is ineficient [sic]." Blacks' presence in the city, he suggested, augmented these traits, breeding "both sloth and inefficiency." As a result, Clyde continued, "the most well-to-do and ambitious" black people eschewed urban life, leaving only "the worst and poorest Negroes" in New York. Clyde's study emphasized that these behaviors emerged specifically in the urban context.[46] The sociological studies seemed to confirm that black people's lack of self-discipline and inability to adapt to an industrial regimen relegated them to a life of destitution. These findings implied that black people could only achieve some measure of success performing the physical, mindless labor of agricultural field work.[47]

Concerns about the influence of the city on blacks (and of blacks on the city), led white New Yorkers to the forefront of a philanthropic effort to aid black people—*southern* black people. In 1868, Samuel Chapman Armstrong began the first markedly successful industrial education program for former slaves with the creation of the Hampton Institute. Like other white northern missionaries in the South, Armstrong brought a conservative racial bias to his reform efforts, emphasizing the value of industrial education to combat the "shiftlessness, extravagance, and immorality" of "dependent" black people. He held a deep conviction that the freedmen and women were "slothful, backward, lascivious, and inferior" and needed skills and training in order to become productive members of an industrial society. The program of industrial education at Hampton University appealed to southern whites eager to maintain a subordinate black population and to northern capitalists desirous of a docile labor supply. Armstrong's call for black people to remain in the South and in the fields, with their "best friends," southern whites, held special attraction for Yankees.[48] William Pickens contemptuously noted the hypocrisy. "The other class which strongly opposes the Negro's coming into town," he wrote scornfully, "is the good white inhabitants of our Northern cities who have so much sympathy for the handicapped Negro that they cannot bear to live near him. They think he is all right at a great distance; and if he will only remain in the South they will strenuously advocate his freedom and equality through their magazines and missionary publications."[49]

Negro industrial education confirmed black people's inferior position in society. It placed the onus on black people to behave morally and adopt middle-class virtues, making them into a tractable labor force. In 1883, the John F. Slater Fund began appropriating thousands of dollars to southern trade schools "that will enable colored youth to make a living, and to become useful citizens." Within four years, the fund was spending more than forty thousand dollars annually to aid up to forty-one schools, and by the 1890s industrial education had eclipsed liberal educational offerings for black students throughout the South. Black students at southern industrial schools received both behavioral and technical instruction under the tutelage of white teachers. They were encouraged to preserve those characteristics that had made black slaves "excel" as agricultural laborers.[50] "Docile, obedient, cheerful, unresentful, of remarkable strength and unusual powers of endurance," the black laborer under proper supervision appeared ideally suited to a life in the fields or performing service tasks for a superior race. But once freed from the restraints imposed by the South's agricultural system, common logic held that he succumbed to "the impulses of his own weakness." Northern cities, therefore, imperiled black people, because in the relative freedom found there, they relinquished their chances for personal betterment. Only southern black men and women, having received careful training from "just and thoughtful" white employers and overseers, maintained the servile traits necessary for their survival at the margins of industrializing America.[51]

Once blacks arrived in the city, they came under increasing scrutiny from reformers concerned with preserving the moral integrity of their city. During the late nineteenth century, numerous organizations undertook the daunting task of cleaning up vice districts, setting their sights on New York City's sex trade. The Committee of Fourteen, the Committee of Fifteen, the Society for the Suppression of Vice, and the Society for the Prevention of Crime all sought to eliminate prostitution from the city. Yet even as many New Yorkers became convinced that sexual evil could be exterminated by effective and vigorous action, they maintained that this applied only to whites. Black women's seemingly natural proclivity for prostitution made them poor candidates for redemption. The popular perception of black women as willing participants in the sex industry emerged at precisely the time in which victims of the "white slave trade" became the targets of sympathy and protection.

Crusaders eager to eliminate red-light districts from the city struggled to understand the reasons why young women would turn to this nefarious occupation. By the 1870s, they increasingly came to view "captives" of the white slave trade as helpless and innocent victims, powerless to make rational choices. Most sensationalist tracts of the period portrayed diseased and despondent "fallen women" whose participation in the sex industry led quickly to their untimely deaths. Conversely, black women were regarded as innately predisposed to a life of prostitution. Their mercenary and libidinous natures made the sex trade particularly appealing to them. In contrast to white prostitutes, black women were viewed as the aggressors, not the victims, in the sex trade. In a direct reversal of gender conventions, white reformers held that morally bankrupt black women enticed unsuspecting white men to behave immorally. Where virginal white girls needed protection from the evil designs of corrupt men, honorable white men needed to be guarded from the provocation of lascivious black women.[52]

Shut out of factory, shop, union, and homework and seeking some escape from the drudgery and hardship of service jobs, some black women fulfilled the widespread stereotypes and turned to prostitution. Statistics on black prostitutes are difficult to assess. Two studies of conditions in New York City in 1915 indicate that the number of black women charged with prostitution far exceeded their proportion to the city's population. George Kneeland, conducting the most detailed investigation of prostitution in New York City available for this period, found that in 1913 American-born black women comprised just over 13 percent of the total number of women incarcerated for soliciting at the Bedford Women's Reformatory. Two years later 19 percent of those arraigned for prostitution in New York's tenements were black. Blacks at this time made up less than 2 percent of the city's overall population. But these numbers, though offering some guidelines on prostitution, need to be treated cautiously. The overwhelming belief in black women's immorality may well have contributed to their disproportionate arrests for this crime. Furthermore, as occurred in the incident sparking New York's

1900 race riot, white police officers regularly presumed black women's engagement in prostitution, causing them to make false arrests on this charge. The presumption of guilt surrounding black women calls into question the statistics about their engagement in prostitution.[53]

Nonetheless, some black women did become prostitutes, creating an underworld of illicit economic activity in the black community. Facing a life of drudgery that proved little better than what they had left behind in the South, some chose prostitution as the best of the meager options available to them. Domestic servants and laundresses earned, on average, between four and six dollars per week for grueling and time-consuming work. Black prostitutes, though almost invariably at the lowest end of the earnings scale for the city's streetwalkers, still could charge fifty cents for their wares. "How can you do it?" demanded a black woman when she encountered a childhood friend who had taken to prostitution. "I would rather kill myself scrubbing!" The other woman remained unmoved. "There is the difference between us," she replied. "I am not willing to die, and I cannot and will not scrub."[54]

Black women set up shop in the tenements, either renting rooms in lodging houses or living in brothels run by a madam. Hattie Ross operated two brothels in the Tenderloin. For each house she paid police officers fifty dollars a month for protection from police raids. After business success there, she moved her house into San Juan Hill, where she boasted a "high-toned" house employing only white women. Within a couple of years she had garnered more than forty-seven thousand dollars in profit from her various brothels. Hattie's case was rare, however. Far more often, whites proffered the capital for prostitution in black neighborhoods, leaving the women with only a percentage of their earnings.[55]

First class prostitution houses often hired black women as the house servants, primarily to distinguish between the types of workers living there. Black servants opened the door to admit customers, served drinks, and tended the rooms. Employment offices regularly sent black women to work in these "disorderly" houses, facilitating their eventual choice to become prostitutes themselves. Still, few black prostitutes could command the kind of wages earned by white women in elite brothels like these that catered to an exclusive and wealthy clientele. In these parlor houses women received between five and ten dollars for their services. Black women, most often working out of the tenements or walking the streets, serviced the poorest classes. Though claiming no monopoly on brutality, many of the men in these classes who were looking to buy sex reportedly treated prostitutes viciously.[56]

Certainly, not all black women came to prostitution willingly. Social reformers, both white and black, warned repeatedly of black women's

unsuspecting entrapment into a life of sin. While reformers undoubtedly exaggerated the extent to which black women had been unwitting
victims of men's "evil designs," some women indeed had come to the
profession involuntarily. Elite women of both races, urgently seeking to
mitigate the forces leading black women into the sex trade, targeted
unscrupulous labor agents who reportedly lured black women out of the
South with promises of riches and an easy life. Upon signing a labor contract, some of these women found themselves committed to working in
a "vice resort." The superintendent of the Bedford Reformatory
informed investigators that the majority of black women incarcerated
there had been brought North by employment agencies that had shep-
herded the women into brothels and other "questionable places."[57]

Regardless of the method by which black women became prostitutes,
white reformers believed that blacks plied their craft with a facility that
demonstrated an underlying willingness to engage in the trade. In addition, black prostitutes' degree of depravity supposedly surpassed that of
white prostitutes. A former police officer, recounting his experiences in
New York after thirty years on the job, remarked that the black population "furnish[es] more examples of lewdness than any other in proportion to their numbers." He targeted black women in particular, noting
that "their native indolence, their emotional natures, all tend to make
the colored woman a free and easy one in her habits." Their migration
from the South had disastrous results; in the urban setting black women
"took to prostitution for a living, preferring naturally that mode of earning a living to entering our kitchens. . . . [Th]ey set themselves up with
an eye to the barbarous, and when they have reached the lowest grade,
are filthy and beastly beyond belief."[58] In contrast, even in their strongest condemnations of white prostitutes, reformers never suggested that
their occupation came as a matter of choice. By the end of the nineteenth century, white "slaves" had become tragic figures in American
consciousness. That sympathy by no means extended to their black sisters.[59]

White reformer Frances Kellor's actions against immorality in New
York City represent the ways in which whites condemned black people
for the city's ills. In a wide-ranging study of unemployment published in
1915, Kellor devoted a long discussion to New York's black population.
Though blacks had limited economic opportunities and experienced
the most serious unemployment problems of any group in the city, in
this section of her book Kellor focused almost exclusively on the growth
of black employment agencies that secured black female "inmates for
disorderly houses." She blamed government malfeasance for the failure
to eliminate these bureaus, emphasizing in her final conclusions that
the presence of black brothels had a deleterious impact on white men

and women who came to the houses as both patrons and workers. Her disgust stemmed not from the consequences of vice in black communities, but from the mingling of white and black people in the sexual arena. Though the purported intent of her study was to mitigate the hardships of unemployment on poor families, Kellor's only discussion about black people—among the most impoverished in the city—aimed at containing illicit activities within their communities.[60]

As with Kellor, most reformers ignored black people unless their actions impinged directly on whites. George Kneeland, in an extensive investigation of prostitution in New York City, made special note of the white children who observed black women soliciting their wares. Two black prostitutes plied their trade in a Harlem tenement adjacent to a public school. Young schoolchildren in the area "noticed the two colored girls and laughed at them, pointing their fingers." Inside the tenements, white children "stood a few feet away listening to what was said." Concern that their tender ears would be abused by listening to "vile remarks and oaths," Kneeland called for the removal of these offenders from the area.[61]

Interracial sex proved to be among the most contentious issues in turn-of-the-century New York City, directing reformers' spotlight onto black participants. The specter of sexual relations between black men and white women raised the particular ire and concern of New York's white population. Outrage at "mixed prostitution" and its demoralizing influence on the "character and reputation of our own homes, and our own children," drove the efforts to clean up vice districts in black neighborhoods and to eliminate "Black and Tan" clubs, which catered to an interracial clientele. George Walling, police captain during the 1880s, described his "horror" upon seeing a Black and Tan. "Vice is not resplendent here," he declared. "It is the resort of the black men as well as white, but the girls are all white!" Exaggerating the physical distinction between whites and blacks, another critic described the "revolting" scene inside a Black and Tan. "White and black mingled indiscriminately in the dance," he explained. "A huge negro swung, with great force, a young white girl." The image of a diminutive, delicate white woman, in the clutches of a black brute was sure to incite antiblack sentiment. Police Commissioner William McAdoo vilified Black and Tans and encouraged fellow officers to maintain "constant surveillance" over the "mixed-race resort," which, besides "running counter to violent racial prejudices and traditions, is an unmitigated and disgusting evil." No other form of vice in the city received such uncompromising wrath.[62]

The image of black men coercing white women into a life of prostitution terrified and outraged white New Yorkers (though similar outrage proved far less vehement when white men consorted with black women).[63] In his sensationalist antiprostitution tract *The Story of Nellie Conroy*, H. B. Gibbud demonized black men for their role in entrapping innocent white women in a life of shame. He described meeting Nellie Conroy on the streets of New York. "She had no hat, no shoes; a dirty calico dress was all the clothing she had on. . . . [h]er hair was matted and tangled, her face bruised and swollen." A "huge negro" who held Conroy "as his slave, and had beaten her because she had not brought him as much money as he wanted," prevented the repentant prostitute from escaping her degradation. Gibbud nearly succeeds in whisking her away from the streets when "we were confronted by the very negro we sought to escape." The kind-hearted white man, saving the hapless white female victim, steps in to protect Conroy, though he admits it "was a fearful moment. . . . I expected every moment to have him strike me. I was no match for him." The reader is relieved to learn that he succeeds in his effort to save Nellie Conroy from her tragic fate as both a fallen woman and prisoner of a black brute. Once freed from her prison, Gibbud assures us, Conroy lived the remainder of her life as "a faithful Christian."[64]

The portrayal of black villains helped to explain white women's involvement in the sex trade. Furthermore, the vision of a physically imposing, irrational, animal-like black man abusing a terrified Christian white woman served to undermine any advances black people had made in the arena of race relations. White people became increasingly concerned about the incidence of interracial sex as New York's black population grew. Images like those portrayed in *Nellie Conroy* cultivated whites' latent fears of the urbanization of black people and fostered racist sentiments. Black people, Gibbud implied, were to blame for the city's ills. Agreeing, white reformers sought to minimize the damage blacks inflicted on their city.

The Committee of Fourteen, established in 1905 to combat vice in New York City, spent years fighting against clubs that catered to white and black patrons. They made countless visits to dozens of night spots, repeatedly condemning places that "disregarded . . . [a]ll laws of common decency and order." Investigators referred to "black and tan joints" as "dance hall[s] of the lowest type," where "niggers" and "coons" mingled with white guests. On the other hand, "nigger dump[s]" that served an exclusively black clientele, generally received no complaints from committee investigators.[65]

Much of the committee's energy centered on closing the most popular and elite clubs open to black people in New York City, including Baron Marshall's Hotel, Wilkins' Café, and Walter Herbert's Criterion Club Café. Marshall's was located in San Juan Hill, the other two in the Tenderloin district. Though legally permitted entry into any restaurant or club in turn-of-the-century New York, in practice black people were often refused service. These clubs provided social centers for blacks interested in a night of dancing and music. But white people's interest in frequenting these clubs as well raised the concerns of reformers eager to keep the races separate. In 1910, a committee investigator reported on finding white women openly consorting with black men in the Marshall Hotel. A group of white women, in the company of black escorts, began a dancing contest to determine who could kick the highest. "They raised their skirts so high, their person could be seen," he wrote with disgust. His conclusion that the hotel served as a "meeting place for white women and their colored lovers" led to his recommendation that it be closed.[66]

Using this and other reports as ammunition, in the following two years the committee made various attempts to repeal the hotel's excise license and effectively shut it down. They sent numerous investigators to find further evidence of wrongdoing. George O'Neill reported that he spent an evening at the establishment, noting to his surprise that "at no time was I solicited while in the premises, although one colored woman did smile at me." He ignored her, and admitted somewhat grumpily, "I wasn't honored further by her fond glances!" He spent some hours at the club, and when he left well after midnight "it was in full blast, coon singers shouting and liquors being served." He insisted that he "entered Marshall's thoroughly without prejudice." Despite the absence of any illegal activity, O'Neill encouraged the committee to shut the Marshall down.[67]

W. E. B. DuBois, founding member of the National Association for the Advancement of Colored People (NAACP), questioned the committee's decision to deny a liquor license to Marshall's, arguing that he consistently found the hotel well run. Furthermore, he stated, Marshall's offered "about the only place where a colored man downtown can be decently accommodated." The general secretary of the committee, representing many of the city's wealthiest and most respected white citizens, responded quickly to DuBois's complaint. "It is a place," he wrote of Marshall's, "which if it could be conducted for either your race or mine, undoubtedly would not be objectionable." The hotel had become the focus for the committee's efforts not because of any legal misconduct, but because "it has that unfortunate mixing of the races which when the individuals are of the ordinary class, always means danger." DuBois admonished the committee that if the objections to Marshall's were grounded in the "races being served together," then it was "seeking to violate the laws of the State of New York, which expressly declare that discrimination between races must not be made in places of public entertainment." The committee, recognizing the NAACP's willingness to bring the case to court, quietly dropped its opposition to the hotel receiving a renewal of its liquor license.[68]

Though the hotel managed to retain its license, reform organizations wielding a great deal of political influence fostered the containment of the black population into increasingly confined city spaces. As the black population in New York grew, the Committee of Fourteen gradually drove black people out of the Tenderloin and San Juan Hill districts. Despite regular contentions of prejudice made by black New Yorkers, the committee worked tirelessly to close "colored resorts." They effectively forced black residents out of tenement houses in downtown and midtown Manhattan. White immigrants quickly filled the empty apartments, pushing black people into Harlem.[69]

In 1915, the Committee celebrated a number of victories in the Tenderloin. It reported that the house at 336 West Thirty-seventh Street, owned by a black proprietor and serving black "customers," had been transferred to white "families" and a tinsmith. That year, the committee found an increase in the number of prostitution cases in Harlem, while a decline was noticed in the old Tenderloin. "This latter decrease," concluded the committee, "as well as the increase in the Harlem district, is probably explained by the movement of the negroes from one section to the other. The block on 37th Street west of Eighth Avenue, in which there were formerly a great many negro prostitutes is now practically cleaned up, there not having been a case from that block during the past year." Between 1911 and 1915, the committee successfully removed black residents from at least nine houses in lower Manhattan and Brooklyn. An observer noted delightedly that much of the area notorious for "vicious negroes" had been "so far as it is possible or can be reasonably expected, purged of the vicious classes." The "resorts," he continued, had moved uptown (presumably to Harlem), "and the colored element is under control." The rigorous efforts of the Committee of Fourteen had effectively helped to force black people into Harlem. The remainder of Manhattan became relatively free of a black presence after 1915.[70]

Furthermore, reformers shaped public response both to vice and to black people. By treating black people as habitual degenerates, reformers allowed other white New Yorkers to discount blacks as morally irredeemable and therefore unworthy of sympathy or concern. Worse, black people faced condemnation as the root of the city's moral decline. The black "invasion" of New York appeared to coincide with the rise in crime and vice within the city. At the end of the twentieth century's first decade, a young white New Yorker, when asked about the North's participation in the Civil War, affirmed, "If we had it all to do over again there wouldn't be any war." His views summed up the changes in northern whites' racial perceptions. In the aftermath of the Civil War, white north-

336 WEST 37TH STREET.

This building was a notorious resort. Its proprietor and customers were negroes. It is now occupied by families and a tinsmith.

Figure 6. A "redeemed" house. Committee of Fourteen, *Annual Report 1915* (New York, 1916).

erners had demonstrated at least a limited willingness to protect black people's civil rights. Within forty years, that commitment had been thoroughly retrenched. Black people came to be viewed as scourges of urban society; when allowed to leave the controls and restraints of the South they succumbed to their "natural" tendencies for violence, immorality, and indolence. The incipient myth of dangerous urban black men and women gave northern whites the tools with which to control black people and exclude them from the opportunities available to other newcomers in the city.[71]

The deterioration of race relations and the increased presumption of black immorality led some of New York's black elite to denounce the migration and dissociate themselves from the newcomers. "Oh, is there no way to keep these people from rushing away from the small villages and country districts of the South up to the cities, where they cannot battle with the terrible force of a strange and unusual environment?" lamented Paul Laurence Dunbar in his novel about the migration experience, *Sport of the Gods*. "Is there no way to prove to them that woolen-shirted, brown-jeaned simplicity is infinitely better than broad-clothed degradation?"[72]

Black people drew dividing lines not only between longtime New York residents and newcomers but also between "respectable colored citizens" and "disgraces to the colored race." Susceptible to being judged monolithically regardless of actual behavior, blacks openly maligned those who might, they suggested, embody the stereotypes. "We are not to be judged by the street loungers and drunkards of our race," a black New Yorker insisted in 1895. Her denunciation of "the lowest grades . . . of blacks" whom "no respectable negro would want to associate with" allowed her to assert common cause with white people also disparaging the black "riff-raff." Other black elites followed suit. "Respectability is too frequently victimized by men and women who compose the 'flashy,' 'impudent' element of our people," warned Dr. William Howard Griffiths, the minister at the Tenderloin's Bethel African Methodist Church. "This element, unfortunately, is a large one," Griffiths continued, "and does us more solid injury than any other agency of evil. It is 'loud' to dress and 'loud' in speech. On the cars, in the streets, or in the drawing-room, their vulgarity mortifies quiet colored people and scandalizes the race."[73]

Worse still, this behavior directly undermined any attempt to improve conditions for blacks in the city. "There has been of late a remarkable increase of crimes against person and property by Afro-Americans," acknowledged the *New York Age* in 1907. The editorial implied that much of this transformation resulted from "the large increase in the Afro-American population, among which there necessarily would be some bad characters[.]" While the paper laid some blame at the feet of white employers unwilling to hire black workers, it saved the harshest rebuke for the migrants "who come into the greater New York [area] with the hope to better their condition only to find that they have jumped out of the frying pan into the fire." The behavior upon arrival "is to be deplored," the *Age* avowed, "as sentiment toward the entire Afro-American population is being affected for the worse."[74]

But black elites' efforts to distinguish themselves from the unwelcome masses failed. Whites had no interest in acknowledging the presence of different groups of black people. When Robert S. Brown and the "Respectable Colored People" in his building complained about the constant noise there, they were "told to go to H——, and called black b——s, or, black Sons of B——."[75] Consequently, a number of members of the black elite joined white reformers in denouncing blacks' weak moral resolve, hoping to at once create common cause with whites and to mitigate the overwhelmingly negative perceptions of black behavior. Despite pressing economic concerns for blacks in late nineteenth-century New York, members of the elite who formed self-help organizations emphasized the need to diminish the incidence of black female delinquency. The "criminal class," argued *Crisis* magazine in 1912, "who are a millstone around the necks of self-respecting citizens, should be kept by force off our streets and thoroughfares." By spearheading those efforts, blacks could demonstrate to critical whites that the two races shared a common set of values. As whites' perception of blacks deteriorated at the end of the nineteenth century, New York's black elite began to develop organizations to undertake the task of uplifting the degenerate of the race.[76]

As early as 1890, a number of New York's most influential black residents, among them the newspaper editor T. Thomas Fortune and the Reverend Alexander Walters, called for the "organizing of societies, or the establishment of homes reclaiming fallen women." This goal was realized in 1897 when Victoria E. Matthews opened the White Rose Mission on East 97th Street. The following year, she incorporated the organization as the White Rose Industrial Association, the first of a number of organizations formed specifically to deal with the particular needs confronting black women in New York City. Like later organizations, White Rose recognized the connection between the migration experience, working conditions, and the home lives of the young women coming to New York. Consequently, it offered travelers' aid, temporary lodgings to black women arriving in the city with no place to stay, and a job placement service with the organizing philosophy of training young black women in the "principles of practical self-help and right living."[77]

Through her work, Matthews also hoped to mitigate the widespread belief in black female immorality caused by the visibility of "these women haunting these certain portions of the city in such an unfailing stream." She complained that whites "take it for granted that all black people—all Afro-Americans—are naturally low." By diminishing the presence of black prostitutes in the city and by simultaneously demonstrating that a cadre of black women held white middle-class values, Matthews intended to demonstrate "that there is another class than is represented by the depraved class commonly met with on the streets and in certain localities." The mission tempered the "dangerous" influences of the tenements by refusing to secure jobs for women that did not permit workers to lodge at the employers' residence. In its first ten years of existence, the home provided temporary room and board to more than five thousand women and met countless boats at Norfolk, Virginia, and New York City's docks in order to steer single women to reputable homes and employment.[78]

The National League for the Protection of Colored Women (NLPCW) also sought to "start the [female] traveler aright" in New York City. In tones evocative of the criticisms made by whites, members of the NLPCW cautioned that the urban environment placed naïve black women at particular risk. "Degrading influences" such as dance halls, lodging houses, and the streets themselves threatened the moral fiber of the "untrained Southern woman" and indicated a need to persuade black women not to come to the city. When they did arrive, the organization provided workers at the docks, an Amusement Club for girls that offered lectures and wholesome amusements, and addresses of reputable homes.[79]

Despite black elites' efforts to demonstrate similar values to those of white elites, race relations in the city continued to worsen. By the turn of the twentieth century, most white New Yorkers refused to acknowledge any distinction among their black neighbors, preferring to denounce the group as a homogeneous mass of depravity. James Weldon Johnson assessed the transformation: "[I]n the fight waged on the Negro battle front," he asserted, the South "had conquered the North; and all through the old free states there was a tendency to concede that the grand experiment [of freedom] was a failure." Warming to this theme, the New York press, reporting on the 1900 race riot, stressed that the man who had killed a white police officer had only recently arrived from the South.[80] This only confirmed white New Yorkers' worst fears of a lawless, uncontrollable, and dangerous urban black population invading and threatening the well-being of their beloved city. The only solution, they found, lay in diminishing the injurious impact of the black menace by keeping whites and blacks separate. "[D]o put those [coons] where they belong for the safety of my children," pleaded a "Mother"

to the mayor in near panic.[81] An early twentieth-century coon song,
"Stay in Your Own Back Yard," captured this same sentiment:

> Now honey, yo' stay in yo' own back yard,
> Doan min' what dem white chiles do;
> What show yo' suppose dey's a gwine to gib
> A black little coon like yo'?
> So stay on dis side of de high boahd fence,
> An honey, doan cry so hard;
> Go out an' a play, jes' as much as yo' please,
> But stay in yo' own back yard.[82]

If blacks refused to abide by this vision of a separate society, then white
New Yorkers would impose it by force.

Chapter 3

To Check the Menacing Black Hordes

Of all forms of prejudice evident in New York City at the turn of the twentieth century, few proved more enduring than the color line imposed on the housing market. Until real estate agent Philip Payton opened Harlem to black residents, most black people living in New York City faced near-squalor living conditions. "Hedged in by prejudice," wrote the *New York Times* in 1889, blacks occupied the "meanest tenement districts" that had "outgrown their availability for any other class" of tenants.[1] Until the early twentieth century, black people lived within integrated Manhattan neighborhoods. With the passing of each decade, black New Yorkers of all classes became progressively more segregated from whites and concentrated into fewer neighborhoods as the city's police officers, white reformers and landlords, and white ethnic inhabitants slowly compelled blacks to seek refuge from constant harassment. To black people's dismay, once Harlem had been transformed into a virtually all-black district, white people permitted (and encouraged) vice to follow and thrive there, though jobs did not. Blacks found themselves isolated from the rest of the city, distant from prospective workplaces, and virtually forgotten by municipal authorities or urban reformers.

Throughout the nineteenth century, as they searched for better, more affordable housing, the black population of New York inexorably pushed uptown from the lowest tip of Manhattan and eventually into Harlem. For a time, a variety of residential options remained open to black people. In 1889, the Reverend Hutchens C. Bishop, rector of St. Philip's Protestant Episcopal Church, tried to rent a home in a quiet residential neighborhood. When the landlord discovered that the light-skinned pastor was in fact black, he refused to lease the building to the clergyman. To his profound relief, Bishop finally convinced the landlord that he and his wife would be exemplary tenants. "If I had not succeeded thus I would have been compelled to go into a noisy tenement house among a class of people that I do not care to be particularly identified with," Bishop commented.[2] But Bishop's victory in 1889 proved increasingly difficult to replicate with the passing years, as white New Yorkers became more strident in their refusal to live in proximity with black people. They pressured landlords to rent exclusively to white tenants, leaving only the dregs of the housing market available to the growing black population. "Before a neighborhood is opened up for colored settlement in New-York," explained Reverend H. A. Monroe, the pastor of St. Mark's Methodist Episcopal Church, "it must have been made untenantable for white people." His own housing situation on West 47th Street illustrated the difficulty. All of the buildings on Monroe's block had been "disorderly houses" until a series of police raids finally ousted the prostitutes. The proprietor advertised the buildings for nine hundred dollars apiece, but "respectable white people would not live in them, and the landlord refused to rent them to colored occupants." Eventually, the persistent vacancies convinced the owner to "throw open" the apartments to the black population, though he first raised the rent to one thousand dollars. Restricted in their options, black residents quickly moved into the buildings, though the landlord compelled the new tenants to sign waivers against any potential damages. "The annoyances to which we were subjected for months after we moved in were something terrible," complained the pastor, "and yet it is to such houses and such neighborhoods that we are limited in our choice of homes."[3]

During midcentury, the black population was centered in a "red hot" portion of Greenwich Village that included the "Minettas" (Minetta Lane, Minetta Street, and Minetta Place), along with Thompson and Sullivan streets. The police referred to this neighborhood as "Coontown," though more sympathetic observers dubbed it "Little Africa." Black people had lived there since the seventeenth century, when freed slaves created a small agricultural community in this northern outpost of the Manhattan settlement. By the second half of the nineteenth century, it had developed a reputation as an area rife with "immoral resorts . . . vicious negroes, and resorts for sporting men and politicians." The squalor there made it a haven only for the most impoverished in the city. According to a report on sanitary conditions, the "filth . . . and the effluvia arising there from are extremely offensive. The privies are generally full nearly to overflowing," and refuse accumulated in empty yards. Some of the alleys had no sewers.[4] The journalist Jacob Riis described the tenement houses in "Little Africa" as "not even fit for pigs." He reproached the building owners for exploiting the racial prejudice that limited black tenants to few housing options, permitting price gauging by landlords who reaped exorbitant profits while "allowing [the tenements] to stand and rot."[5]

Dank, drafty, or unventilated apartments that provided no fresh air or faced garbage-laden alleys not only created cheerless living quarters but also promoted health problems. The Dinzey family, immigrants from St.

Christopher, quickly encountered the worst that New York's deplorable conditions could throw at them. Although they arrived in the city in fine health, nearly all of the members of the family soon contracted recurrent illnesses undoubtedly caused or exacerbated by their unsanitary basement apartment. After months in those rooms, Mr. Dinzey became too sick to work, forcing the family to apply for relief. The Charity Organization Society (COS) helped them secure a better apartment, but Mr. Dinzey never fully recovered. Within a year, Mary Dinzey became a widow.[6]

Despite the dilapidation of Greenwich Village's housing, the growing immigrant population put pressure on the housing market, and an "Italian incursion" helped to oust black residents. One white observer, explaining the transformation of the neighborhood, implied that interracial violence had precipitated the change. "[T]he razor is not so hot against the stiletto," he noted tersely. With the growth of the ethnic white population, reformers directed greater attention to the district, eventually driving most of the Village's black residents out of the area. By the end of the century, the more northern Tenderloin and San Juan Hill neighborhoods claimed the densest concentrations of black residents in the city.[7]

The few stalwart black holdouts in lower Manhattan lived in a racially heterogeneous world. On Minetta Lane in 1900, for example, six out of eight buildings on the north side of the street housed both black and white (mostly Italian) tenants. A number of interracial couples were listed in the federal census. However, black Village residents faced a growing employment crisis. By the turn of the century, all but one elite white family in the district had abandoned the longtime practice of hiring black domestic workers in favor of the trendy choice of ethnic servants. Compounding the economic pressures, blacks now endured outright antipathy from their neighbors and from police "protectors." In 1913, Rebecca Musgrave wrote to Mayor Gaynor, protesting repeated "annoyance by police." She claimed that police harassment had forced her to move from her apartment on Minetta Street. Three weeks later, police again tried to run her out of the neighborhood. She begged the mayor to "stop this that i have got to be drove arround like a dog and cant live no place . . . im almost Crazy." Inspector John Daly, reviewing the accusation, discovered that Musgrave had a history of arrests for prostitution and soliciting. Daly denounced the woman and her daughter who lived with her. "Both are strong, healthy and well able to work," he inveighed, "but choose to make their living by prostitution." Daly commended the officers' actions even as he reinforced the belief that black women preferred prostitution to "honest" labor.[8] Many, including Musgrave, capitulated to the pressure exerted by those who hoped to rid the area of black people and abandoned the Village. The Tenderloin became an alternative destination in the late nineteenth century, as New York's black residents sought a more congenial environment. However, the Tenderloin offered little improvement over the conditions that black people had hoped to leave behind.

In 1908, the Reverend Adam Clayton Powell moved to New York City to accept a commission as the new pastor of the Abyssinian Baptist Church, located in the Tenderloin at Fortieth Street between Seventh and Eighth Avenues. Powell settled in across from the church and prepared to become a member of the community. To his surprise, he found himself unexpectedly immersed in an underworld of "pimps, prostitutes, keepers of dives and gambling dens." Distressed by the depravity he witnessed in the district and shocked by the defiance of the "harlots" who "would stand across the street on Sunday evenings in unbuttoned Mother Hubbards soliciting men as they left our service," Powell began a campaign of "gospel bombardments" directed at the sinners. When preaching failed to elicit the changes that he sought, Powell organized a neighborhood reform movement to eliminate the rampant vice that existed openly on the streets. With a group of like-minded citizens, he called first on the city's vice squad, then the police commissioner, and finally Mayor Gaynor himself for assistance. The mayor, according to Powell, "practically told us to go to hell." During the terse exchange between the city's highest official and the group of neighborhood representatives, Powell received his first lesson on the relationship between New York City's black population and its municipal government. Seasoned black New Yorkers already knew what Powell was just discovering: neither the city's police officers nor city authorities saw fit to protect black people. Much to the contrary, many members of the city's police force actively perpetrated the vice that proliferated in areas of dense black concentration such as the Tenderloin. Eventually, the Abyssinian Baptist Church surrendered to the harassment. After years of encouragement from its pastor, in 1923 the church relocated to Harlem, following a congregation that had long since fled.[9]

As in Greenwich Village, black people in the Tenderloin lived in tenements interspersed with immigrants, mostly Italian and Irish. But savvy landlords who recognized that black people enjoyed only limited housing options charged black tenants higher rents than their white counterparts paid. In 1899, a reporter from the *New York Tribune* described a typically dilapidated Tenderloin building that housed black tenants: "It is situated in the rear of the lot, and is entered from an alleyway. Its only safety, from a sanitary point of view, is in the ventilation which it obtains from the court-yard running through the centre and the open space running all around. The western wall is practically barricaded from the light, with the exception of small windows sufficient to give air to the sleeping rooms. The front rooms in the courts are almost pitch dark." The neighborhood also became notorious as one of the most vice-ridden in the city. "I am a colored man," wrote N. R. Ashley to Mayor Hugh Grant that same year, "and being a colored man I am compel to stay . . . and to live where ever I can get a place." He implored the mayor to improve the "disgraceful" conditions in the Tenderloin, but to no avail.[10]

As racial tolerance deteriorated in the late nineteenth century, white residents began a campaign of harassment that gradually led to blacks' flight from this area as well. Journalist Jacob Riis recounted black settlers' attempts to "make a stand against the intruders" as "hostile camps" battled each other for residential preeminence. "Vain hope!" Riis declared. "Perpetual eviction is the [Negro's] destiny." Rosanna Weston experienced some of the tough times. "They used to go out . . . with bats and things," she recalled. "The Irish would call 'em bad names, niggers and everything like that, and they'd be out there fightin'." The worst violence occurred during the 1900 riot, but smaller skirmishes erupted with regularity. In 1911, New York City mayor William Gaynor received an anonymous letter complaining that black people had suffered repeated attacks by white men in the Tenderloin district. Despite assurances made to the contrary, the police department never investigated the complaint. Similarly, when a pair of white men assaulted a young black girl, police officers and city authorities refused to take any action. Encouraged by police complicity, whites continued their aggression until blacks finally abandoned the Tenderloin to the growing immigrant population.[11]

In the midtown San Juan Hill district, black people found their world less racially diverse than it had been in the Village or the Tenderloin. Though immigrants and blacks lived in close proximity on adjacent blocks, individual tenement buildings and even entire streets tended to be racially homogeneous. San Juan Hill became one of the most congested residential areas in the city as southern and Caribbean migrants crowded into its dilapidated apartments. By 1910, the bulk of Manhattan's black population, which had reached more than sixty thousand, had settled in this region. And the tension between blacks and their white immigrant neighbors made this among the most contested neighborhoods as well. According to New York lore, San Juan Hill received its moniker not to honor the famous battle of the Spanish-American War but to satirize the constant clashes that erupted there between black and white residents.[12]

Housing conditions in San Juan Hill proved no better than they had been in the Tenderloin. Mary White Ovington characterized the massively overcrowded tenements as "human hives, honeycombed with little rooms thick with human beings." A single block in the district accommodated upward of five thousand people. The tiny apartments often opened into air shafts or narrow courtyards that admitted no fresh breezes, only the smell of the garbage below. Many rooms had no windows at all.[13] The congestion also created a serious health risk to an already vulnerable population and compounded residents' fear of strangers. Disease ravaged all of the impoverished communities of New York City's overcrowded tenements. But malnutrition and blacks' inability to rent anything but the worst tenements in the city exacerbated the impact of their poverty. Blacks could little afford the cost of medications, prolonging illness and increasing the possibility of contagion. Though infectious diseases impacted whites and blacks alike, they struck blacks with disproportionate frequency. Jessie Sleet, visiting nurse for the COS, found in 1900 that the mortality rates from a wide range of diseases were far higher among blacks than whites. Nationwide statistics demonstrated that six times as many blacks as whites died from diphtheria and croup, two times as many from whooping cough, typhoid fever, heart disease, pneumonia, and dysentery, and nearly three times as many from consumption.[14]

Inside New York City's tenements, tuberculosis was the most common and dreaded of the contagious diseases threatening the city's residents. Municipal officials and private organizations sought to eradicate the scourge, though most ignored its disproportionate impact on the city's black residents. An often-fatal illness, the ironically dubbed "White Plague" killed twice as many of the city's black residents. Responding at last to blacks' alarming susceptibility to tuberculosis, in 1905 a group of white and black reformers organized the Sub-Committee on the Prevention of Tuberculosis among Negroes. And the *New York Age*, the city's weekly black newspaper, made numerous efforts to educate its readers about the contraction, spread, and treatment of the disease. But educational efforts met with little success, while overcrowding exposed even the most mindful to the contagion.[15]

Infectious diseases hit babies the hardest. A mother's absence, a frequent occurrence when women worked as domestics, meant that infants could not breastfeed, contributing to problems of malnutrition in the black population and making babies more vulnerable to disease. Though white and black reformers strove to supply modified milk to black infants, the quantity never fulfilled the extensive need and the quality never matched mother's milk, explaining in part the high black infant mortality rate in New York City.[16] In 1908 an investigator reported that the black infant mortality rate in New York approached three hundred to every thousand births, with an average of two black babies out of seven dying under one year of age. The corresponding rate for white babies was less than half that for blacks: 127.7 per thousand births. Naomi Washington's parents often told the story of her birth while she was growing up. "My father said I was so small the midwife put me in the palm of her hand," Naomi remembered. "My mother said when she saw this little rat, she turned her head to the wall and asked God to let me live. She promised God that if I would live, she would raise me for him." Naomi survived, but seven of her eleven siblings did not. In fact, through the first decade of the twentieth century, the growth of New York City's black population resulted exclusively from migration. More black people in the city were dying than being born. Conditions failed to improve despite the concerted efforts of organizations struggling to confront the problem. In 1915, New York's Department of Health reported a black mortality rate of 26.31, almost exactly double that of whites.[17]

Experiencing chronic illness in dank, fetid apartments, families understandably moved in search of better lodgings as often as economic circumstances permitted. But precarious finances forced many to make the reluctant return to cheaper, less salubrious apartments. Seeking to forestall the recurrent cycles of poverty, many black New Yorkers instead resorted to lodging arrangements. Under the best circumstances, families subleased to a tenant who not only helped them pay the rent but could also replicate kin or community ties. When the Johnsons found themselves unable to afford their monthly rent of eleven dollars on Sixty-ninth Street, they invited a West Indian friend, Theodore Lytton, to room with them. His monthly contribution of five dollars became essential to the family's solvency and permitted them to remain in their residence for nearly half of 1901. But the choice to retain a lodger in order to rent a pleasant, better-quality apartment with four "very nice light airy rooms on the top floor" came at the expense of family privacy. Lytton, though a friend from home, nevertheless put a strain on the family. When he secured a live-in service position that obligated him to relinquish his room, the Johnsons resolved not to seek another lodger. Their decision forced the family to find less expensive rooms in the heart of San Juan Hill's crowded neighborhood.[18]

Although lodging offered a degree of escape from economic desperation, by opening their homes to people with whom they had no intimate ties, black people exposed themselves to myriad dangers. Lodgers sometimes caused serious trouble for their landlords; court records reveal numerous cases of theft and rape committed by boarders. When she made the decision to accept a lodger into her home, little could Frances Fischer imagine the havoc he would soon wreak on her life. Needing some help in making ends meet, she agreed to rent the man a bed for a weekly sum of $1.50, though he often failed to pay on time. Her apartment in an old tenement building—a so-called railroad flat—had no hallways, forcing her lodger to walk through the front three rooms, including her daughter's, in order to reach his room at the back. He often returned home after midnight, waking her up as he went to his bed, and he frequently disturbed her on Sunday mornings when she was trying to catch up on some sleep. His disruptions finally made the situation intolerable for Frances, and she decided to end the arrangement. "I stayed up to see if I couldent catch him" when he came home one night, she explained, "and finely did and when I asked him for some money why he cursed me and told me that he would get even." Days later, two policemen arrived at her door claiming that they had received a tip about drug sales from her apartment. Upon conducting a search, the officers found cocaine in the residence and arrested Fischer. "Now Judge," she insisted, "do you think that man could have done that nasty trick?" Frances spent more than six months in jail for a crime that she adamantly maintained had been fabricated by her lodger.[19] Josephine Brown claimed that her lodger, Charles Albright, "works on my nerves." When Albright refused Brown's request to terminate the living arrangement, Brown's husband forcibly removed Albright from the premises. Resentful about the eviction, Charles returned later that day with a pistol and shot his former landlord.[20]

The volatility of the lodging relationship also made it an unreliable solution to black New Yorkers' housing and financial crises. Mary Downes spent years in New York struggling to make ends meet. After her husband's death in 1889, she pulled two of her children out of school in order to find jobs while she washed laundry. Her failing health and insufficient income forced the woman to accept two lodgers into her home. The family managed to eke out a living when both of the lodgers abruptly left in favor of other arrangements. The loss of this income pushed the family into destitution. On the brink of eviction—the rent had been paid every month with the lodgers' contributions—Mary was obligated to appeal to the COS for emergency relief. They offered temporary support, but without lodgers, Mary and her family continued to hover on the brink of penury.[21]

Compounding the problems of unsanitary and overcrowded housing, the residential restrictions that pushed the majority of the black population into San Juan Hill by the turn of the twentieth century also forced all classes of black people to cram together in uncomfortably close proximity. The relatively well-to-do intermingled with the destitute; the most morally conservative lived adjacent to the depraved. The "virtuous and vicious," explained white journalist J. Gilmer Speed in 1900, live so near to one another that they "elbow each other." The "respectable elements" of the race struggled to highlight their elite status. "It has long been a problem," the *New York Age* complained in 1908, "to separate the hoodlum element from the respectable class of colored people." One "respectable colored woman" categorically demanded that "[e]very man who cannot give a good record of himself or as to where he works . . . be sent to jail, or [be given] some such punishment."[22] Doctors, artists, teachers, elevator operators, prostitutes, preachers, domestic servants, thieves, and the unemployed all found themselves sharing neighborhood space, with no group able to escape the influences of the others.

As the overcrowding worsened, police neglect caused a further decline in neighborhood conditions. San Juan Hill quickly evolved into one of the most violent and dangerous regions of Manhattan. The New York Central Railroad's open tracks, "which maimed black and white impartially," offered neutral ground between blacks in San Juan Hill and "white enemies" to the west. Anna Murphy, a black woman, described the uneasy game played out on the Hill's streets. "The Irish kids wouldn't let the black kids cross St. Nicholas to go into the park and sleigh-ride," Murphy recalled. The conflicts became part of the neighborhood culture. "One Saturday the Irish would run, and the next Saturday the blacks would run across that street. It was almost a ritual." This rite had dangerous consequences. An anonymous informant wrote to Mayor Mitchell in 1914, complaining about "a bunch of white boys" in the area who demanded money from any black passerby. Refusal to proffer a dime resulted in physical retribution; one woman had been struck over the head with a milk bottle. These episodes occurred only four blocks from the station house, and the writer admonished the mayor that failure to halt the attacks would cause "blood shed up here because the people is getting very tired of it." Rosanna Weston's parents warned her away from the Irish side of the street. "That was forbidden territory. You weren't supposed to go over there. They used to come over on this side and they would fight."[23]

Police officers' refusal to protect black people from violence left blacks constantly vulnerable to assault, especially from the ethnic white enclaves living in the vicinity and vying for opportunities to improve their own status. Guido "Bullets" Bressan described how the Italians living in midtown Manhattan would "fight the niggers down on San Juan Hill." He acknowledged that whites always initiated the aggression, entering black neighborhoods with the intention of starting a fight and expecting few official repercussions. "We were up on 69th or 68th," Bressan explained, "then we come down, beat 'em, throw rocks, plenty of that. They never come up there, we usually went down there." Bressan admitted that his buddies often crafted a story that would vindicate

Figure 7. A black child near San Juan Hill, 1895. Museum of the City of New York, The Byron Collection, 93.1.1.17115.

the violence. "One guy might say that some colored guy hit this guy, and we'd all go down, and they'd be on the corners here. We'd throw rocks, cans, everything. We didn't care if they were ready or not, if they were black, we'd go after 'em." Despite the public attacks, policemen never interfered.[24]

Not content to simply turn a blind eye on the physical assaults against the city's black residents, New York's policemen often initiated or aggravated the violence. In each racial conflict that occurred in New York City in the early years of the twentieth century, black people accused the city's police officers of inciting or abetting the attacks. During a heat wave in July 1905, a race war exploded in the San Juan Hill district that was reminiscent of the Tenderloin's riot of five years earlier. Tensions had been brewing since the previous year, when black witnesses testified that a white police officer had killed a black man. The following summer, policemen in the district conspired to "crack some of the negroes' heads." Fighting finally broke out after a scuffle on the street between a white man and a black man. Officers quickly joined the fracas, clubbing any black person they could find. In the aftermath, charges of police brutality reached the highest levels of city government, and countless black men and women testified to their mistreatment at the hands of the city's officers. Arthur Moody, shot by police after receiving a beating at their hands, later died. Another officer who "indulged in promiscuous shooting" struck a black carpenter with one of his bullets and succeeded in breaking the man's leg. And dozens of black men arrested and sent to station houses experienced vicious beatings and were forced to "run the gauntlet" in the squad room with the lights turned out. According to witnesses, each man was led "like an ox to the slaughter pen" and shoved into a long corridor where police officers with billy clubs "proceeded to beat them upon the head and bodies until they were nearly dead."[25]

Police Commissioner William McAdoo quickly responded to the outbreak by ordering the black population to disarm. He issued no corresponding order to whites in the neighborhood. Black people in the city vociferously clamored for an investigation; instead Commissioner McAdoo left for his vacation home, admonishing blacks to "deposit their revolvers, blackjacks, and razors" with the police. Although McAdoo approved the transfer of Police Captain Cooney from the San Juan Hill precinct, he assured "the lawless colored element of the Twenty-Sixth Precinct" that they "must not construe my act as any change of policy on my part with regard to dealing with them." The new captain received direct instructions from the commissioner to "fearlessly" enforce the law and to "suppress promptly any disorder in that section." Once again, the city's police protectors treated black people as the aggressors rather than the victims of violence. Even the *New York Times*, which had actively covered the 1900 riot, buried its few articles on the 1905 disturbance deep within the paper. White New Yorkers were becoming desensitized to and more accepting of violence against black people.[26]

Lower and midtown Manhattan became emblematic of the failures of coexistence in a racially intolerant climate. Frustrated black New Yorkers perpetually sought residential alternatives. After real estate agent Philip Payton founded the Afro-American Realty Company in 1904 specializing in acquiring rental property for black tenants in Harlem, this once off-limits neighborhood became an exciting alternative to San Juan Hill. The elite outpost on the northern tip of Manhattan held the prospect of spacious, modern, clean, and even elegant living quarters. It also provided an escape for the middle class, who hoped to distance themselves from the crime and vice rampant in other black neighborhoods. The broad, tree-lined, and well maintained boulevards of Harlem offered a dramatic improvement over the congestion of San Juan Hill or the squalor of the Tenderloin. Well-to-do blacks fled uptown trying to escape both the deplorable condition of San Juan Hill's tenements and the law-lessness in their midst.

But many of the same conditions that black people hoped to leave behind were quickly transplanted into the formerly upscale neighbor-hood as more and more blacks found their way into Harlem. Many of the landlords who made the decision to lease to black people did so with the full knowledge that their new tenants had few housing options. Con-sequently, they raised prices and neglected their buildings, replicating the deplorable conditions found elsewhere. The New York Colored Mis-sion reported in 1912 that its investigators and social workers regularly discovered that black people lived in "filthy and revolting" apartments. The organization sharply criticized landlords for their neglect of tene-ment buildings, arguing that the "adverse influences of untidy, ill venti-lated, uncomfortable homes" undermined the health and general well-being of its constituents.[27]

Residential overcrowding rapidly reoccurred as black families were once again forced to accept lodgers in order to pay Harlem's high rents. At the same time, residents of Harlem relinquished one of the greatest advantages of life in midtown: geographic convenience to potential employment opportunities. With so many black people reliant on ser-vice and domestic jobs for their economic survival, proximity to elite whites could be essential not only to finding work but to minimizing the transportation costs that ate into a family's meager resources. For some, the carfare alone could preclude the acceptance of a position. When a real estate agent offered William Montgomery twenty-five dollars a month to work as a hall man, the unemployed husband and father eagerly considered taking the position. However, when he learned that the job did not include board and would necessitate daily carfare, Mont-gomery had second thoughts. "I don't see how I can work for that know-ing what I have got to do and other expences [sic]," he concluded dejectedly. Mrs. Armstrong complained to a charity worker in 1912 that the cost of transportation that had to be paid before she received her first wages nearly prevented her from taking piecework sewing coats. Her training as a seamstress in the West Indies made her one of the very few black women at the time who had the opportunity to engage in homework. Nevertheless, she needed to pay for transportation to pick up the material, to return the finished garments, and to receive her wages on the scheduled payday. "I am asking for the last time," she implored a charity worker. "[A]ll I have work for up to now is 75 cnts which I wont receive before Monday and I want that for car fear [fare] to go out next week to work." Struggling to avoid eviction for not paying the rent and with no money for food, the cost of transportation became an insurmountable burden for Mrs. Armstrong and for the growing numbers like her who did not live near their place of employment.[28]

As black people moved into Harlem, they found a world gradually devoid of whites except for the police officers. The black vanguard that made its way into this exclusive section of Manhattan faced a barrage of Negrophobic attacks. White church leaders insisted that blacks form their own congregations. The Reverend Dr. Van de Water, pastor of a Harlem church and a self-proclaimed "friend of the Negro race," encouraged St. Philip's Episcopal church to move to Harlem in 1907 to minister to the growing black population there. "[I]t is not for the best interests of either the whites or the blacks that they should attend the same Sunday schools, or the same churches," he explained. "I hold that it is much better for all concerned that the races should worship by themselves."[29]

Angry white residents demonstrated less restraint in their opposition to the black "invasion" of Harlem as they desperately sought to defend their neighborhood from the black "enemy." The Harlem Property Owners' Improvement Corporation (HPOIC), active from 1910 to 1915, led the charge. "It is the question of whether the white man will rule Harlem or the negro," HPOIC founder John Taylor cautioned in 1913. "When will the people of Harlem wake up to the fact that they must organize and maintain a powerful anti-invasion movement if they want to check the progress of the black hordes that are gradually eating through the very heart of Harlem?" demanded an editorial. In 1915, a group of secular and religious Harlem leaders protested against opening a moving picture show at Lenox Avenue and 129th Street, afraid that it would bring "an influx of colored people." They argued that "130th Street ought to be the dividing line between colored and white people." But economic self-interest undermined even their most strident efforts. Landlords earned greater profits by renting to black tenants, promoting the rapid integration of Harlem. As blacks continued settling in Harlem, panicked whites either struggled to adjust or fled altogether. The *New York Times* captured the image of a neighborhood transformed. "A constant stream of furniture loaded with household effects of a new colony of colored people who are invading the choice locality are pouring into the street. Another equally long procession moving in the other direction is carrying away the household goods of the whites from their homes of years."[30]

Failing to halt the influx through private efforts, whites turned to city authorities for help. Joseph S. Fried, who dubbed himself a "citizen in distress," protested the "constant danger" his son faced on his way to and from school in Harlem. The "negroe guerilla hands that infest the section," Fried wrote to the mayor, "pick out as their prey weak and unprotected individuals . . . mostly plying their nefarious trade in the morning, when the boys have a few pennies for lunch." Whereas working-class Irish and Italian youths in the San Juan Hill and Tenderloin districts had vented their frustrations with violence against their black neighbors, the relatively elite whites in Harlem felt less inclined to engage in street fights. Instead, they demanded that the city's police officers shield them from the "menacing" black "hordes." White "citizens" beseeched the police to "afford this dangerous and prejudiced section of the negroe colony, adequate protection for the whites." Officers rushed to comply, quickly arresting eight black youths for juvenile delinquency. They also increased the police presence in the area around the Harlem vocational school that served white children.[31]

Nonetheless, by 1930 almost all of Harlem's white population had fled, leaving the neighborhood to black residents. The remainder of Manhattan witnessed a corresponding decline in the number of black people living outside of Harlem. Between blacks' desire for decent housing and respite from whites' harassment on the one hand, and growing antiblack sentiment among the city's other residents on the other, Harlem became nearly the only area in which black Manhattanites could easily reside. But the move to Harlem, one more step in the perpetual migration of black New Yorkers, became their last. With blacks now hemmed in by geography, the city's white population quickly moved to confine the black population within this single area, thereby ensuring that the remainder of the city would remain free of the Negro "menace." The city's police patrolmen, the most visible arm of municipal government and long antagonistic to blacks, served on the frontlines of the battle to enclose blacks in a world of violence, crime, vice, and poverty, thereby transforming a once-elite neighborhood into an urban slum and ghetto.[32]

Overwhelmingly Irish Catholic, members of New York's police force came from a group that had historically contentious relations with black people. Since the earliest years of sustained Irish immigration to the United States in the first half of the nineteenth century, black people had complained of the newcomers' access to citizenship while they, American born, remained outsiders. Tensions between the groups mounted as the Irish moved into the few working-class occupations open to black men and women and quickly asserted their privileged "white" status. Frederick Douglass noted acerbically in 1853 that "[t]he Irish, who, at home, readily sympathize with the oppressed everywhere, are instantly taught when they step upon our soil to hate and despise the Negro." During the New York City draft riots of 1863, Irish conscripts demonstrated against the Union Army's draft policy. Their anger soon shifted to the city's black population, culminating in the mob burning down the Colored Orphan Asylum. Though relations between the two groups stayed relatively calm throughout the remainder of the century, the 1900 riot, another in 1905, and frequent smaller episodes confirmed that the animosity had not dissipated. More than fifty years after Douglass's criticism, a black New York educator made a similar observation about Irish attitudes. "Pat O'Flannagan does not have the least thing in the world against Jim from Dixie," he remarked, "but it didn't take Pat long after passing the Statue of Liberty to learn that it is popular to give Jim a whack."[33]

As police officers, Irish New Yorkers gained the authority to translate their antiblack prejudices into sanctioned behavior. In his 1906 memoir reflecting on his time as the city's highest-ranking police official, Irish American commissioner William McAdoo unequivocally disparaged New York's black residents as "troublesome and dangerous characters." In a lengthy diatribe, McAdoo alleged that nefarious and subhuman "coons" posed an insidious threat to the innocent and unsuspecting (white) residents of the city:

In the male species this is the over-dressed, flashy-bejewelled loafer, gambler, and, in many instances, general criminal. . . . They never work, and they go heavily armed, generally carrying, in addition to the indispensable revolver, a razor. When in pursuit of plunder, or out for revenge, or actuated by jealousy, they use both weapons with deadly effect. In one case, one of these desperadoes almost literally cut a man in two with a razor, and in several instances they have inflicted fearful wounds on policemen. . . . The negro loafer . . . is subject to violent fits of jealousy, and, when filled up with the raw alcohol which is dispensed in the neighborhood, murder comes naturally and easily to him.

According to McAdoo, his patrolmen also faced the constant risk of violence at the hands of an innately savage population. The suggestion of police vulnerability justified the harsh treatment used by his subordinates to restrict black people's actions.[34]

Equally ominous to white New Yorkers, McAdoo implied that "coons" insinuated their degradation into every facet of urban life. Rather than earn an honest living, they appropriated the earnings "from a life of shame" of the "one or more women in their train." "If they sleep at all," McAdoo continued, "it is in the daytime, for they are out at all hours of the night. In the afternoon they can be seen sunning themselves in front of their favorite saloons and gambling-houses, like snakes coming out of their holes." Exposing his underlying preoccupation, McAdoo stressed the upheaval caused by blacks' subversion of the accepted racial order. "They are impudent and arrogant in their manner," he complained, "and will block the sidewalks until white women have to go around to get past them, running the risk at the same time of being insulted." And, McAdoo warned, their numbers were growing. While "decent colored people" arrived daily from the South, "one of these [coons] will get hold" of the newcomer "and not only will he rob him, but before he is through with him he will probably make him as bad as himself." No black person, McAdoo implied, could be trusted for long. In the liberal urban environment, free from white control or rigid discipline, even honest members of the race would soon succumb to their basest natural instincts.[35]

Black women, too, faced the police commissioner's censure. Like her male counterpart, McAdoo declared, "the vicious and drunken colored woman . . . in a paroxysm of passion, and under the influence of liquor, is likely to use a weapon very freely, and not a few of them carry revolvers and razors."[36] Encouraged by the attitude of his commanding officer, patrolman Cornelius Willemse referred to black women as "Amazons" who yielded to their violent inclinations with sometimes fatal accuracy. According to his hyperbolic description, black women preyed on white men, robbing them "with impunity, especially those who look respectable and well-dressed." They relied on white men's humiliation at having been caught consorting with a black woman, virtually guaranteeing that the crime would remain unpunished. This scheme succeeded, according to the police officer, due to the "natural" facility with which black women practiced the craft of prostitution. Using sex as part of a calculated plan for getting rich came easily to black women unwilling to work in legitimate occupations for their money. Black women, both McAdoo and Willemse insisted, were promiscuous, materialistic, and dangerous to the city's collective morality. Like their male counterparts, they threatened to inflict their vices on the city at large.[37]

The integration of these pervasive stereotypes into routine police interactions with the city's black residents had a devastating impact on black New Yorkers, leaving them vulnerable to assaults from within and outside their neighborhoods. Cornelius Willemse, while a fresh recruit to the New York City police force in the late nineteenth century, received clear directives on how to treat the black people within his patrol area. Early in his tenure on the force, Willemse found himself in conflict with a group of black men who loitered on the street corners and allegedly made offensive remarks to white female passersby. He attempted to disperse the group. "At my order to move along," Willemse wrote in his memoirs, "they shuffled off slowly, dragging their feet on the sidewalk, in a way which seemed to say, 'Feet, we'll be back as soon as this fool cop is gone.'" Angered by their perceived insolence, Willemse decided that they were "ripe for a lesson."

Without warning, Willemse began beating any black man in his proximity, "work[ing] with the old nightstick as hard as I could." Within minutes, "Negroes were lying all over the sidewalk, some of them half conscious, others bruised and bleeding." He had no intention of arresting the group, nor did he believe he had grounds since the men had broken no laws—their only "crime" had been the subversion of racial norms—so he left them "to scamper off to the best of their ability." Willemse smugly evaluated his success at ridding the streets of the black menace and asserting his authority on his post. "I had made good on my threat of 'skull trouble.'" He expected no further difficulty from them.

To his surprise, the next morning Willemse received a message to report to his boss, Inspector "Smiling Dick" Walsh. Several of the black men whom Willemse had beaten the previous day had come in "with their heads swathed in bandages" to register a formal complaint against him. As Willemse nervously entered the station house, the sergeant "gave me a broad wink . . . and I knew instantly that he was going to guide me through the mix-up." Speaking loudly, the sergeant instructed Willemse to "grab that bunch in there, charge them with disorderly conduct and throw them down in the cellar." The complainants immediately fled, "no one stopping them, of course."

Inspector Walsh then offered some advice to his subordinate. "I certainly gave instructions to keep those corners clear," Walsh began, demonstrating that he too worried about protecting white women from affronts by black men. But he cautioned Willemse to be more careful in the future. "Go back to your post, protect women from interference and show them all that you're boss on that corner." Walsh concluded the meeting with a commendation to the patrolman for his actions, certain that "the complainants we've just had here will give your post a wide berth." He approved of Willemse's tactics as well, but made one suggestion: "[W]hen you use your stick," he recommended, "always make a collar with it because, you understand," (here Walsh "smiled knowingly") "you can always use force to overcome unlawful resistance. Don't forget that 'unlawful resistance' covers a multitude of sins."[38]

The actions of both Officer Willemse and Inspector Walsh illustrate the ways in which city authorities tolerated and fostered a climate of racial subjugation in New York City. Through the criminal justice system, whites imposed pseudo-legal controls on New York's black population. With the tacit (and sometimes explicit) encouragement of municipal authorities, police patrolmen brutalized black people and subverted their civil rights, leaving the victimized population with few avenues for remediation. Over time, police harassment gradually helped to contain the black population within specific physical spaces in the city as they sought respite from the abuse. The police also shaped the economic and social endeavors in which black people could engage without molestation. Increasingly, the police molded black neighborhoods to conform to popularly held stereotypes about blacks. They supported the growth of vice industries in areas with heavy concentrations of black residents and used physical force to ensure that vice (and the black people themselves) did not stray from these districts. And through subterfuge like that practiced by Willemse, Walsh, and the desk sergeant, the city's men in blue obstructed black people's efforts to find recourse or escape the conditions that ensnared them in a life of poverty and racial subordination.

Black people were not alone in experiencing contentious relations with the city's police force. Jews and Italians, for example, often protested their mistreatment by New York's patrolmen. Nevertheless, although other ethnic and immigrant populations within the city also periodically became police targets, none faced the overwhelmingly uniform condemnation that black people endured. And while members of each of these groups complained about poor treatment at the hands of the police, most could expect better relations once they had mastered the English language. Perhaps more importantly, unlike blacks in the city, who experienced more rigid residential segregation over time, second- and third-generation ethnic New Yorkers could move out of their immigrant enclaves, virtually guaranteeing improved interactions with all levels of municipal officials.[39]

The relationship between New York's black population and its police officers was unique in the comprehensiveness of the mistrust. By the end of the nineteenth century, police had begun the indiscriminate use of physical harassment and intimidation as a staple of control and authority in black neighborhoods. In 1890, T. Thomas Fortune, editor of the New York Age and one of the most elite members of the city's black population, found that his status and political savvy could not save him from police harassment. Challenging pervasive discriminatory practices, Fortune registered a complaint about a restaurant that had refused to serve him. The officer on the scene, rather than accept Fortune's sworn statement, placed the black newspaperman in a jail cell for disorderly conduct and refused him the opportunity to either call a lawyer or send for a bondsman to provide his bail money. Only after three hours did Fortune manage to secure his release. Fortune successfully prosecuted his charge against the restaurant, though he never managed to secure redress for the abuse he received at the hands of the police officer.[40] This kind of petty aggravation and humiliation became a pervasive component of the methods used by police officers to control and restrain the city's black population.

Over time, police brutality became almost standard procedure against black suspects in custody. In 1913, Samuel Booth, a black man, was arrested on the street after a police chase. Oscar Hague, the arresting police officer, testified against Booth at the ensuing assault trial. "He did not say anything after I arrested him," Hague informed the court, "because I beat him up a little bit. In other words I put him out of commission." Upon cross-examination Hague became more specific. "I hit the defendant with my fist," he admitted. Samuel Booth told his own story of being assaulted at the police station. "They beat me all up," he explained of the officers. "I was hit with the butt of a gun or something. I don't know what they hit me for." When Booth threatened the officers that he would inform the District Attorney about the attack, Hague smugly responded that "I wouldn't have a chance. . . . He said when he got through framing me up I wouldn't have a chance." The jury convicted Booth; Hague never faced charges for his mishandling of a suspect in custody.[41]

The tendency to subdue black suspects first and ask questions later became ingrained in police culture. Responding to mounting pressure to address the rampant corruption in the police force, early in the twentieth century the mayor's office commissioned an investigation into police behavior and ways to improve the relationship between patrolmen and their constituents. During the inquiry, one officer who worked in a black district offered telling testimony: "What chance has a cop without a club against a couple of mad niggers?" he questioned bluntly. The policeman rejected any suggestion that black neighborhoods could be patrolled with anything other than brute force. The investigating panel did not challenge the underlying assumption of this testimony. Deeply imbued with stereotypes about blacks' violent and immoral proclivities, police officers operated under the prevailing philosophy that black people needed to be controlled, not protected.[42]

For some officers, the lax enforcement of police behavior offered an exciting opportunity to be "boss on the job" and rule "with an iron hand." This attitude encouraged police brutality to abound in New York's black neighborhoods. Cornelius Willemse recalled the heady days in the early twentieth century, before police reforms had been implemented and enforced, when he was authorized to use his nightstick freely on black people. His sergeant cautioned him to "[h]ave your eyes peeled" and preserve the peace with physical force whenever necessary. "They don't know what talking means down there," the superior officer confided. The patrolman spent his shifts "smashing heads" at will and instilling fear in a population that had almost no access to legal recourse. Willemse reveled in this freedom.[43]

Nevertheless, as long as black people lived in racially mixed neighborhoods and shared the city streets with the rest of the populace, the police faced a daunting challenge in fulfilling one of their most important—albeit unspoken—mandates: to keep blacks from interfering with whites. The growth of the black population in the late nineteenth century led to the increased visibility of black people around the city. James McCabe described a Manhattan street scene in 1881. "Well dressed men and women are brushed in the throng by . . . grotesquely attired negroes with huge advertising placards strapped to the front and back . . . in happy ignorance of the inconvenience they give to others by taking up a double share of room." Over time, blacks' presence became more evident and took on more sinister connotations. Much to the consternation of unhappy whites, black men seeking respite from the crowded tenements frequently gathered on street corners. Their unyielding presence threatened to upset the social order. "Negroes congregate on the sidewalks and white people are compelled to take to the middle of the street," Francis Legrange protested to Mayor Gaynor in 1912. Most disturbing, however, was the decline in deference that black men demonstrated toward white women. "My wife came home from church on Sunday night," a white man complained, "and as she passed the place [where black men were standing], one of them niggers said some Bad word to her & she sat down and cried." Accustomed to black servility and virtual invisibility, this defiant rejection of traditional symbols of black subordination undermined whites' sense of well-being and superiority.[44]

White people frequently registered complaints with city officials about the presence of blacks in their neighborhoods, obligating the police to devote time and energy to ensuring that blacks did not molest white people in racially mixed residential areas. George Weekes protested to Mayor Gaynor in 1912 that a police officer pursuing a group of black men through the streets of San Juan Hill struck him and used "profane language" when ordering him to leave the area. Officer Henry Egan vehemently denied any wrongdoing, insisting that the men who had gathered on the street corner were behaving intemperately and needed to be dispersed. The block where the chase occurred, Egan explained, "is one that is receiving the special attention of the police, [because] it is entirely populated by negroes, who are mostly of a disorderly character." Inspector Hayes, investigating the incident, concluded in his report that the officer had responded reasonably to the conditions he encountered. Black men's appropriation of city space, tantamount to a declaration of equality, offended whites' sensibilities. The patrolman received public commendation for his success at curtailing the menace of black "corner loungers."[45]

Black women became special targets of police manipulation and control. From working-class immigrants to wealthy socialites, white people denounced black women for their supposed depravity and the threat they presented to the moral well-being of the city's white citizens. It

Figure 8. Delivery men taking a break on Thirtieth Street, 1903. Museum of the City of New York, The Byron Collection, 93.1.1.15401.

became nearly impossible for black women in New York to persuade whites of their moral rectitude. Edith Williams, arrested in 1910 for grand larceny and felonious assault, sent a letter to Mayor William Gaynor from New York's Tombs Prison. She complained that Officer John Nekola intentionally humiliated and degraded her. He viciously beat her and spit in her face during her arrest and "cull [me] awful mane [names]." Nekola's use of slurs revealed his personal contempt for Williams specifically and black women generally. The investigating inspector, however, ignored the officer's breach of professional conduct and discounted Williams's allegations. Arguing that she had accosted a white man for the purpose of prostitution and later stabbed Officer Nekola with a hat pin, the inspector concluded that Nekola had behaved appropriately in subduing Williams. As an immoral woman, he asserted, Williams's "opinion is unworthy of belief." He found "no grounds for complaint."[46]

The specter of sexually promiscuous black women enticing innocent white victims to behave disgracefully offered "proof" that black women could not be left to their own devices, but instead belonged in white people's kitchens. Confronting a shortage of domestic servants in the latter decades of the nineteenth century, whites used the claim of depravity to assert that black women benefited from the training and "systematic repression" provided by their constant interaction with white superiors. Whites' civilizing influence on morally lax black women helped to mitigate the terrifying alternative: permitting unrestricted black women to unleash their licentiousness on the city at large. When black women refused to accept the tutelage of whites, police officers then became responsible for overseeing the protection of whites from black women's degeneracy.[47]

Stereotypes of black female immorality provided the rationale for denouncing a wide range of behavior. In a court case involving an altercation between two white men, police investigator Daniel Curtayne took advantage of the opportunity to censure black women and raise fears about their ability to entrap unsuspecting white men. He admitted that he was drawn to the scene by the presence of black women, not by the fight itself. "[T]he moment I saw these women," Curtayne explained, "I saw the similarity of this case to other cases. It is the way things usually happen." Exaggerating the extent of the menace, the officer described the women's strategy. "These prostitutes bring in drunken white men. . . . I find that to be the case in hundreds and hundreds of cases, and they find easy money. They go through the white man and get everything he has." Curtayne's account reflected whites' deep-seated fears that blacks were weaving nefarious plots that would ensnare unsuspecting whites into a web of immorality. Though the police offered no specific evidence of prostitution, and despite the irrelevance of this testimony to a case about a fight between two men, the judge convicted the defendant and sentenced him to five years in the state penitentiary in part because of his association with the black women.[48]

Whereas policemen used physical force to keep blacks from interfering with whites, they otherwise ignored black neighborhoods almost entirely. In a study conducted in 1915, social workers found blatant police neglect of both San Juan Hill and Harlem. Inspectors and captains told investigators, "without mincing their words," that they "considered the colored people worthless." According to police testimony, it was "useless to bother" with black neighborhoods. So long as black residents did not murder each other or commit crimes against whites, the police "let them do as they pleased." In these two districts, almost exclusively populated by black residents, violence, crime, and vice thrived freely. From all directions, blacks faced danger. White civilians or police officers could attack with impunity or underwrite the development of red-light districts. And black criminals roamed these neighborhoods at will, unchecked by the city's sworn protectors.[49]

Black-on-black crime came in many forms, from petty theft (though far from insignificant to those who struggled just to feed their children) to murder. Robberies habitually occurred in the crowded tenements, facilitated by the prevalence of nontraditional housing arrangements. When strangers roomed with one another and moved often, opportunities to appropriate others' belongings frequently presented themselves. James Corrothers, during his first months in New York City, spent time as a lodger on Eighteenth Street. A few dollars behind with the rent, he gave up the room and left a trunkfull of his possessions as collateral. When he returned some weeks later ready to pay and collect his things, Corrothers was outraged to learn that his trust had been poorly warranted; in his absence, someone had stolen all of his belongings. The regularity with which black people's jobs forced them to be away from home for extended periods exposed them to the possibility of becoming victims of theft. Ada Montgomery struggled to save enough money to move her family away from New York, but after leaving her daughter in a nursery in order to take a domestic position, she returned home to find that during the day someone had broken into her rooms and had stolen all of their clothing. Annie Graves's mother, visiting from Virginia to help care for her grandchildren during her daughter's protracted illness, had an "unpleasant experience" during her first encounter with the city. Mrs. Trent was robbed of some money while lodging in an apartment being used as a rooming house. She left "rather hurriedly," anxious to return home.[50]

The police made no effort to impede the rampant theft plaguing black neighborhoods. A black man in Harlem told incredulous investigators that so many of his neighbors' apartments had been robbed that he placed his best suit in pawn during the week. Each Saturday night he removed the clothes for Sunday use, repeating the cycle the following week.[51] Violent crime also regularly went unchecked unless white people became victims. Sterling Green, accused of shooting at his wife, killing his brother, and seriously wounding another man, remained free until he fired at two detectives, neither of whom even knew of the previous crimes, while dining at a restaurant. An "epidemic of murders," three committed in broad daylight, took the lives of four black people during the course of just one week. In another instance, a police officer chased Samuel Jones, accused of inflicting a minor wound on his friend with a bread knife, through city streets. The officer opened fire during the pursuit, despite the presence of innocent bystanders, fatally shooting the man.[52] This climate of violence put everyone in the neighborhood at risk. The police might leave crimes uninvestigated altogether. Alternatively, police intervention could be equally perilous to the innocent.

Police neglect also encouraged vice to flourish within black communities. Policemen actively abetted the development of red-light districts in black neighborhoods, helping to make the stereotypes about black people become a self-fulfilling prophecy. Like other northern cities, vice thrived in black neighborhoods to a greater extent and with greater success than in other districts, primarily because they were permitted to do so. "In more than one city," Richard R. Wright Jr. noted in his 1908 survey of Negro housing in the North, "the distinctively Negro neighborhood is the same as, or next to, that district which seems, by consent of civil authorities, to be given up to vice." Like Cleveland, Philadelphia, Detroit, and Chicago, the white police force of New York City and white reformers refused to allow red-light districts to develop anywhere except areas with heavy concentrations of black residents.[53]

Police officers coveted assignments in vice-ridden districts, especially those that received little attention from reformers. Bribery schemes run by the city's police department had long helped officers supplement their civil servant salaries. "I had the best Christmas and New Year's I had had in years," one officer admitted after telling about the bribes he received for protecting a gambling ring. "The kids got nice toys and mama could buy things for the house." To his tremendous disappointment, when a new police captain came into the precinct, this officer lost his privileged position.[54] Captain Max F. Schmittberger, testifying in the mid-1890s, before the Lexow Committee investigating police corruption, confessed that blackmailing was "a matter of common understanding" in the police department. The captains of the city's various districts, Schmittberger added, "[took] advantage of any opportunity that presented itself to make money out of their respective precincts." Blackmail worked more effectively in some areas than others, and wards where vice was prevalent became preferred assignments for members of the city's police force. No appointment had greater appeal than one in a black neighborhood, where few reformers, politicians, or white elites would complain about the presence of vice.[55]

As the police commander of the Nineteenth Precinct in the Tenderloin district, Schmittberger vigorously encouraged and shielded the numerous illegal activities taking place under his watch, making it a lucrative business for himself and his subordinate officers. He testified that policy shops in his district paid twenty dollars a month, liquor dealers about eighty, pool rooms two hundred dollars, and "disorderly houses" anywhere from ten to five hundred dollars, depending on their quality and clientele. He personally earned nearly four hundred dollars each month from the vice industries in his precinct. Regular patrolmen involved in collecting the monthly "dues" each earned approximately one hundred dollars of blackmail money per month. Anyone who spent time as a precinct captain in the Tenderloin, according to one officer, "could live on tenderloin steaks the rest of his life." Local police inspectors became known as "Czars of the Tenderloin."[56]

When Cornelius Willemse received a desirable transfer to the Tenderloin in 1902, he began his new commission "excited and eager for adventure." By his own account, the four years he spent on the Tenderloin beat were among the most enjoyable of his long career in law enforcement. "Altogether," he later recalled, "there was something to be done every minute I was on post." His antics caught up with him, and in 1906 Willemse was transferred "as a grafter" to the Minetta Lane district. Willemse, though intending to "toe the mark" after the change, discovered to his delight that "there was a good bunch on my platoon and we had a lot of gambling, skylarking and good bosses. . . . So, happy days were here again!" Willemse admitted to sleeping on the job, leaving the area entirely unprotected. When a "Citizen" complained that the police officer assigned to Minetta Lane "stands in with the [sporting] men & women," Willemse's own admissions affirmed the veracity of the grievance. He explained, "[Y]ou never heard the word 'taxpayer' from complaining property owners and that was a great relief." This area of Greenwich Village, comprised predominantly of poor black people who had resisted moving northward, had almost no influence on New York's political machine. Similarly, the Tenderloin district had long been ruled by blackmail, with police officers permitting prostitution and illegal Sunday liquor sales in exchange for substantial bribes. In every Manhattan neighborhood with heavy concentrations of black residents, white police officers enjoyed free license to preserve their own economic interests by ensuring the survival of prostitution and gambling rings. Reformers working to clean up the city increasingly associated the presence of black people with the existence of vice. They overwhelmingly blamed the illicit activities on black residents, implying that police corruption only facilitated the natural tendencies of an immoral population. Reformers therefore viewed black people as legitimate targets of repression, not assistance.[57]

The universal abandonment by white people—municipal authorities, police, or reformers—consigned black neighborhoods to became breeding grounds for prostitution, gambling, drugs, and crime. Policy playing, a form of gambling, was popular in black neighborhoods. Players selected numbers, much like a lottery, and the winner was determined by legitimate lottery drawings in other states. Gambling was illegal in New York State at the turn of the twentieth century, but policy playing thrived in back alleys and tenements. Illicit policy shops catered to a range of patrons, mostly from the poorest groups in the city. In one, an investigator found "three negroes, two Irishmen and four Germans . . . all of them bucking the tiger furiously."[58] Despite the popularity of policy among diverse elements of the city's population, many whites associated policy playing with black people. "In every district where they live," noted James McCabe, "you will find dingy little lottery offices, patronized mostly by them." Annie Connelly complained numerous times to the police about a policy shop in her neighborhood frequented by "the lowest kind of colored men and women," to no avail. Desperate to remove this blight from her community, she finally made a direct appeal to Mayor Van Wyck in 1901, denouncing the police for their failure to close the place down and begging the mayor to remove "this Den of Vice." The investigating officer dubiously claimed to find nothing illegal at the address in question, and the police commissioner reminded the mayor in his report that "it is customary for malicious or evil-minded people to charge the police with being in the pay of this, that or the other person."[59]

The police-protected gambling rings in black neighborhoods lured workingmen and women to risk their wages in the hopes of a quick fix for their persistent economic privation. An anonymous complainant wrote to Mayor Gaynor about a group of "loafers" who "hang around all day long play[ing] that 3 card monty and shoot[ing] craps." They lured passersby to join in the games and gamble away their earnings while the "new cops on the beat" who "are worse than the old ones used to be" did nothing to interfere. The families who relied on that money struggled to force the city to rid their neighborhoods of the problem. "I want to ask you," implored "a poor woman who needs her husbands earnings," to "break up these two gambling clubs here in 59th Street." Her husband spent "a good portion of his weeks earnings" there and "don't have enough left to support me and my little children." She too blamed the police who "could get them very easily if they only tried but I am told that the men who run these clubs pay them for protection." The captain of the police precinct assured the mayor that "no evidence of a gambling house nature could be observed, or cause for police action found." Furthermore, the investigator "failed to find any person who had any cause for complaint or who would substantiate the statements made in this communication." The problem continued unabated and moved uptown to Harlem as the black population began its relocation. There, too, gambling was openly enjoyed "without any interference from the police," and men visited the "dives . . . after working hard all week and loose [sic] every cent of their hard earned wages, leaving their wives and children in want and distress and hungry."[60]

With limited occupational alternatives and with police complicity, prostitution, gambling, and other illegal activities became occupations of choice for some black New Yorkers who eschewed the drudgery of washing laundry or running an elevator. Still, black people discovered that they could not keep all of their earnings even from illicit endeavors. During the Lexow Commission's vice hearings, for example, a black prostitute complained to the committee that she had been forced to pay the police a portion of her proceeds from streetwalking. By charging extortionist's fees in exchange for protection, police officers in black neighborhoods diminished the available supply of disposable income for black people. Even when engaged in underworld activities, black people found their ability to succeed inhibited by whites' obstruction.[61]

The emergence of a black ghetto in Harlem permitted police and reformers' work to at last coincide. White reformers, eager to eliminate vice from the city, found an acceptable repository for illicit activities. Alternatively, the police found a place where they could leave black people to their own devices and not worry about whites' complaints. The only victims in this process hailed from a population without political or social clout. The emergence of an urban ghetto made the strategy of containment simpler to pursue and more easily sustained. The "Harlem tragedy"—its transformation into a slum after the population there became predominantly black—occurred not only because of overcrowding and high rents but because the police patrolling this district worked to ensure that it became Manhattan's vice and crime headquarters.[62]

White people in New York provided the capital to develop vice in Harlem. They owned most of the saloons, clubs, and prostitution houses, though they often hired black managers to run them. In 1914, only five of the saloons serving the black population of Harlem had black proprietors. The Committee of Fourteen, an antivice organization, found in its investigations that white-run institutions created "one of the chief sources of trouble" in Harlem. Through whites' investments, Harlem became a "wide-open city" for all forms of vice. The transformation of Harlem into a virtually all-black community corresponded with its recognition as the leading prostitution center of New York. Ninety percent of the "daughters of joy" institutions were owned and managed by whites. By the 1920s, with the enthusiastic infusion of white capital, more prostitution houses could be found in Harlem than in four other New York districts combined.[63]

Having a central hub for illicit activities served white New Yorkers very well. They could enjoy forbidden temptations at will, yet rest assured that vice would remain contained in an area far removed from their own families. And vice in Harlem was public and easily accessed. The "openness of vice conditions in this district" distressed Ernest R. Alexander, a Negro lawyer hired by the Committee of Fourteen to conduct a secret study of unlawful pursuits in Harlem. "There is a larger amount and more open immorality in Harlem than this community has known in years," noted George W. Harris bitterly. Though unwilling to invest in legal economic endeavors, whites used black Harlem as their illicit playground.[64]

In 1910, S. S. Hall wrote to the mayor with a suggestion for ridding Harlem of the growing presence of crime and vice. A "small force of good [black] men," he argued, should be hired to the police force as "special officers." Their specific task would be to combat the illicit activities prevalent in the Harlem neighborhood. Police Commissioner William Baker quickly submitted a report to the mayor on this question, urging Gaynor to deny the request. "The situation in that particular locality is being taken care of," he assured the mayor. "I do not believe it would be good policy to employ colored men . . . to work in that locality." White police officers had no interest in receiving assistance to combat vice. Much to the contrary, they expended a great deal of energy protecting the illegal activities that offered welcome opportunities for graft. In an area like Harlem, vice could easily thrive in the absence of interference from politically powerful white reformers.[65]

Hall's suggestion, however, exposed the glaring exclusion of black people from the city's police force. Without officers who had specific ties to the black community, none of New York's protectors had a vested interest in cleaning up those districts. The refusal to hire black people onto the police force through the first decade of the twentieth century permitted the creation and perpetuation of police brutality and graft within black neighborhoods and fostered the deep mistrust between those two groups. Police stereotypes of other populations were partly mitigated by the incorporation of members of those groups into police ranks. Though predominantly Irish Catholic, by the late nineteenth century the force included a small German presence, more than one hundred Jews (actively recruited by Theodore Roosevelt during his tenure as commissioner in the mid-1890s), and a small cadre of Italians. Those numbers had all increased substantially by the end of the first decade of the twentieth century. Like other ethnic groups who felt unfairly targeted by the city's policemen, the black population had long agitated for an appointment of their own to the city's force as a way of mitigating the prejudicial treatment they experienced. Their demands repeatedly fell on deaf ears until 1911, when Samuel J. Battle became the first black man to serve the city in that capacity. His token presence, however, did little to alter the fundamentally suspicious view that black people had of the city's police force.[66]

In 1873, the New York police department caused tremendous scandal in the city when word spread that it had made plans to appoint a number of black policemen to the corps. The *New York Times* quickly dispelled the rumor, reassuring its readers that, "as a recognition of the claims of the colored people, twenty-five able-bodied negroes have been offered positions as street-sweepers." Whites in the city, having been startled by the "revolutionary" plan to "equip the negro in the uniform of the force," breathed a collective sigh of relief.[67] The issue of black police officers did not disappear, however, and through the turn of the century black men sporadically made attempts to gain admission to the force. Samuel C. Craig, a Georgia-born black New Yorker, applied to the Municipal Civil Service Examining Board in 1886. His petition was quietly denied. The *New York Age* demanded the inclusion of a black officer to the ranks in 1891, threatening political action if no changes took place. "The Afro-American voters and tax-payers have the power to break down the official prejudice which keeps them off the police force, and they should use that power." But blacks' relatively small presence among the city's voting ranks diminished their ability to pressure the city effectively.[68]

No other sustained effort was made until Samuel Battle spent two years fighting for a chance to join the force in New York City. A southern migrant, Battle had been working at Grand Central Station as a Red Cap, carrying passengers' bags and earning decent money in tips. On good days, Battle pulled in upward of twenty dollars. Still, knowing that the job would not last forever, he began searching for alternatives. "I thought of the Police Department," he explained in an interview. "I thought of this Irish policeman, a little fellow, a fine old fellow, but I never saw him do anything except stand around and talk. . . . I thought to myself; now, this is the kind of a job I would like."[69] Battle took the Civil Service examination in 1910 and passed with a percentage correct slightly above eighty-four and earning a rank of 199 out of a roll of 638 names. He was repeatedly passed over for appointment, however, and asked Fred Moore, editor of the *New York Age*, for help. Moore spearheaded the fight for Battle, who finally became a member of the force in 1911. Still, his struggles had not yet ended. After a thirty-day training period, Battle received his first assignment. He was placed in the San Juan Hill district, where he experienced hazing from his colleagues. No one spoke to Battle, and the white officers refused to have him sleep in their quarters. They tried to block his admission to the Policeman's Benevolent Association. One day, Battle found a note pinned over his bed "with a hole in it about the size of a bullet hole." The message on the note stated, "Nigger, if you don't quit, this is what will happen to you." Only after a tense two years did the ice finally break for Battle. In 1913, when he was transferred to a Harlem precinct, his white fellow officers at his new post accepted him into their ranks.[70]

Battle's addition to New York City's police force made some marginal changes in the balance of power between the police and the city's black population. He recalled some rioting that occurred in the San Juan Hill precinct in 1911 while he was still in training. By the time he reached the neighborhood, "the whites and the Negroes were battling." He saw white officers "beating up the colored people" and thought, "Here's my chance to get even with them. I saw them whipping black heads, and I was whipping white heads. I'll never forget that." Though temporary and limited, for a brief moment a black man had the legal right to wield physical authority over white people without fear of retribution. Still, Battle alone could not cure all of the ills facing black people at the hands of the white police force. Because he refused to cooperate with the graft in San Juan Hill, his superiors removed him from that post. So blackmailing and vice continued nearly unmitigated in black neighborhoods.[71]

Black people's mistreatment at the hands of the city's police force created a climate of fear and fundamental mistrust. Blacks viewed the police as perpetrators of violence, not as protectors. They complained about police brutality and corruption and struggled to combat it. The police, blacks told an investigator, "did not make raids on the 'dens' but only came down when there was a robbery, stabbing, or a fight; they are brought down by results but do not remove the cause." Even murders might be ignored by the police, as long as no white people had been hurt, leaving black people constantly vulnerable to crime and violence. In the heart of San Juan Hill, witnesses saw a black man thrown from the roof of a building known to house a gambling ring. The perpetrators were notorious among the neighborhood's residents, and "fear of injury" prevented many from speaking out. "An American" begged the mayor to open an investigation because "the cops are of no use." The author then provided specific assistance, naming the offenders as Mr. Cooker and August Hill. Police Inspector Richard Walsh issued a brief report on the episode, confirming the death of William Powell in the "thickly populated colored section" of town. None of the tenants in the building offered any information about the episode. "I believe," Walsh concluded, "the man accidentally fell from the roof." The case was closed, leaving the neighbors uncertain about their own safety.[72]

Frustrated by the constant abuse they received at the hands of the police, some black people sought revenge. Relying on their own vigilante justice, the black community found ways to protect their own. White officers periodically complained of having "missiles"—bricks, bottles, and rocks—thrown at them from the anonymity of the tenements. In 1903, San Juan Hill residents launched a successful offensive

against area patrolmen. Witnessing the arrest of a black man, black tenement dwellers sent a volley of bricks onto the policemen below. When
officers opened fire on the assailants, a number of the residents
responded with their own gunfire. Despite a prolonged chase, the police
failed to capture any of the harassers. Just as peace seemed to be
restored, a black woman in an apartment above the street emptied a pail
of dirty water on a crowd of officers, drenching them "to the skin." She
too managed to escape. Some years later, the *New York Age* warned that
harassment "is a game that two can play at." Directing its attention at
"the police who single out Afro-Americans when there is a riot for the
purpose of smashing their heads," the traditionally conservative newspaper unexpectedly promoted self-defense. "A razor properly handled,"
cautioned an editorial obliquely, "leaves hurts that talk a long time. . . .
[When] Afro-Americans are put on the defensive it is right that they
fight to a finish in holding up their end. Cowardice under any circumstances is the basest sort of thing." Despite any temporary victories, however, in the long run these efforts merely provided policemen with
greater ammunition with which to excuse their treatment of black people—both the criminal and innocent alike.[73]

Gradually, black people learned not to openly complain about police
misconduct. Fear of reprisal forced many to keep silent or attempt to
circumvent the police altogether by making their appeals for intervention directly—though often anonymously—to the mayor. "I would prefer that my name should not be mentioned," Hattie Williams wrote to
Mayor Gaynor in her complaint about a gambling ring, "as I fear . . .
some means of revenge." Disregarding her concern, the mayor sent the
letter to the police commissioner, who ordered Lieutenant Daniel Costigan to investigate. When the officer contacted Williams at her home, she
quickly dissembled, suggesting that she had no personal knowledge of
wrongdoing but had made an assumption based on the amount of noise
emanating from the apartment in question. Costigan reported to his
superiors that he "found no evidence of gambling or other violations
of law on the premises." The mayor's blatant disregard for Williams's
apprehension about her personal safety undoubtedly taught her an
important lesson about the wisdom of trusting municipal authorities.
Costigan returned to question her at least three more times; on each
occasion she assured the officer that she had no more complaints. With
the mayor unwilling to protect complainants or seek independent cor-
roboration of their grievances, expressing dissatisfaction with police
conduct proved to be a dangerous choice for already vulnerable black
people.[74]

Among patrolmen's arsenal of weapons that could effectively silence
assertive black people was the ability to arrest them for nebulous infrac-

tions such as resisting arrest or disorderly conduct. Once caught in the criminal justice system, black people found their rights and freedom further endangered by those charged with issuing blind justice. Blacks vainly begged for fair trials. But judges, like policemen, often regarded blacks with palpable contempt, at times bluntly referring to black defendants as "niggers." Still, some blacks tried desperately to beg for mercy. "I am a colored man, poor and almost friendless," Sydney White wrote from Sing Sing prison in his appeal for clemency, "and therefore my word may seem of little value, but, nevertheless, I assure you that when I regain my liberty, I shall lead an honest life." Judges receiving these requests from black people rarely took them seriously. Most often, they ignored the pleas outright.[75]

Black defendants struggled to mitigate the prejudice of juries and the racism embedded in the judicial system. Flimsy evidence against black suspects regularly served as the basis for convictions. Once found guilty, blacks often received long sentences and stiff financial penalties that few could afford to pay. Frank Miller wrote to Judge Norman Dike in 1913, complaining of the injustice of his conviction; the five white men implicated in the robbery had been acquitted. "[It] would seem," he understated, "that an unwarranted discrimination was made against me on account of my color." Miller explained that the district attorney prosecuting the case "was very insistent that I plead guilty, so much so, that he intimated that if I did not he would see that I got a life sentence." His own court-appointed attorney never entered any defense. Despite the egregious mishandling of the case, Miller received a harsh ten-year sentence at the state prison for allegedly stealing $125. Judge Dike, who often referred to black defendants as "coons" and "niggers," refused to either reconsider the conviction or reduce the sentence.[76]

Eager to remove the "black menace" from city streets, white judges and juries required little proof in order to return a guilty verdict against black defendants. After Nelson Browne was arrested in 1913 during a domestic dispute, his fiancée, against whom the assault occurred, testified on Browne's behalf, insisting that the cut she received from him "was very slight" and warranted no punishment. The Reverend Edward Wainwright also served as a character witness, informing the court that Browne had regularly attended church for the previous seven years. Even the probation officer investigating Browne's background confirmed that the defendant had been steadily employed and had a decade's worth of strong references. Furthermore, Browne had no prior criminal record. Despite the overwhelmingly positive testimony and the absence of any witnesses against him, Judge T. C. T. Crain sentenced Browne to the state penitentiary for one year, calling him "a dangerous character" who obviously "inten[ded] to assault other people." Richard

Boyce similarly received a prison sentence for a crime he apparently did not commit. In 1914, the twenty-five-year-old man was arraigned on a rape charge. Court transcripts revealed that "[n]o correct facts were laid before the Judge . . . to corroborate this allegation." Despite persistent doubts about the truth of the accusation, the jury spent little time deliberating the evidence and convicted Boyce of the crime. Judge Dike commented in his trial notes that the defendant "[s]eemed to be a clean cut young colored man" whose guilt had not been confirmed. Because the facts "remained open to doubt," Judge Dike "imposed only a light sentence" of three months' incarceration.[77]

Complaints from scores of imprisoned black convicts exposed a pattern of prejudice within the criminal justice system. Walter Saunders challenged the decision returned against him, questioning the reliability of the prosecution witnesses. He implored the judge to explain how two women who could not determine either the color or sex of the person who had assaulted them could then identify him as the attacker. "I have not been treated fair and honest in my case," Saunders complained. "[A]lso my jury were prejudiced and did not render a fair and impartail [sic] verdict." Violet Jones's appeal was denied when the judge charged her "pimp" with bringing drugs to the jail for her. John Place, a twenty-five-year-old black man convicted of assault and sentenced to one year in jail and a five hundred dollar fine, insisted that the case against him had been based on the testimony of a "bad woman . . . whose evidence sent me away." He begged the court to reconsider his case "and to intercede in behalf of one who is deserving a little consideration." The judge, in his review of Place's case and prior record, determined that "the 'nigger' is in the right place and ought to remain there." Unable to afford an appeal (had he been able to, he would simply have paid the fine and secured his release from prison), Place had no further recourse. Francis Fischer, though receiving the intercession of the penitentiary chaplain and having finished her six-month sentence for selling drugs, was refused the diminution of her fine because, when convicted, "she walked out of court smiling." For the white judge, this impudence was enough to prolong her incarceration.[78]

Like Place and Fischer, many black people convicted of crimes found the monetary punishment they received more daunting than the prison time they faced. Judges repeatedly added fines, typically five hundred dollars, to jail sentences. Failure to pay the fine meant remaining in custody even after the prison sentence had been completed. This became an effective method of extending prison terms when the legal system restricted the length of jail time that could be imposed for particular crimes. Isaac Glasper began an eleven month and twenty-nine day prison term for assault on January 15, 1912. In January of the following year he began a series of letters to the judge pleading for forbearance from the five hundred dollar fine that forced him to remain in prison. Six months after his term had expired he remained incarcerated, unable to pay the insurmountable fee. Intractable, the judge determined that "Glasper is a loafer and does not deserve much consideration. A couple of years in prison might teach him to work." Unable to impose a long prison sentence for a minor assault charge, by forcing a black person to procure a sum equal to nearly the entire annual income of the average black family, the judge guaranteed him a long stay in jail.[79]

The imposition of heavy fines kept black people off the streets. It became one of the legal methods by which judges incorporated popular stereotypes of black people into their decisions about the fate of black defendants. The sense that the white city was under siege, threatened by criminally predisposed and immoral black men and women, persuaded judges to find mechanisms for confining blacks and limiting their presence and influence in the city. Black people faced the constant anxiety of becoming ensnared in the criminal justice system and being removed from their families, friends, livelihoods, and freedom. For families with loved ones in jail, they confronted a desperate choice between paying the rent and putting food on the table or securing a relative's release from prison. Black people in New York City had a torturous relationship with all elements of the law enforcement system. Invariably, they lost.

At all levels, New York City's criminal justice system conspired to relegate black people to an inferior status in the city. Officers on the streets, police captains and commissioners, judges, and juries demonstrated that black people should not be treated as equal citizens. Though legally they may have laid claim to that status, their inability to demand fair and equitable treatment effectively removed them from the body politic. They were harassed and brutalized by police officers, convicted of crimes based on negligible evidence, and slapped with harsh prison sentences and fines for the express intention of keeping them in jail and minimizing their threat to white people. Police officers' treatment of blacks as a monolithic group undermined the attempts by the majority of this population to differentiate themselves from pervasive racial stereotypes. Growing residential segregation that corresponded with increasingly widespread beliefs about black criminal behavior entrapped blacks in neighborhoods that were being gradually overrun by vice and crime. The amalgamation of the underworld with the honest, of the legally employed with the prostitutes, gamblers, and thieves, allowed white people to rationalize their perception of all black people as criminal. Eventually, the growing fear of a violent and immoral black population led to the emergence of a black ghetto in Harlem far removed from the center of Manhattan's thriving economy, hampering blacks' efforts to find jobs, raise their children in an environment free from pernicious influences, and achieve full incorporation as welcome members of the New York metropolis.

Chapter 4

Jobs Are Just Chances

Frederick Challenor left his home in Barbados at the turn of the twenti-eth century, bound for New York City. Like most immigrants, he expected to find greater opportunities in his adopted home than in the one he had left behind. In 1907, he married Aletha Dowridge, a fellow Barbadian whom he had met in America, and the newlyweds set out to establish a life together in Brooklyn. They welcomed the birth of a daughter, Elise, in 1908. Just about a year later, however, mother and daughter returned to Barbados as Frederick struggled to find a steady job to support his family. The couple's separation lasted until late 1910, but Elise remained on the island permanently to be raised by her grand-mother. Finding themselves in dire financial straits once more, exacer-bated by Aletha's failing health and inability to work the long, hard hours required of domestic servants, Aletha returned to her mother's home in Barbados at the end of 1911. She did not join Fred again until 1913 as he tried repeatedly and unsuccessfully to make ends meet and bring his wife back to Brooklyn. "I am kept without any money but hope for better days," he wrote in one of his earliest letters. They were a long time coming.

The nearly fifty letters Fred sent to Aletha during their periods apart reveal his constant, overwhelming concerns about money. The contents are replete with his agonized apologies for sending so few "greenbacks" to her and Elise, his tales of ever-changing jobs that always proved disap-pointing, and his efforts to get himself out of debt. "I just want to pay all who I owe then I will feel better to myself and be a little indepen-dent," he admitted nearly a year into their first separation. In the months since his wife and daughter had left, Fred worked in one apart-ment building earning twelve dollars a month, then as an elevator opera-tor for four dollars a week. He quit both. He subsequently took a job at a shoe factory, but explaining he was "weary with it" continued search-ing for a good janitor's position. Unsuccessful, he reluctantly left the factory during the summer to work on leisure boats. Frederick found boat work demeaning and unpleasant but he could not pass up the chance to make enough money in tips to bring Aletha back to him.

During their second separation, Fred found work for a time as a domestic servant with a family in the city, though he finally gave up that job in February 1912. "I just couldn't stand the worry any more," he apologized in his letter to Aletha. "I have been gaining nothing by the house so what's the difference." Instead, Fred made plans to go back to the shoe factory, and for once his prospects seemed relatively promising. "The old man at the factory wants me to stay with him altogether and he will pay $12.00 a week," he wrote Aletha optimistically. He also had another offer to work as a janitor for fifty-five dollars a month. Fred chose the janitorial position and quickly regretted his decision. "[A]fter going to work on the 1st of April I saw where it would not suit me to keep the place . . . somebody has to be in all the time and the houses were not together." He quit. Having "lost out" on both opportunities, Fred decided to return to the boats for the summer. "I shall beg you not to feel any discontented [*sic*]," he pleaded with his wife.

A summer serving as a waiter on the boats and a protracted illness left him with only forty dollars to take the family through the difficult winter months, forcing Aletha to remain in Barbados still longer. "All thoughts of coming home are abandoned until later," he wrote. Fred "met with a great disappointment" when he could not secure a job on one of the passenger ships that ran between New York and the Caribbean. "What little [money] I did have is gone. . . . I am back in the shoe factory now in a week. . . . You better spend Christmas with your mother and Elise and then I will get you over." Fred tried once more to take an apartment job, this time running the elevator. He soon gave up the position though, claiming "it was giving me [a] cold." Finally, he returned to the factory, though sickness severely diminished his hours. In addition, his annual forays onto the ships kept him from securing his regular position. "[T]hey would not give me the job I was always working at as they say I wont stop [stay] with them in summer so I have to be contented and do the best I can until its time for me to go back on the boats." He wrote again of his hope of getting the family out of debt. "I am still trying to find a good janitors job as I feel my success depends on it more than anything else." But mid-1913 found him still empty-handed. "I will be going back on the boats in a couple of weeks," he said resignedly. He wrote his last letter to Aletha on May 4, 1913. She joined Fred in New York soon after.[1]

Fred Challenor's work experience illustrates the precarious economic circumstances confronted by black people in New York City in the decades prior to World War I. Though black New Yorkers had long faced difficulties breaking into the skilled trades, in the post–Civil War era black men and women became increasingly excluded from all of the city's economic and industrial endeavors. As the nation embarked on its journey toward industrialization, blacks remained on the periphery of America's progress. Even as hundreds of thousands of immigrants poured into the city in the half-century following the Civil War, fueling New York's growth as the nation's principle metropolitan center and spurring American industry, the city offered its black residents bleak prospects for achieving the American dream.

By the latter decades of the nineteenth century, the stream of immigration that had once hailed primarily from western Europe now came overwhelmingly from the southern and eastern parts of the continent. Far more than older generations of immigrants, these newcomers typically settled in cities as they began their life in America. Most arrived in the United States without skills or capital and entered the labor market at its lowest level, carving niches in emerging industries and infiltrating jobs long held by black workers.

Employers took advantage of the abundance of unskilled workers among the European immigrants and hired them for longshoring, paving, shoe shining, and other occupations that had formerly welcomed black workers. Between 1900 and 1910, for example, the number of black hostlers decreased by 18 percent—from 633 to 518—as immigrant white men stepped in to fill the demand. Black porters faced even greater infringements on their jobs, witnessing a dramatic decline in their numbers during the first decade of the twentieth century, from 2,143 to 1,645. White male immigrants took these positions with growing frequency; their ranks increased in that period from 5,020 to 6,202.[2] The tensions between black and immigrant communities in New York mounted as black people tried to assert their claim to a birthright being denied them in favor of newcomers who often could not even speak the language.[3]

The most devastating form of occupational eviction and competition came in unskilled positions, especially domestic service, which had proven to be the cornerstone of black men's economic survival in the city. The number of black male servants and waiters failed to keep pace with the dramatic growth of the black population in the city, remaining virtually unchanged between 1900 and 1910 as the black population increased by nearly one-half. At the same time, the number of white male immigrants engaged in service work almost doubled during that decade, from 18,178 in 1900 to 32,825 in 1910. To hire black servants as chambermaids, coachmen, waiters, chefs, footmen, or valets had been a mark of stature in nineteenth-century New York City, harkening back to slavery days. But by the last decade of the century, the white elite's custom of using black servants had begun yielding to the practice of employing white foreigners or Asians to work in their homes. Consequently, by 1900, black men found themselves virtually driven out of the

TABLE 1. OCCUPATIONAL CATEGORIES AND SELECTED OCCUPATIONS OF THE
MALE AGGREGATE AND NEGRO PAID LABORERS OF NEW YORK CITY, 1890–1910

	Aggregate Population	% of Total Employed	Aggregate Negro Population	Negro % of Total Employed	Negro % of Negro Employed
1890					
Total	753,678	100	13,453	2	100
Professional	21,367	3	112	.5	.9
Domestic	132,995	18	8,118	6	69.5
Trade & Transport.	259,829	34	2,695	1	23.1
Manufacturing	248,779	33	755	.3	6.5
Janitors	2,416	.3	366	15	3
Servants/ Waiters	22,261	3	4,434	20	33
Porters	16,739	2	886	5	7
Launderers	2,175	.2	1,612	74	12
1900					
Total	1,102,471	100	20,395	2	100
Professional	60,853	6	729	1	3.6
Domestic	206,215	19	11,843	6	58.8
Trade & Transport.	406,675	39	5,798	1	28.8
Manufacturing	419,594	38	1,774	.4	8.8
Janitors	6184	.5	800	13	4
Servants/ Waiters	31,211	3	6,280	20	31
Porters	11,322	1	2,143	19	11
Hostler	5,891	.5	633	11	3
1910					
Total	1,566,240	100	33,110	2	100
Professional	75,122	5	1,526	2	4.7
Domestic	141,843	9	16,224	11	49
Trade & Transport.	612,351	39	9,797	2	30.3
Manufacturing	580,880	37	4,504	.7	13.9
Janitors	9,039	.5	4,788	15	14
Servants/ Waiters	47,237	3	6,458	14	20
Porters	13,834	.8	3,912	28	12
Elevator Op.	7,554	.4	3,067	41	9

Sources: *Eleventh Census of the United States: 1890. Population,* II (Washington, D.C., 1897),
pp. 640, 704; *Twelfth Census: 1900. Special Reports: Occupations* (Washington, D.C., 1904),
pp. 634–40; *Thirteenth Census: 1910. Population,* IV (Washington, D.C., 1914), pp. 571–74.

first-class hotels, restaurants, and elite homes, supplanted by whites and Japanese who had "poache[d] defiantly upon the black man's industrial preserves." Black men were then relegated to lower paying, less desirable domestic positions in poorer homes and hotels. A black southern migrant in New York City noted the marked decline in opportunities above the Mason-Dixon line. "For the black, it was more friendly in Georgia than here, because of the competition for jobs here," he explained. Southern whites left menial work to black men. "But here in New York the white man put you up against the wall."[4]

The mushrooming immigrant population in New York City also sparked a dramatic transformation in the city's textile trades. By the late nineteenth century, custom tailoring of men and women's clothing had given way to ready-to-wear apparel. From 1880 to 1910, the number of clothing establishments in the city jumped from 966 to 6,145. The fierce competition forced manufacturers to underbid each other, with the workers absorbing the narrow profit margins in their low wages. Many employers contracted out the assignments for workers to perform at home. Others set up workspaces inside the tenements, creating crowded "sweatshops." By 1895, roughly six thousand sweatshops operated in Manhattan and another nine hundred in Brooklyn, employing in the vicinity of eighty thousand workers. Virtually all of them were white, and many were women.[5]

The road from the Ellis Island ferry to the rest of the United States led literally through the garment district. Once through customs at Castle Clinton, most newcomers walked up Broadway until they arrived at Canal Street, the heart of the wholesale trade district. Two blocks north, at Grand Street, they found the city's retail center. As they settled in neighborhoods surrounding the garment district, different immigrant groups came to control particular industries, and women often held subspecialties. Southern Italian women, for example, dominated the field of tailoring men's clothing. They also controlled the production of artificial flowers and cleaning of ostrich plumes. Syrian women made most of the kimonos and lace and dominated the fields of crocheting and embroidery, while Germans sewed custom vests. Jewish women flooded into garment industry sweatshops and also concentrated in the home production of straw hats, women's neckwear, and fancy bows. Irish and native-born home workers made men's neckties. Many native-born white women secured jobs in stores around the city.[6]

Black women, on the other hand, were virtually shut out of both factory and homework. White women refused to work alongside black women and persuaded factory owners to preserve the racial homogeneity of the city's female-dominated workplaces. The prejudices extended so far, explained reformer Mary White Ovington, "as to prevent a colored woman from receiving home work when it entailed her waiting in the same sitting room with white women." While a very few black women managed to overcome the racial barriers (a white reform worker reminisced about seeing "paper tags threaded with string by an old Negro dying of tuberculosis on Cornelia Street"), they found themselves almost entirely excluded from the garment industry that permitted white women to preserve their maternal roles even as they contributed to the family's coffers.[7]

Because of their exclusion from New York's industrial sector, black workers, far more often than members of any other group in the city, found themselves consigned to unskilled, menial, and service jobs. Between 1890 and 1910, more than half of employed black men over the age of ten worked in domestic and personal service, as opposed to less than one-fifth of white men.[8] Similarly, black women found work almost exclusively in domestic service, hovering around 90 percent throughout the period 1890 to 1910, as compared to less than half for the aggregate female population. And within the category of domestic service, the vast majority of black women were confined to the least desirable jobs. In 1900, 93 percent of black women engaged in domestic and personal service worked as servants or laundresses. Among foreign-born women employed as domestics in the city (56 percent of the total number of immigrant women employed for wages), 85 percent held these exhausting, unappealing positions. Fewer than twenty-seven thousand of all native white women workers chose laundry or service jobs. U.S.-born white women had far greater occupational options. Most listed in the service category boasted positions as nurses and midwives, housekeepers and stewardesses, or boardinghouse keepers. These occupations were more remunerative, less physically draining, and more prestigious than performing the drudgery of servants' work. (See Table 2.)[9]

The limited occupations available to black laborers tended to be the most dangerous, least reliable, and lowest paid in the city. In 1916 the National League on Urban Conditions among Negroes, an organization founded in New York City in 1911, conducted a study of one hundred black apartment house workers. Despite the variety of positions available in apartment houses, 98 percent of black apartment house employees worked as elevator men, switchboard men, or firemen. Only 2 percent obtained the better-paid position of superintendent. The study noted the "unreasonably long hours and low pay" that came with these jobs, held by 9 percent of gainfully employed black men in the city as compared with only two-tenths of 1 percent of whites. "It is only such undesirable occupations as this," the report concluded, "that the Negro finds open to him to any extent."[10] One building owner concurred. "We can't keep a decent white fellow when we get one," he complained. Hard-

TABLE 2. OCCUPATIONAL CATEGORIES AND SELECTED OCCUPATIONS OF THE
FEMALE AGGREGATE AND NEGRO PAID LABORERS OF NEW YORK CITY, 1890–1910

	Aggregate Population	% of Total Employed	Aggregate Negro Population	Negro % of Total Employed	Negro % of Negro Employed
1890					
Total	251,217	100	8,563	3	100
Professional	9,400	4	78	.8	.9
Domestic	108,073	43	7,455	7	89.9
Trade & Transport.	28,569	11	25	.09	.3
Manufacturing	81,771	33	739	.9	8.9
Laundresses	10,814	4	2,193	20	26
Servants	86,624	34	5,025	6	59
1900					
Total	367,437	100	16,114	4	100
Professional	22,422	6	281	1	1.7
Domestic	146,722	40	14,586	10	90.5
Trade & Transport.	65,318	18	106	.2	.7
Manufacturing	132,535	36	1,138	.9	7.1
Laundresses	16,102	4	3,224	20	20
Servants	103,963	28	10,297	10	64
1910					
Total	586,193	100	26,352	4	100
Professional	45,278	8	603	1	2.3
Domestic	189,619	32	22,654	1	86.0
Trade & Transport.	131,724	22	365	.3	1.4
Manufacturing	166,785	28	2,428	1	9.4
Laundresses	17,823	3	5,213	29	20
Servants	113,409	19	14,097	12	53

Sources: *Eleventh Census. Population, II*, pp. 640, 704; *Twelfth Census. Occupations*, pp. 634–40; *Thirteenth Census. Population, IV*, pp. 571–74.

working white men often received assistance from the building's tenants in finding better positions and soon quit their lower-paying apartment jobs. "This wouldn't happen once in a dozen years to one of my colored men," the superintendent continued. "Consequently we can keep our decent colored boys."[11]

Elevator men experienced a hard life. They typically worked 168 hours every two weeks—seventy hours one week and ninety-eight the next. They had no holidays or days off, and each Sunday worked a swing shift with their night (or day) counterparts. The man with the fourteen-hour shift, scheduled to work from six o'clock Saturday night until eight o'clock Sunday morning, instead continued working until noon, for a total of eighteen hours. His day-shift coworker then came on duty at noon on Sunday and stayed until eight o'clock the following morning, a twenty-hour stint. The two thereby switched night and day shifts at the end of each week. Combined with the long hours, Harold Ellis, a former elevator man (he preferred to call himself an "indoor aviator"), remembered how cold and drafty the nights could become. Furthermore, elevator men had no private room. "If you had to sleep," Ellis recollected, "you had to take a nap sitting up in the hall." Fred Challenor complained that his brief work as an elevator operator made him ill.[12] One of Langston Hughes's early poems, "Elevator Boy," revealed the tedium of this line of work:

> I got a job now
> Runnin' an elevator . . .
> Job ain't no good though.
> No money around.
> Jobs are just chances
> Like everything else.
> Maybe a little luck now,
> Maybe not . . .
> Only the elevators
> Goin' up and down . . .
> I been runnin' this
> Elevator too long.
> Guess I'll quit now.[13]

Longshoremen faced the added stress of seasonal unemployment. When ships came into port, blacks could often find work loading and unloading cargo (though they often were given only the simple task of trucking on the pier). By moving from gang to gang, each laboring from twelve to twenty hours, some individual men managed up to thirty-five hours of work at a stretch. However, these jobs only existed when ships docked at New York City's wharves, making it impossible to rely on steady employment. The uncertainty of receiving a regular paycheck, along with the long hours of heavy, exhausting toil, made this work undesirable enough to whites that black men could often find longshoring positions throughout the pre–World War I era. Black men could also be seen working on underground excavations, in rock drilling operations and land clearing, or laying down asphalt. Many sought jobs working on the subway during its construction at the turn of the century. Because of the dangerous conditions, employers turned to black workers to fill positions that many whites rejected.[14]

Black women, however, found themselves in the unusual position of being shut out of the most dangerous occupations available to female laborers. Because of the tremendous limitations encountered by all women workers, white women took the jobs that were more dangerous but offered more autonomy and conferred greater respect than domestic service. Mary White Ovington explained black women's confinement to domestic service, noting that while factory work was more dangerous than domestic jobs, and sweatshop conditions often compromised workers' health, still the white job seeker "knows her mind, and follows the business that brings her liberty of action when the six o'clock whistle blows." Single white women disdained service work as demeaning, preferring positions in the city's shops and factories that granted them independence in the evenings and on Sundays. Married white women who continued to engage in paid labor frequently sought homework, allowing them to contribute needed income to the family's reserves while replicating traditional patriarchal structures in the home. These women had the power to keep blacks out of industrial occupations and utilized it, at once diminishing competition and proscribing black women to service roles that popular stereotypes affirmed were appropriate for them.[15]

Domestic service jobs offered little to recommend them. Women working as domestics complained bitterly of the absence of free time afforded them. "Living with our employer," explained one woman, "our free time wasn't so free, the pay wasn't very much, yet we couldn't take a second job in the evenings." A white servant described the hardships in greater detail. "I had a good room and everything nice," the woman admitted, "but I'd have spared them all if only I could have had a little time to myself." Her employer had "no conscience as to hours" and demanded that she remain on call "till eleven to answer the bell, for she had a great deal of company."[16]

In the South, where service work was almost the exclusive purview of black women, live-out work became relatively common by the late nineteenth century. Though single women could be expected to live at their employers' residence, the high incidence of married women with young children in the southern labor force required live-out labor arrangements.[17] In New York City, most employers of domestic workers demanded that their staff live at the workplace. This caused tremendous difficulty for women, who frequently had family responsibilities in addition to their jobs. As the proportion of southern black women in New York's domestic service industry grew, their influence forced a gradual trend toward day labor. "[T]he Southern servant," Mary White Ovington observed, "unaccustomed to spending the night at her employer's, in New York also, frequently arranges to leave her mistress when her work is done." Still, the practice of living out did not predominate until the shortage of domestic workers during World War I forced employers to accommodate the demands of their workers.[18]

Even servants who lived in their own homes or boardinghouse rooms had little time at the end of the day to spend with their families or to enjoy other forms of entertainment. Most employers required servants to arrive by seven in the morning and remain at work until dinner had been finished and cleaned—often until nine o'clock at night. Over 80 percent of New York City's servants in 1894, both live-in and those who left their employers' house at the end of each day, worked longer than ten hours in any twenty-four hour period. Problems with chronic fatigue impinged on their ability to then participate in leisure time activities or fulfill their family responsibilities.[19]

The work itself was arduous. A general house servant's day might include cooking and serving meals, cleaning the house (dusting, sweeping, and scrubbing), answering the door, sewing and mending clothes, running errands, washing and ironing, lighting fires, and making beds. A woman in Barbados sent a letter to her daughter who had recently moved to New York City, pleading that she not wear herself out with domestic work. "[W]e know that nothing can be done without money," she wrote, "but my child you must try not to over work yourself as you ar not very strong and you have a dare little daughter. . . . [Y]ou must cair yourself for her sake," she admonished. The irony for black women, however, was that they needed to work in order to provide for their "dear little daughters" and sons, but the domestic jobs open to black women took them away from their families for days at a time.[20]

When white employers viewed their black servants not only as employees but as subordinates as well, domestic work could certainly become distasteful and demeaning. A blues song captured some of the frustrations that black women experienced when working in whites' homes:

> Black gal, black gal, got some work for you,
> Tell me white folks, what you want me to do?
> Got a big house to clean and scrub,
> Dishes to wash, floors to mop and rub.
> White folks tell me, how much you going to pay?
> Well, lemme see now, seeing it's a rainy day—
> Oh thank you white folks, I done heard that before.
> Get away you white trash 'fore you get me real sore.[21]

White employers, demanding efficiency and a cheery disposition from their servants, complained when the hired help behaved insolently. The Ryder family in Brooklyn hired Loretta Rapalyea, an orphan, as a domestic worker. They fired her for "incorrigible" behavior and for "being out nights in bad company." Only fifteen years old at the time of her discharge, Loretta had never received an education. The Ryders controlled her activities and appropriated her labor while withholding her education and demanding all of her time and her goodwill. Though she had worked for the family a number of years, once she failed to maintain the standard of loyalty and cheerfulness they expected from their servants, the Ryders refused to have anything more to do with her. The House of Refuge, a reformatory in upstate New York, contacted Mr. Ryder with the news that she needed to undergo surgery for abdominal problems, suggesting that she might be pregnant. The man wrote back, telling the institution that he was "not interested in girl." She died alone soon after the operation.[22]

As may have occurred in Loretta's case, sexual assault remained a constant threat in the lives of domestic workers. Though white servants confronted this threat as well, prevailing stereotypes about black women's sexuality limited their ability to defend themselves. New York's legal system denied that white men could sexually victimize black women, and the courts responded to black women's charges accordingly. One domestic servant who pleaded for financial assistance from a municipal relief agency told a story of repeated sexual violations by a variety of white men at her place of employment. At her first application, she was an unmarried mother of an infant. The woman explained that she had endured a yearlong sexual relationship with her employer's white gardener. When she became pregnant, the man denied any involvement with her. She brought suit against him in court, demanding financial assistance for the child. She lost the case. The agency helped the woman find another service position that would allow her baby to accompany her. There a white grocery deliveryman raped her and left her pregnant. She took him to court as well, again seeking child support. She again lost her case. Some years later she returned to the relief agency pregnant with a third child by a white man. Within five years, this woman had given birth to three children, all of whom had been fathered by white men who refused to take any responsibility for them. The courts felt no compunction to intervene, forcing her to support her children in any way she could. She continued to work as a servant for an employer ambivalent about the presence of three small children. When the youngest died both her employer and the reform agency blamed the woman for neglecting the baby.[23]

Black women's overwhelming dissatisfaction with domestic service caused tremendous turnover among the workers. Housework, explained one critic, "does not create much ambition; the mistress moves, flitting, in New York fashion, from one flat to another, and the girl also flits among employers, changing with the whim of the moment." A study of

802 black women in personal and domestic service positions confirmed this account. Sixty-four percent remained with one employer for less than eleven months, with nearly one-fifth of the women changing jobs after fewer than three months. Only 14 percent remained in a single position for more than two years. Like white women who shunned domestic service whenever possible, blacks also sought to escape it. As soon as industrial opportunities became available to them during World War I, they left their servants' positions expeditiously. Until other options were open, however, they simply changed employers often in search of better conditions or wages. They rarely found either.[24]

Hoping to preserve a home life while earning money for their families, black women began to carve niches in the labor market that helped them balance multiple roles. Many became laundresses while others hired themselves out as day workers. Laundry work offered some advantages to servant work. A twenty-six-year-old black woman who had begun domestic service at age eleven and found that "sweeping stairs and carrying slops was hard for her," decided after eighteen months in a commercial laundry that hand ironing was "not as hard work as general housework." Another black woman told interviewers that she preferred laundry work to her experience as a servant because she had "more time to herself, and receive[d] better pay than domestic service."[25] But laundry work was extremely difficult and exhausting, requiring a tremendous amount of physical exertion. Few black women were welcome in commercial laundries; most toiled over washtubs in their own apartments, making them perpetual "steam rooms."[26] Mary White Ovington described the familiar scene in a laundress' apartment. "[T]he little flat would be full of steaming clothes, or the clean smell of ironing; and a mother, with a baby on the bed and another at her skirts, would be taking in washing." One migrant from Virginia who supported herself and her family by taking in washing complained that the work had "aged [her] right much since coming to New York."[27]

Like washerwomen, day workers also had the advantage of being at home with their families at night, but they faced the constant vagaries of an uncertain job market. One week they might find work each day. The following week could find them empty-handed. When Mary Rock first came to New York City she quickly found a job that allowed her to come home to her new husband each night. But her employer only needed Mary for a few days' service at a time. "I was with her two days last week and will have one day there every week Friday to mend and put away her clothes," she wrote to her sister. Mary's letter also conveyed her insecurity about her future. "I may be there all next week as she telephoned to me last night that her Japanese boy would leave to day so she wants me to come and help her until her other man comes[.] [S]he has hired a colored man but he cant come for a week or two." The irregular schedule made day workers' income very unreliable. This was especially difficult for women who depended on day work as the sole means of support for their families. And child care concerns plagued day workers just as they did domestic servants. Though these women returned home in the evenings, they still needed to find supervision for their children during the day.[28]

In addition to the difficult, dreary, and sometimes dangerous working conditions experienced by black workers, their earnings relegated them to a life of poverty. The study of apartment house workers found that the average pay of elevator and switchboard men was $27.50 per month. Doormen earned an average of $32.50, though few blacks held this marginally more lucrative job. Typically, apartment house employees also received in the vicinity of $3 per month in tips, bringing the majority of these workers a monthly salary of just under $31. The average income, then, for one of the largest groups of black workingmen was $2 a week lower than the recommended minimum wage of $9 per week advocated for single women in New York City by the New York State Factory Investigating Committee.[29] While longshoremen earned a slightly more livable salary of $11 per week, the inconsistency of available work left them in at least as precarious a position as that of elevator operators. And even this wage remained well below the $60 per month deemed the minimum necessary for a family living in New York City.[30]

Within the aggregate black population, over 75 percent of men working in twenty-four different occupations earned less than $6 per week. A further 20 percent received between $6.00 and $8.99. Few of these men worked in positions that allowed them to supplement their incomes with tips. Women's work paid poorly as well. A survey of sixty laundresses found that fifty-one earned between $4 and $6 per week. Servants fared the same. Of 979 women employed in general housework, 871 earned salaries in the same range. Overall, of 2,138 black women domestic and service workers studied between 1906 and 1909, 7.7 percent earned less than $4.00 per week, 45.5 percent between $4.00 and $4.99, and thirty-nine percent from $5.00 to $5.99. Only 7.8 percent earned more than $6 a week.[31] A study of forty black families found that their average weekly earnings, including the wages of all workers in the family, to be between $12 and $15. With that income, an investigator found that after regular expenditures a family had only $11 remaining per month to provide for clothing and food. "Such people must be all the time in debt," he concluded tersely.[32] Forced to buy clothes and other necessities on installment at high interest rates, many black families found themselves in a cycle of indebtedness from which they could not easily escape.[33]

Employers, taking advantage of the economic struggle confronting most black New Yorkers, offered lower salaries to their black employees than to their white employees. The contractors for the Catskill aqueduct reported that they hired black workers at $1.75 per day, though they had tried to entice native-born whites with higher wages. "We have paid [white men] as high as $2 and $2.50 to set up forms and at laboring work of that kind," they admitted.[34] In another instance, the owners of several apartment houses in the vicinity of West Eighty-fourth Street sought to replace their black workers with whites. They raised the monthly salary to $40, up $10 from the black workers' wages. When the switch proved unsatisfactory (the owners complained that they could not find reliable white workers) and the black men returned to their jobs, the wages returned to the original $30.[35]

On the meager salaries earned by blacks in New York City, very few families could put any money into savings, making periods of unemployment especially difficult. Workers who left their jobs in search of better opportunities were laid off; those who could not report to work due to illness or injury faced the prospect of destitution. These conditions contributed substantially to the economic uncertainty experienced by most black families and created the impetus for sending so many black women into the work force.[36]

A far higher percentage of married black women worked for wages than white women. For most gainfully employed white women, paid labor served as a temporary interlude between coming of age and entering marriage. The majority of white women left their jobs upon marrying and remained at home, though some continued to perform home work in the tenements. Black women, however, whether or not they had husbands, found themselves compelled to work regardless of their marital status and late into their lives. While only 4.2 percent of New York's married white women held jobs at the turn of the century, nearly one-third of the city's married black women earned an income.[37] By 1910 over half of black women with husbands remained in the work force. In that same year, only 1 percent of married Russian Jewish women worked for pay, concurrent with 5 percent of Irish women, 30 percent of German women, and 36 percent of Italian women.[38]

The economic conditions that required married black women to enter the work force also obligated many to continue working until late in life. At the turn of the century, while young black women under the age of twenty worked at similar rates to foreign-born white women of the same age cohort, a marked disparity emerged after women achieved an age when many married. By their early twenties, less than half of white women of foreign birth or with immigrant parents participated in the paid labor force, as compared with 66 percent of black women. And after the age of forty-five, more than half of black women continued to engage in paid labor, as compared with only 14 percent of white immigrant women. The capriciousness of black men's incomes, the persistent demographic imbalances that precluded some women from ever marrying, the high rates of widowhood, and the inability of sons and daughters to support elderly parents all forced black women to continue working long after most white women had ceased gainful employment.[39]

While most black New Yorkers struggled to make ends meet, a small group overcame the odds and achieved financial success. In 1890, a meager 1 percent of black men worked in skilled jobs, but as the black immigrant and migrant populations grew the proportion increased nearly fivefold, lagging less than 1 percent behind the ratio for white New Yorkers. Still, the composition of black skilled workers differed sharply from that of white men. In 1910, 40 percent of all black male professionals worked either as musicians, actors, or artists. Just over one-fourth of professional white men were similarly engaged. Clergymen comprised another 8 percent of professional black men. Conversely, nearly 15 percent of professional white men worked as lawyers and judges, and over 10 percent as physicians and surgeons; only 3 and 4 percent, respectively, of black professional men held these occupations.[40] At the turn of the century, only forty-two black physicians and twenty-six black lawyers served New York City's black population of more than sixty thousand.[41]

Even as the ranks of skilled workers grew in the early years of the twentieth century, some faced new challenges in New York's changing racial climate. Black barbers, for example, discovered that they had far fewer customers, particularly among white clientele, after the turn of the twentieth century. While their numbers remained virtually unchanged between 1900 and 1910, white male immigrants became barbers in ever-growing numbers. Their ranks swelled from 1,744 at the turn of the century to an astonishing 10,115 ten years later.[42] The increased availability of white barbers, coupled with a growing disdain in New York City for black people generally, forced black barbers and other entrepreneurs to turn more and more exclusively to black patrons for their livelihood.

The advent of civil service reform in 1883 helped to increase the ranks of the black professional class. Clerks working for the municipal or federal government also comprised a relatively large proportion of the black elite. U.S. Post Offices in the city employed nearly two hundred black men in 1909; others could be found at the New York City Custom House and in other clerkships around town. Because so few white-collar jobs were available to black men during this period, clerkships—often mere stepping stones to white workers—were highly coveted positions for blacks that conferred status and relative wealth. Ambitious men studied vigorously for the civil service exam in their spare time, and some

Caribbean immigrants even became citizens just for the chance to join the government's payroll.[43]

Nevertheless, the city resisted blacks' entry into the professions. Between 1873 and 1895, for example, the city of New York appointed no new black teachers to any of its schools. The 1873 law to end school segregation in the city mandated that all public schools be open to any of the districts' residents. Though many of the city's black residents had fought for this change, its adoption brought unexpected hardship to black teachers. The migration of the black population to other districts within the city led to their entrance into previously all-white schools. By 1880, only three all-black schools remained in the city, and the Board of Education voted for their closure. After a vigorous struggle, led in large part by black teachers who feared for the loss of their jobs, only one of the schools was closed. The remaining two maintained their all-black teaching staffs but were open to pupils of any race.[44]

Still, with the exception of these two remaining schools with black teaching staffs, black teachers found themselves virtually excluded from their profession. It was not until 1895 that Susie E. Frazier, after a long battle with the city, became the first black teacher to receive a regular appointment at a white school with an otherwise all-white staff. Despite this breakthrough, few blacks managed to secure jobs in the city's schools. Southerners trained at normal schools and who had taught in black schools there often discovered that their training did not suffice for New York City's more rigorous standards. Howard Johnson and Anna Murphy both recalled that their college-educated parents had been forced to take menial jobs when they could not find work "in the white world." Johnson's father "smashed baggage at Grand Central Station." During his free time, he played on a baseball team "comprised of the [other] redcaps at Grand Central, half of whom were Ph.D.s." Murphy's father, a migrant from South Carolina with a degree earned at the Avery Normal School in Charleston, became the head bellman of a large hotel in New York.[45]

White workers in New York worked hard to ensure that blacks would not compete for more lucrative jobs in the city. In 1909, William L. Bulkley was named principal of Public School 125. The school's white teaching staff railed against a black man replacing the white acting principal. They almost unanimously agreed to request transfers from the school board.[46] Other white workers became violent when confronted with the prospect of competing with blacks. The *Crisis*, a monthly magazine published by the NAACP, complained in 1912 that white chauffeurs in New York were using subterfuge to eliminate competition from their black coworkers. A black chauffeur described the difficulties. White drivers would "put mothballs in our gasoline tanks, short-circuit our ignition system and throw the carburetor out of adjustment. One man put emery into my gasoline tank." Another black chauffeur in New York was physically assaulted.[47]

White employers were often complicit in keeping their labor force free of black workers. When an electric company wrote to the principal of one of New York City's high schools in search of some "bright, clean, industrious boys" to join their business, the principal asked if they would give employment to black youths who met the qualifications. "The next mail brought the expected reply that no colored boy, however promising, was wanted." An editorial in the *New York Call* detailed the breadth of the problem: "The man who has a trade at his fingers' ends finds all forces combined to prevent him from making a living thereby. First, the employer tells him that he has no prejudice against color, but that his employees will object and make his business suffer. If, perchance the negro gets by, is given a chance to make good, the employees in the office, factory and workshop combine to injure his work and to make life miserable for him."[48]

Employers openly admitted that they preferred to hire white laborers, and settled for black employees only when no alternatives could be found. New York City's Police Department confessed as much in 1907 when it requested that the position of cabin boy for the police boat "Patrol" remain in the noncompetitive municipal civil service class. Mr. Blot, a representative of the department, explained the rationale. "The position is a very menial one," he testified before a committee evaluating the request. "It is simply waiting on the crew, washing dishes, and doing odd jobs around of that sort. . . . [I]t is very doubtful if you could get a white man . . . who would take the job." With a salary of just twenty dollars per month for the performance of menial service work, Blot concluded, "It is a pretty hard job to get anybody to take it." The motion was granted, and a black man was hired to fill the position.[49]

A study conducted in 1907 of 528 black men living in New York City determined that of the ninety-four claiming to have trades, only twenty-seven found employment that utilized their training. The remainder worked as unskilled and menial laborers. The National League on Urban Conditions among Negroes found that 26 percent of the apartment house employees interviewed in 1916 had learned a trade before being compelled to accept menial work for their survival. And the rise in immigration continued to exacerbate the problems for black men. "The difficulty of finding desirable employment for colored men and women is increasing and not diminishing," complained members of a reform organization after the turn of the century.[50]

A Caribbean immigrant in New York City, known simply as Panama, recalled his experience when trying to find work. Upon arriving in the city, he went to an employment office in search of a job. Hearing that a company was looking to hire an engineer, Panama applied. "We don't want no porter here," the superintendent immediately told him, revealing his assumptions about black men. Insisting on the chance to prove his abilities, Panama impressed the man with his effective handling of the engine. The supervisor then came to talk with Panama. "I will tell you," the supervisor said frankly, "if you wasn't a black fellow, if you was a white fellow, then you would have a job all your life here. But since you're a black fellow, I can't keep you here." Finally, Panama was forced to take work as a handyman. "No, no, if you were a black man you couldn't get a job as an engineer in this place here," he angrily told an interviewer. "You want them to kill you? . . . That was a white man's job. Do you think that you could go near an electrician's shop? Do you think that you could go near a bricklayer's job? They kill you. Those were white man's jobs."[51]

One of the most effective ways of avoiding competition with black workers was by excluding them from the city's labor unions. The majority of local unions in New York City refused membership to blacks, virtually eliminating them from many fields of skilled work. In 1906, an investigator found a total of 1,388 black men in the city's trade unions. She estimated this to be approximately 5 percent of those gainfully employed. These union men were concentrated in a total of twenty fields, including asphalt workers (320), teamsters (300), rockdrillers and tool sharpeners (250), cigar makers (121), bricklayers (90), waiters (90), and carpenters (60). The remaining thirteen unions had fewer than fifty black members each. An additional 102 different trades on the list of the Central Federated Union, however, claimed no blacks as members.[52] Women seeking jobs in New York's factories faced similar difficulties. The shirtwaist makers' union refused admission to black women, thereby preventing them from working in the city's shops.[53]

Few unions maintained official policies excluding black workers. But white members and union leaders found ways to keep their ranks all white. One black man who had been a mason in Virginia and Washington arrived in New York with high hopes for a bright future. But when he applied for admission to the union in order to find work in his field, he was told he "must have some one to vouch for him."[54] White union members rarely acted as sponsors for black applicants. Other potential black members were repeatedly told that the union was not accepting new members, or simply ignored blacks' efforts to join.

The handful who managed to acquire union cards learned that union leaders often discriminated when allocating jobs. Even as members of labor organizations, blacks could not count on the prospect of steady work. "The Negro," commented a black bricklayer, "has to be extra fit in his trade to retain his membership [in the union], as the eyes of all the other workers are watching every opportunity to disqualify him, thereby compelling a superefficiency. Yet at all times he is the last to come and the first to go on the job, necessitating his seeking other work for a living, and keeping up his card being but a matter of sentiment. . . . While membership in the union is necessary to work, yet the hardest part of the battle is to secure employment."[55] Both from inside and outside labor organizations, blacks found the task of acquiring skilled jobs to be nearly impossible.

Blacks in New York tried to rectify some of the problems of being excluded from white unions by forming their own organizations. Despite some concern that "to draw the color line themselves would be a great detriment," in 1907 a number of black printers joined together to establish the Negro Printers' Association. They cordially invited "all Afro-American printers" to enroll, "and by so doing help a good and necessary movement." Later that same year, New York's black carpenters mounted a successful campaign to organize a black local of the Carpenters' Union. Of the eighty-six black carpenters in the city, only a small number had managed to gain entrance to local unions, "and these few have not been especially pleased with their situation, even after their admission." After initial rejection, the District Council of Carpenters approved the application to establish a black local. Following the carpenters' lead, others formed organizations as well. In 1912, the Colored Public Porters' Association was established with a membership of forty-six. The Elevatormen's and Hallmen's Association, with forty-five members, came into being that same year, along with the Colored Chauffeur's Association. Black longshoremen began exploring the possibilities of creating their own union as well. All of these groups sought to obviate the impact of racial discrimination on black workers.[56]

One of the most active and effective organizations in New York working to ameliorate blacks' economic position in the city was the National League on Urban Conditions among Negroes (commonly known as the Urban League). Formed in 1911, the Urban League brought together three groups in New York City that had been striving to reform blacks' condition: the National League for the Protection of Colored Women (formed in 1905), the Committee for Improving the Industrial Condition of the Negro (1906), and the Committee on Urban Conditions among Negroes (1910). This combined organization provided a variety of services to blacks seeking decent jobs. It helped skilled black workers form associations to increase their bargaining power with employers, opened two industrial schools in the city to provide vocational training, and offered a job exchange program that allowed employers to post open positions and job seekers to list their skills.[57]

The Urban League made direct appeals to white employers, touting the value of black labor. In 1914, for example, J. T. Clark, secretary of the Urban League's Housing Bureau, wrote a letter to the *New York Times* in response to a complaint made about the quality of janitors in the city. Since "such lines of service do not ordinarily attract a very ambitious class of white workers," Clark declared, apartment house owners should look elsewhere for efficient employees. He suggested that they "give some of our colored men an opportunity along this line. . . . I know of many colored men who have special training in janitor work, but have not corresponding opportunities to apply their experience." As a result of its efforts, the Urban League found jobs for a few hundred applicants each year and helped to train many others in skilled trades.[58]

White workers fought to undermine these incursions into their professions. James L. Wallace, one of New York's foremost black labor leaders after the turn of the century and an agent of the International Union of Pavers and Rammersmen, called for black men to apply for jobs as pavers in the city. "I could fill the streets with colored pavers could I get them," he claimed in a newspaper advertisement. Initially, white pavers supported their black coworkers, going so far as to strike against an employer who refused to hire black workers in 1906. But by the following year, white pavers had had enough of the competition. The black pavers' local fell three months behind in their dues payments to the governing body. According to the union constitution, that warranted the local's suspension until full payment had been made. When the black local presented their dues in full three days later, "the treasurer not only refused to receive the dues, but the white union immediately got an injunction against the colored pavers." This injunction prevented the black local from appealing to the executive committee or to the national meeting. After more than three years of legal battles and the assistance of the NAACP, the court finally lifted the injunction on the condition that the black local pay $348 to the white union as reimbursement for expenses. In 1911, the black pavers were still working to win back all of their rights as union men.[59]

·Facing so many obstacles from organized labor, some blacks took advantage of opportunities to break into new occupations by acting as strikebreakers. A white journalist warned his readers that "[i]n this matter of excluding colored men from unions, skilled mechanics must remember that they run the risk of building up in the United States a great body of justly indignant and always available STRIKE BREAKERS."[60] Some blacks, frustrated by their inability to find skilled jobs, actively encouraged blacks' participation in breaking strikes. Referring to a lockout of union workers by New York City's Building Trades Alliance, one man commented, "[W]ere there 38,000 colored men skilled in these branches, the exclusion from membership, heretofore so potent, would lose its power and they could secure work in spite of the attitude of the several trade unions."[61] In 1886, a black newspaper encouraged blacks to answer the Third Avenue Railroad Company's appeal for workers to replace its striking employees. The *New York Age* repeatedly rebuked whites for their disruptive strikes and attacked unions for their discriminatory practices. It went so far as to censure the practice of honoring picket lines.[62] While not all blacks viewed strike breaking so favorably, for ordinary black men and women trying to earn a living, strikebreaking offered one way to better their condition.

By the 1880s, newspapers around the country regularly reported black strikebreaking activities. Dock workers, steelworkers, cloak makers, meat packers, and coal miners throughout the North all felt the effects. In New York in 1887, 1893, 1895, 1903, 1904, 1907, 1910, 1911, and 1912, black strikebreakers played a role in labor conflicts involving the city's longshoremen, laborers, subway workers, street cleaners, baggage handlers, hod carriers, waiters, and garment workers.[63] One black man in New York City, himself an active union supporter, admitted that unless more white unions in the city began to accept black workers in their ranks, blacks would be forced to continue their role of strikebreaker. "I find that discrimination on the part of unions is still made," he remarked, "and with Negro mechanics and workmen steadily coming into New York . . . and being forced into idleness by the attitude of the trade unions," conflict between white and black workers could be the only outcome.[64]

White and black longshoremen on New York City's docks had a long history of racial strife. In June 1863, for example, three thousand Irish longshoremen lost a strike for higher wages in large part because of the introduction of black strikebreakers. Tension between the two groups ran high, and sporadic violence plagued the docks throughout the spring and early summer. A month later, many of the defeated Irish longshoremen were among those participating in the brutal draft riots in which uncounted numbers of blacks were murdered or driven out of the city. In 1887, shipping companies in New York again turned to strikebreakers when the Knights of Labor organized the "big strike" on the city's docks. The National Steamship Line brought in blacks and Italians to replace the strikers, but while the Italians were retained as dock workers, when the strike ended blacks found themselves again without jobs. Six years later, in a widespread strike in Brooklyn, blacks brought from the South helped to break the strike.[65] One black member of the longshoremen's union explained bluntly some years later, "[W]e are in the union today because the white man had to take us in for his own protection. Outside the organization the Negro could scab on the white man. Inside he can't."[66]

Despite their relatively frequent use as strikebreakers, black men did not gain a permanent foothold in the city's longshoring industry until 1895, when the Ward Line used them to break a local strike. The company subsequently hired blacks exclusively for a number of years. Strikes in 1899 and 1907 further strengthened blacks' position on the New York waterfront. The *New York Age* editorialized about the 1907 walkout, asserting that strikers who prevented others from working "should be put in jail." In that labor conflict, Italians on the picket lines mobbed six black strikebreakers. Four of the strikebreakers were locked up for disorderly conduct. They "should have been commended rather than punished," continued the newspaper article.[67] Ultimately, however, this strike helped blacks secure jobs on the waterfront. Some years later, a white New Yorker recalled that in the 1890s, black longshoremen and roustabouts were "still a novelty." Shipping companies soon discovered, however, that "the colored man's brawn was peculiarly fitted for this class of labor" and began hiring blacks in large numbers. "Many of these had been roustabouts on the Mississippi cotton wharves and could handle 400-pound bales without great inconvenience," he exaggerated, and they "brought their levee songs with them," delighting the passersby.[68]

White unionists in New York struggled to keep "the race question" out of labor conflicts. In 1912, members of the all-white International Hotel Workers' Union in New York walked off the job and ran immediately into the problem of black strikebreakers. The manager of the Plaza "took the strike leaders entirely by surprise and brought up a situation that they had not anticipated." He began bringing black waiters from the South to break the strike. The news of his action "was greeted as a sinister and ugly move," and even within the realm of labor strife the strikers considered this move as outside the boundaries of fair play.[69]

Responding to the industry's new strategy, the union contacted the Colored Waiters Association, urging them not to become involved in the labor struggle. They also appealed directly to black waiters and cooks in the city, inviting them to join the Hotel Workers' Union. When these efforts achieved only marginal successes, a committee of strikers visited a number of black preachers, begging them to advise their congregations against strikebreaking. Despite these efforts, many black men took advantage of the relatively lucrative opportunity to work in some of the city's finest hotels. Many had just arrived from the South in anticipation of the summer resort season, planning to head soon for Saratoga and other popular summer vacation spots. Encountering the strike, a number chose instead to try their luck as strikebreakers, with the hopes of turning that opportunity into more permanent jobs. The presence of so many workers ready to cross the picket lines had ominous implications for the white strikers. "There are two negro waiters available for every white waiter," the manager of the Hotel Majestic warned his white employees. He and others soon demonstrated their willingness to change the complexion of their work force. But as white hotel workers began returning to their jobs with the resolution of the labor conflict, the black strikebreakers again found themselves closed out of both the hotels and the white union.[70]

Like black men, black women took advantage of the opportunities presented by strikes to try and secure jobs otherwise not available to them. On November 22, 1909, one small local of the International Ladies Garment Workers Union called a general strike of all of the shirt-waist makers in New York City. Known as the Uprising of the Thirty Thousand in reference to the number of workers who responded to the call, this strike gave black women a rare chance to obtain work in the city's garment industry.[71]

At the time of the strike's inception, almost no black laborers could be found in New York's garment factories. Only 803 black women were listed as dressmakers in the entire city, and most of those worked independently. While black women could receive training in sewing, dressmaking, millinery, and artificial flower making from two trade schools in New York, rarely could they find jobs in those industries. Mary White Ovington explained why this was so.

[Black women] meet with repeated difficulties; white girls refuse to work in shops with them, private employers object to their color. . . . [D]espite her efforts and occasional successes, the colored girl in New York meets with severer race prejudice than the colored man, and is more persistently kept from attractive work. . . . Occasionally an employer objects to colored girls, but the Manhattan Trade School repeatedly, in trying to place its graduates, has found that opposition to the Negro has come largely from working girls. . . . [A]n aggressive, combative minority [of white women workers] is quite sure that no matter how well-educated or virtuous she may be, no black woman is as good as a white one.

Fanning racial tensions in an effort to undermine the walkout, clothing manufacturers took advantage of black women's exclusion from the industry and the union by hiring them as strikebreakers.[72]

Union officials, concerned about black women's role in weakening the strike, invited the strikebreakers to instead join the union. The *New York Age*, however, rejected this plea, asking, "Why should Negro working girls pull white working girls' chestnuts out of the fire?" The newspaper went on to recruit black women as ironers in factories facing a walkout. An editorial explained the rationale: before the labor troubles began, "Negro girls were not asked to join the union." The newspaper felt confident that the union would discriminate again after the strike, whether or not black women worked as scabs. In the meantime, black women should take advantage of the opportunity presented to demonstrate their capabilities as factory workers and to make money while they could.[73]

In response to the escalating tensions between the union and black workers, a crisis meeting of the Cosmopolitan Club, an organization comprised of white and black men and women "for the discussion of present day problems," convened to discuss the strike. Held at a church in Brooklyn on January 21, 1910, the meeting passed a long resolution regarding blacks' relationship to the union:

> *Resolved,* That the citizens of Brooklyn in mass meeting assembled, protest and urge the women of color to refrain from acting in the capacity of strikebreakers in the shirtwaist making concerns of New York, because we regard their action as antagonistic to the best interests of labor.
> We further urge that, in the event of the successful termination of the strike, organized labor exercise a proper consideration of the claims and demands of the men and women of color who desire to enter the various trades in the way of employment and the protection of the various labor unions. . . .
> Those familiar with negro opinion will feel the significance of this appeal from the leaders of the race. The colored girl is urged, not to enter the market and underbid, accepting any chance to learn a trade, but to refrain from injuring other women, and whenever possible, to ally herself with the cause of union labor.[74]

Members of the Women's Trade Union League (WTUL) tried to reinforce these attitudes, pointing to blacks' participation in the Waist-Makers Union. Elizabeth Dutcher, an officer in the WTUL, claimed that "[i]n New York, colored girls are not only members of the union but they have been prominent in the union." She provided no numbers, mentioning only one woman who served as the secretary of her shop organization during the walkout. Dutcher further asserted that at meetings held at the Fleet Street Methodist Memorial Church in Brooklyn and St. Marks Methodist Church in Manhattan during the strike, "members of the Ladies Waist-Makers Union said definitely and publicly that colored girls were not only eligible but welcome to membership."[75] Despite these claims, after the strike ended the union did little to welcome black women into their organization or the factories. Like other labor unions in the city, the WTUL did not actively recruit black members until after World War I.[76]

Compounding the economic toll exacted by exclusion from New York's industrial sector, white employers of black workers reinforced and aggravated deep divisions within the black population. Employers manipulated regional stereotypes in their drive to employ "ideal" servants and laborers, giving preference to southern- and Caribbean-born black men over native northerners. Distinct geographic groups clung together to ensure their own economic survival and identity, exposing widening schisms within the black population. These practices bred conflict and tension among members of different regional and cultural groups even as these same members faced common challenges because of their race.

Geographic origin played an especially critical role in determining who would succeed in finding skilled work. Northern-born black men's difficulties in finding skilled positions stemmed largely from whites' stereotypes about urban blacks and from competition with better-trained black migrants and immigrants. In the Caribbean, black workers performed most of the skilled manual labor needed on the islands. Southern black men also had opportunities to receive industrial training and work experience before migrating to the North. As a result, of the 13 percent of black workingmen in New York City who claimed a trade, three-fourths hailed from the South. Just over one half of Caribbean immigrants were skilled craftsmen.[77] A survey of black business enterprises in San Juan Hill found that Caribbean immigrants owned and managed fifteen while Americans claimed only five—a restaurant, three poolrooms, and a saloon. While the majority of all blacks worked in unskilled jobs, the cohort of black skilled workers and professionals in New York City were disproportionately natives of other places, contributing significantly to the growing tensions between different groups of blacks in New York's crowded tenements.[78]

Employers' hiring practices, in addition to limiting the opportunities for black workers, exacerbated the differences between black northerners and other black job applicants. Racial stereotypes suggested that urban black men had none of the discipline necessary even for the most menial tasks. Southern blacks, on the other hand, were typically viewed as tractable and subservient, qualifying them for domestic positions, or brawny and strong, making them well suited for physical labor. C. J. Harrah, president of the Midvale Steel Company in Philadelphia, for example, chose to import eight hundred southern black laborers in 1900 to work for him. "We do not take colored men from Philadelphia," he explained. "[W]e find the colored men we get here are accustomed to being brought up as waiters or in domestic capacities . . . so we prefer to get them from Virginia." Southern black men, he claimed, "are lusty fellows . . . with shoulders twice as broad as mine. . . . The men come up here ignorant and untutored. We teach them the benefit of discipline." The general manager of the Pullman Company testified before a Senate committee that his company avoided hiring northerners because "the younger colored man that is found around in the slums . . . [is] not always altogether of the right caliber." To employ porters, the Pullman Company sent representatives into the South who found "men of a desirable class."[79]

Caribbean immigrants received employers' favor more often than southerners. The Urban League, studying the conditions of elevator operators in New York City, discovered that apartment house superintendents had a strong preference for immigrant black workers. Out of fifty superintendents surveyed, twenty-nine favored Caribbean men while twenty-one claimed to have no opinion. None expressed a partiality for native-born blacks. "I prefer the West Indian," explained one employer. "He is more dependable. While he 'talks back,' nevertheless he doesn't get 'sore' and leave the job. The American Negro, on the other hand, if reprimanded, does not flare up like the West Indian, but becomes sullen and the next day leaves the job."[80] Harold Ellis, himself an immigrant from the Caribbean, recalled that newspaper advertisements for porter jobs would state, "'West Indian preferred,' because the West Indian was considered a foreigner, and he was more industrious than native-born blacks. He never had to borrow money before his payday." Native-born blacks resented the preference for foreigners. "There was bad blood between the two," Ellis continued. "The West Indian was getting along better. There were more colored lawyers who were West Indian, more West Indian colored doctors."[81]

Furthermore, immigrants tended to concentrate in small enclaves in the city, helping newcomers find housing and jobs. Two or three countrymen would often room together, and when one was out of work the others would help support him until he secured another opportunity. Frederick Challenor wrote to his wife in Barbados that he stayed with friends during a period of unemployment "so as to prevent me from paying any rent until I can see further." In the meantime, "the working members strain every effort to obtain positions for their comrades." West Indians were "ever on the alert to place some countryman" in available jobs. Their concentration as elevator operators offered them some leverage in interpersonal recruiting—over 60 percent of apartment house superintendents surveyed stated that they hired new workers through the suggestions of their current employees. This kind of cooperation did not occur as often among American-born blacks. As a result, Caribbean immigrants had greater success finding jobs in the city.[82]

Like New York's black residents, members of other ethnic groups in the city also experienced many occupational and economic hardships. Italian men, for example, suffered from low wages, chronic unemployment, and poor working conditions. But unlike black men, their positions in skilled trades, factories, or retail trades offered them the future promise of moving up the economic ladder through promotions, better pay, and on-the-job-training, while the diverse job options open to Italian men gave them a certain degree of control over their work experience. Furthermore, immigrant men typically found themselves in occupations conducive to contact hiring. Migrants often secured job opportunities through the intercession of family members already at work. Employers' willingness to hire their workers' relatives and friends gave immigrant men power and esteem within their kin and ethnic groups.[83]

Black men, more than any other group of men in the city, found themselves overwhelmingly concentrated in dead-end, demeaning jobs. Positions as elevator men, waiters, cooks, and servants offered few avenues for advancement. They also gave black men little chance to assist others in finding work. While in some service industries, such as hotels or restaurants, the concentration of black employees may have been high enough to allow for interpersonal recruitment, most service jobs for black men were found in the nonservice sector and formed a relatively inconsequential proportion of the work force. When these ranks were filled, no other black employees were wanted. Black men, therefore, in dramatic contrast with the experience of immigrant men, found jobs as individuals, often going from workplace to workplace in search of opportunities. Their inability to help others in the search for employment denied black men an important source of power and status within their communities.[84]

In addition, black men often worked alone, which prevented them from developing bonds of friendship with coworkers. Servants, elevator operators, and doormen worked in isolation. They spent hours in solitude, broken only by the presence of white people demanding that they perform a service. This isolation precluded black men from forging emotional connections with others sharing their same experiences. The talking, singing, joking, smoking, and "merry makings" that were an integral and crucial element in the creation of social cohesion within the city's factories did not exist for black men. Neither could black men work at home, as many Jewish and Italian immigrants did, where family units stayed together and men could assert their patriarchal authority. Excluded from factories and even from performing outwork within the confines of the tenements, black men remained on the fringe of America's industrial culture.[85]

"Coon" imagery worked explicitly against black men's attempts to enter the industrial labor force. Factory supervisors in Pittsburgh, for example, made clear that they considered black men to be "inefficient, unsuitable, and unstable" for the heavy pace and highly disciplined nature of millwork. Worse still, employers accepted the popular image of black men as "idle loafers" who sought "easy money." On the other hand, immigrant Slavs' "habit of silent submission, their amenability to discipline, and their willingness to work long hours and overtime without a murmur" made this pool of workers far more desirable as industrial laborers. Though Slavs (and many other immigrant groups) faced condescension and even racial antipathy from whites, this never excluded them from the nation's burgeoning industries.[86]

For black men, the workplace became a source of emasculation rather than a way of demonstrating and asserting manhood. Service work imposed more than economic hardships on black men; it undermined their ability to fulfill the patriarchal role enjoined by white middle-class ideals. Being a good provider was the cornerstone of white middle-class masculine identity in the late nineteenth century. Service jobs, by their very nature, contradicted white masculine ideals of manly independence and responsibility. One man bitterly declared that because of racial prejudice in New York City he could only legitimately be considered "half a man." Black men, like Frederick Challenor, struggled to provide for their families and to become, as Challenor succinctly explained, "independent." Low wages precluded most from doing so. Frederick Challenor's best job prospect only paid fifty-five dollars per month, for example, and many of the positions he took paid well below that figure. Unable to act as the sole—or even primary—breadwinner, few black men in New York gained respect or status as a result of their labor.

None of the traditional symbols of manhood were easily available to black men. The camaraderie and kinship ties that linked so many immigrant men on the job did not exist for most black workers. And in a world in which work in large part defined manhood, black men could not be considered "manly" if they worked in service positions. These jobs were the antithesis of masculinity; the ideal servant, after all, had to be submissive, subservient, and docile and needed to follow orders. "Men are not valued in this country . . . for what they are," declared Frederick Douglass. "They are valued for what they can do. It is vain if we talk about being men, if we do not do the work of men." Yet in New York City, black men were unwelcome in occupations that gave them independence, responsibility, power, or prestige. It was a profound struggle to be, as W. E. B. DuBois described his own experiences, "a man and not a lackey."[87]

William L. Bulkley, the principal of a nearly all-black public school in New York City, described the conversations he frequently had with black boys who came to him seeking authorization of their working papers. "What kind of work will you do," Bulkley would ask. "I am going to be a door-boy, sir," came the typical reply. "Well, you will get $2.50 or $3 a week, but after a while that will not be enough; what then?" The job seeker often expected to become an office boy next, then probably a bell-boy. When prodded to see the culmination of their careers, many expressed their desire to achieve the position of head bellboy. "He has now arrived at the top," explained the principal, "further than this he sees no hope. He must face the bald fact that he must enter business as a boy and wind up as a boy."[88]

In his collection of essays, *Darkwater*, DuBois wrote about the psychological toll that service work took on black men. He struggled as a youth to avoid menial labor that he hated "instinctively." Instead he performed odd jobs and chores "that left me my own man." He clung to his independence, making it central to his sense of dignity and self-respect. Once, however, he needed money and took a waiter's job at a large hotel. "Our work was easy, but insipid," he recalled. The absence of mental challenge was compounded by the recognition that whites encouraged black servants to behave submissively.

I saw that it paid to amuse and to cringe. One particular black man set me crazy. He was intelligent and deft, but one day I caught sight of his face as he served a crowd of men; he was playing the clown,—crouching, grinning, assuming a broad dialect when he usually spoke good English—ah! it was a heartbreaking sight, and he made more money than any waiter in the dining-room. I did not mind the actual work or the kind of work, but it was the dishonesty and deception, the flattery and cajolery, the unnatural assumption that worker and diner had no common humanity. It was uncanny. It was inherently and fundamentally wrong. . . . Then and there I disowned menial service for me and my people.[89]

Nevertheless, because of the disdain with which whites held service work, black women were virtually assured of a job—if they were willing to accept the low wages and difficult working conditions that corresponded with domestic service. Throughout the end of the nineteenth and early twentieth centuries, the demand for domestic servants in New York City far exceeded the supply of women willing to take these positions. And black women seemed to whites to be particularly well qualified to fill domestic jobs. Prevalent stereotypes of black "mammies," suggesting an eagerness to serve white families and cook hearty meals, confirmed for white people that black domestic workers would well care for whites' homes and children. Even as black women were scorned for their supposed insensitivity toward their own children, they were renowned for their capabilities in white people's homes. The New York Colored Mission offered a free employment office where they annually secured domestic service jobs for hundreds of black men and women, with the numbers increasing each year. In the annual reports, the mission often noted that the "demand for good servants is constantly in excess of the supply."[90]

This situation provided something of a safety net to black women and conferred on them a degree of authority and influence within their social and kin networks that was rare for women of other groups. The shortage of servants in the city enabled black women to assist friends and relatives in finding jobs. Although a woman's employer may not have required other servants, she often knew of someone else who did. Black women could offer personal recommendations to fill available openings, thereby securing positions for others. At a time in which black men suffered in esteem and respect because of their labor, black women attained a degree of status due to their ability to assist others in finding jobs. Informal recruitment remained the preferred hiring method among white employers of servants at least until World War I.[91]

Black women's overwhelming presence in the workplace undermined traditional relationships in a patriarchal society. Confronted by the competing pressures of family and financial concerns, black women sought ways to raise children, preserve marriages, and bring money into the household. Many faced these responsibilities alone, the result of either widowhood, abandonment, separation, or choice. With or without partners, black women, with extremely limited employment options available, struggled to balance the many roles they had to play. At the same time, black men's frequent inability to provide economic security for their families had profound consequences as they sought to establish their masculine identity and endeavored to keep their families from destitution. Finding ways to preserve and maintain their families proved to be among the greatest challenges black New Yorkers faced.

Chapter 5

The Anxiety of Keeping the Home Together

The everyday struggle for economic survival wrought havoc on black people individually and collectively. Poverty exacted its toll in the number of lives lost to disease, undernourishment, poor health care, and dangerous jobs. Its price was paid in mental anguish, the separation of children from parents and husbands from wives, and the vulnerability of unsupervised children. With few resources at their disposal and only a limited number of organizations providing services to them, black people endeavored to develop support networks from among strangers and sought creative ways of enduring their hardships. But imminent (or actual) destitution could devastate families despite the most strenuous efforts to preserve them.

Mary Rock, a newlywed, moved to New York City with her husband from Canajoharie, New York, early in 1903. Soon after arriving, she sent an optimistic letter home, letting her family know that "I got here all right and am all settled and Harry has a nice place running an elevator." Mary understood that she too would need to work and soon found temporary employment as a servant. Despite the bright prospects, she hinted that New York did not feel like home. "We will stay here until spring . . . but no longer," Mary confided to her sister. But August of the following year found them still in the city, and the outlook now seemed grim. Neither she nor her husband could find steady jobs, and Harry would be forced to leave New York and accept work on a passenger ship if conditions failed to improve. "I dont want him to go," Mary lamented, "as I will be alone so much then but times are dull now and they cut his wages down at the place he is working so if he cant do better he will go to sea again." The constant battle for survival had drained her optimism. Mary had become "tired of it" and wished "to come out home to live so much." She described her sense of entrapment. "We cant get one cent ahead here and both of us work all we can do is pay it out in rent and get something to eat . . . we pay $12 where we live now just think $6 every other Saturday night and you better have it or out on the sidewalk go your things." Harry too, she wrote, "is crazy to get in the country away from this old New York he hates it here."[1]

Mary's letters to her sister speak to the tremendous strain and pressure caused by the threat of destitution. Family stability and cohesion often bore the brunt of poverty's wrath as husbands and wives struggled to make ends meet, keep a roof over their heads, and care for each other and their children. In New York's unwelcoming environment, these could be Herculean tasks. Black women shouldered an especially heavy load. Alone and lonely, with no family support in the city, it fell to Mary to pay the rent, perform the daily tasks of maintaining a household, and await her husband's return as she prayed that her marriage would not be sacrificed to the difficult process of earning a living.

Economic proscriptions in New York City severely undermined the stability of black families, creating hardships and challenges that other ethnic communities did not encounter. Because of the racial lines drawn in New York's job market, black men and women often found themselves required to leave their homes and families in order to bring money into the household. Many black men left during the summer months when job opportunities became available on leisure boats touring the coastline or in the resort hotels of popular vacation spots like Saratoga, Newport Beach, and the Bahamas. New York City's cold winters, with their accompanying high fuel bills and fewer job opportunities, often could only be endured if black men had earned enough during the summer to carry them and their families through the hard winter months. The New York Colored Mission, one of the few philanthropic organizations in the city serving black people, regularly reported near penury during the winter months. Wood yard tickets that allowed black men to work for a day or two in exchange for economic assistance were "most thankfully received, especially where there has been a wife and little children to support, and no steady employment during the severe months of the winter."[2] One man told investigators that he faced this problem every year. A husband with four small children, he found that he could earn enough money during the summer to get the family "fitted out." But as the colder months approached, "work slacked up but expenses went on; sometimes there was sickness and almost always in winter he got into debt."[3] The promise of good tips lured men like Harry Rock away from their families, as they scrambled to find remunerative positions that would pull their families out of debt and ensure economic stability during leaner times.

The transience of the black male population in New York resulted in part from increased job competition with white immigrants in the late nineteenth and early twentieth centuries. European newcomers forced blacks out of the city's better hotels and compelled many black men to spend two or three summer months employed as waiters outside of the city. One man, originally from Richmond, Virginia, spent part of the year working as a porter at Grand Central Station. During the summer, however, he left for the Bahamas, where he acted as manager of the wine room at one of the hotels on the island.[4] Two studies, one conducted in 1911 and a second in 1913, confirmed the individual accounts and revealed that even wintertime could be a season of instability. Men left for "country hotels" in the summer and to warmer climes such as Palm Beach in the winter. A white traveler on a tour through America marveled at the scene in Saratoga. "To see one of these negro waiters in a white apron, a tin tray, covered with small bird-seed dishes, poised upon the upraised palm of his right hand, steering his way through the maze of chairs, tables, and other waiters down the long dining-room, was to see a rare sight," he wrote in his travel account. "These black servants, and the dress and ornamentation of the [white] women, made one feel as though one were wandering about in a mammoth aviary, peopled by birds of paradise attended by Africans."[5] Many of these waiters who created such entertaining spectacle remained in Saratoga only seasonally, coming and going with the flow of money to the resort.

While the practice of following wealthy whites to their vacation spots helped add money to a family's coffers, it strained the resources of the few black-owned boardinghouses in New York City that depended on a steady stream of black lodgers. A black Brooklynite who supported herself by renting out rooms wrote to a friend in the West Indies in May 1910, "you know my hardest times are coming now, boys going off and big rent, but I trust God to get as many as will pay it." A month later, one of the lodgers revealed that the house remained only partially full. "Since Will left his bed has been vacant & I suppose Mr. Best will be going to the country in a week or so," she explained. "Howie has come to be with us today. I dont know if he means to stay. You know the boys are birds of passage in summer."[6]

The impact of black male transience on businesses dependent on black patronage paled in comparison to the strain it created on familial relationships. While many men did not like working on the boats or leaving to take jobs elsewhere, the women and children who remained in New York often suffered more severely. Left without husbands and fathers, they faced loneliness and the uncertainty of whether or not money would arrive in the mail at critical moments. The Montgomery family routinely experienced long separations during the summer months when William left his wife and children for Saratoga. Early in 1906, both of the couple's daughters became ill, the elder with tuberculosis and the younger with the measles. The cost of the medicine nearly exhausted the family's resources. Worse, the quarantine sign placed on the door by the Board of Health frightened away potential employers. Unable to find steady work in the city, William decided to leave for

Figure 9. Black waiters at the United States Hotel, Saratoga Springs, N.Y., 1890s. Collection of Brookside Museum, Saratoga County Historical Society.

Atlantic City in March, far earlier than his usual forays to upstate New York. He needed all of the family's savings to pay for his transportation, leading Mrs. Montgomery to fear dispossession from their apartment for failure to pay the rent. While she typically worked outside of the home and left her younger daughter in the care of her older sister, Golden's illness forced Mrs. Montgomery to stay with the children, compounding the economic strife. In April, only a month after her father's departure, Golden's condition deteriorated dramatically. Mrs. Montgomery became so concerned about her daughter's health that she implored her husband to return home. Despite his anxiety about Golden, William chose to continue working, explaining that as he expected to be laid off at the end of the month, he "would remain in Atlantic City until that time." His absence wore heavily on the family as they grappled with illness, hunger, and imminent eviction. Nevertheless, William had little choice if he hoped to earn enough to support his family.[7]

The possibility that a temporary separation might become permanent existed as an ever-present fear for families who endured the absence of one of their members. Not all men chose to return after a summer away at the resorts or a stint on the ships. When Charles Higgens suddenly stopped sending money to his family after a year and a half of intermittent separations, his wife, Emily, had no idea how to feed and provide for her three children. During his recurrent absences, Charles had regularly mailed a portion of his wages to his wife. The abrupt silence left her panic-stricken; she did not even have an address at which to find him. Charles eventually returned after this interlude, but his absences became more frequent and prolonged over the next few years. Finally, in 1915, Emily wrote to the New York City police department asking them to "please find my husband," who had apparently returned to the city but had absconded again. At that point, he had been missing for eight weeks. She described his appearance in detail and offered some suggestions as to his possible whereabouts. "He is likely to be found at pool rooms or houses of ill repute," she admitted. She bluntly outlined her need. "Babys been sick. I am not able to work, and [it is] his business to care for us." This time, however, her husband stayed away permanently.[8]

Further compounding the impact of voluntary separations for economic or personal reasons, black men's contentious relationship with the city's criminal justice system exacerbated the prospect that black families would be fractured. Unsympathetic white judges rarely showed leniency to black men convicted of crimes and often imposed long sentences and heavy fines or bail, keeping black men away from home. "I want to beg your Pardon for my mistake," Emanuel Travis wrote desperately from his jail cell to Judge Dike of Brooklyn. "For the sake of [my] family I would like to be forgiven as I have a wife & three little children whom I would not like to leave in distress. I again beg your pardon promising you that it will never happen again So help my god Hoping you will help me to get out and work for my little ones." The judge summarily denied his request, leaving Travis in jail and his wife grappling with the responsibility of being the family's sole provider and caretaker.[9]

A couple's separation, especially a protracted one, could undermine the bonds that had originally brought them together. Women learned to survive and even grew accustomed to life without a partner; men who worked outside of the city enjoyed the freedom of not having to deal with daily responsibilities to a wife or children. After months of being apart, Frederick Challenor wrote to his wife, Aletha, in 1912, admitting that "things have not been bright at all" economically. He found himself "much straitened up for money" and deeply in debt to friends and creditors. He felt his failings profoundly, pleading with his wife to understand that "I am doing the best I can for you." Frederick desperately sought to fulfill his responsibilities to his wife and child; his failure to do so not only kept the family apart but also weakened his wife's esteem for him. Aletha confided to a friend that the separation and Frederick's inability to buy the food and clothes they needed put tremendous strain on their relationship. She confessed that she was losing confidence in her husband and worried that he would never have the money to reunite the family in New York City. Only the persuasion of a female friend convinced Aletha that Fred genuinely made every effort possible to bring her back to him.[10]

Even when men and women both found work in New York City, the likelihood of at least one adult's removal from the home far outpaced that for white families. The limited job market for black men pushed many into the most dangerous jobs, precipitating a higher mortality rate than that for any other group of men in the city. The preponderance of widowhood among black women was correspondingly high. Nearly 10 percent of all black women in New York City between the ages of twenty-five and thirty-five reported being widowed on the 1900 federal census. Throughout the period from 1890 to 1915, a larger percentage of black women than white native or foreign-born women experienced the death of their spouse, compounding an already pernicious demographic imbalance within New York's black population. Because they had an easier time finding jobs, more black women than men migrated to the city from the South. As a result, in 1900, 124 black females lived in the city for every one hundred black males. Nearly 20 percent of black women in New York could not find a partner, leaving them alone in the city and increasing the pressure on them to enter the work force.[11]

With or without husbands, black women's work experiences, like men's, contributed significantly to the physical separations of black families. Since the earliest days of colonial slavery, white people had demanded black women's labor. This expectation did not change in the aftermath of emancipation, despite patriarchal challenges mounted by black men and women fighting to keep black women out of the fields and white people's kitchens. Whereas white women who remained at home were celebrated as "paragons of the domestic ideal," black women who did likewise faced whites' ridicule and condemnation for being lazy. In the Reconstruction South, white landowners undermined blacks' efforts to emulate white feminine standards by insisting on black women's continued participation in fieldwork. And in the North, white employers' virtual refusal to hire black men and the widespread demand for female domestic servants both obligated and permitted black women to fulfill the role of provider.[12]

But the primary source of income available to white women in New York City, outwork, remained closed to black women. This form of labor permitted white women to participate in the labor market while preserving traditional gender roles by remaining at home. More importantly, by staying at home, white mothers continued to supervise their children even as they brought money into the household. Black women, virtually shut out of home industries, faced impossible choices that often had devastating consequences for black families. When black women left home to work as domestic servants, they typically had to leave children behind. Though some employers permitted servants to bring infants, few domestic positions allowed women to bring older babies and children, especially those old enough to walk (and potentially destroy whites' property), forcing many mothers to rely on alternatives that rarely proved satisfactory. The absence of adequate supervision for black children left at home reinforced white social workers' suspicions about the weakness of the black family and justified whites' pressure to remove black children altogether from their parents' household.

The growing numbers of immigrant white women entering the paid labor force near the end of the nineteenth century spurred the creation of a variety of day nurseries for New York City's white children. In one rare example of a nursery that also accepted black infants, an investigator discovered that the two black babies had been abused by "a vicious nurse who had all the prejudice of many of her kind concentrated in her." The woman repeatedly pinched the black children, though their dark skin had prevented doctors from easily identifying the cause of their persistent crying.[13] But these institutions more typically rejected black babies altogether, leaving black parents to scramble to find someone to care for their children. In this early period of black migration into the city, many faced the challenges of urban life without familial support. Bereft of older relatives who traditionally would be called upon to help with child care duties, some black parents hired elderly women in the neighborhood to act as surrogates. Also suffering from the absence of kin networks—adult children who would traditionally support elderly parents—these women who no longer had the stamina for service work might scratch out a meager existence by watching other people's children. The arrangements rarely satisfied any of the parties. In 1898 the New York Colored Mission reported that these women earned about twenty-five cents each day per child. Not enough to live on, still the $1.75 weekly cost to hire someone to care for a child represented nearly 30 percent of a servant's wages.[14]

The caregiver, "some poor old woman who has not sufficient to keep her own body nourished," often tried to watch a number of children at a time in order to meet her own expenses. Alternatively, younger women who watched other people's children as a strategy for avoiding outwork might ignore their paying charges while caring for their own children. Lizzie Davis, who placed her two girls with a neighbor woman while she performed day labor, found that the woman neglected the Davis children. According to an investigator, the caretaker "seems to be very lazy and apparently has not given the children proper care." The woman left Lizzie's infant "lying in bed and [would] never take it up during the day," while she obliged the older girl to hold "her own child while she would do her own work and would hardly ever give the child food."[15]

Sarah Watson's efforts to work and provide for her daughter reveal some of the challenges facing both parent and caregiver when women relied on virtual strangers to look after their offspring. Sarah became a single mother in 1910 after her husband succumbed to his battle with tuberculosis, leaving her "the only support for my little girl." Despite her own illness ("she was unable to hardly crawl around"), Sarah sought work and finally secured a steady position. Nevertheless, between meager wages and insurmountable expenses, Sarah finally turned to the Charity Organization Society (COS) for assistance in 1915. At that time, her daughter, Mildred, was living with Mrs. Peck, a neighborhood woman. Mrs. Peck told the COS investigator that "it would be a cruelty to ask [Sarah] to care for [Mildred]. She would undoubtedly lose her present position and in her feeble state of health is not in a condition to take care of anyone." Though Sarah was "anxious to have the baby with her," she could find no job that would permit it. Her live-in position only allowed her to go home on Sundays. Two months later, Sarah placed Mildred in the care of another woman, Mrs. Jones, who charged three dollars a week for the overnight board. But Mrs. Jones had plans to work in Asbury Park, New Jersey, for the summer. In addition, Sarah was frustrated by Mrs. Jones's refusal to wash the child's clothes. For her part, Mrs. Jones complained that she had not received full payment from the child's mother, claiming that Sarah "has paid something but not enough." As Sarah was planning to join her employers at their country home for the summer, she begged the COS for help in finding a new live-in arrangement for her daughter. "I want to take good care of her and this help would make me glad and greateful," she implored the organization. Already facing the painful prospect of not seeing her daughter throughout the summer season, Sarah sought a place where she could confidently leave Mildred for a number of months. Despite her pleas, the COS ignored the particular challenges confronting this single mother struggling to juggle multiple responsibilities. The organization closed the case, arguing that Sarah was fully able to pay for her daughter's care on her own. The action left Sarah in desperate straits and Mildred the victim of circumstances created by her mother's inescapable poverty.[16]

For a woman with small children needing constant supervision, domestic service could prove agonizing. It was often impossible to adequately balance the persistent demands of a baby with the unceasing labor required of servants. Unsympathetic employers, concerned first with their own needs, often obligated servants to neglect their children and care for white babies and households. Employers could be stingy with food for either the employee or her offspring, and certainly babies spent a great deal of their time without parental care. But the mother's ability to hear her child cry for attention or food might create a painful, irreconcilable dilemma for her. In a poignant example of this conflict, a relief organization compelled a single black woman with a newborn baby to place her infant in a boarding home and accept a live-in domestic position. Devastated by the separation and at risk of losing her job because of the amount of time she devoted to visiting her baby, she counted among the lucky ones—she found a situation that permitted her infant to accompany her. After the birth of her second child, her employers began to complain of her "continual fret about the children." When the youngest fell ill and died, the woman "was much grieved and reproached herself that it had not had proper food and care." Her employers, however, seemed relieved. "[A]s her work and conduct improved after the death of the child," the employment agency reported, "they were willing for her to continue in their service." [17]

As children grew out of babyhood, white employers who had permitted domestic servants to bring their infants to work might spurn the presence of more mobile and destructive youngsters in the house. After having her baby with her since birth, in 1892, Annie Holland was forced to board her six-year-old daughter at the Riverdale Orphan Asylum. Annie performed service work, and her employer refused to permit the rambunctious little girl to stay in the home any longer. In the crowded group environment of the orphanage Ella contracted pneumonia and acute tuberculosis. Within a month of being placed at the institution, Ella died.[18] Despite the trauma caused to black mothers by their separation from their children, employers rarely sympathized with their employees' predicament. Prevailing stereotypes of black women as irresponsible and uncaring mothers helped whites rationalize their insistence on keeping black women away from their families. The economic realities that forced black women away from their homes permitted unsympathetic whites to justify their suspicions that black women failed to uphold the ideals of motherhood.

Desperate black parents, unable to find reliable and affordable care for their children within their own neighborhoods, turned to Riverdale (formerly the Colored Orphan Asylum) or the Howard Orphan Asylum, the only two social agencies offering assistance to black children. Each year scores of black families boarded their offspring at these institutions. The Howard Orphanage, founded in 1866 to serve black children who had been excluded from the New York Orphan Asylum, housed more than two hundred black children each year. Of this number, nearly one-fourth were children with at least one living parent. Mothers needing to "go to service" often boarded their children at the asylum for three dollars a month. While this resolved a critical child care concern for people like Maggie Thompson, who turned to domestic service after her husband's death in 1889, the cost of boarding cut into workingwomen's meager earnings and diminished their ability to save enough to ever remove their children from the institution. Boarding also led to long separations that could cause a range of consequences, from the diminution of parental authority to a weakening of emotional bonds. For Maggie and her daughter the impact was immediate; Riverdale authorities reported that the child cried incessantly as a result of being abruptly weaned from breastfeeding.[19]

Perhaps most importantly, having children in an orphanage caused an even greater assault on parent-child relationships than existed when children remained in the tenements. Decisions about a child's upbringing became the prerogative of orphanage authorities rather than the parent's. For example, when Frida Johnson placed her two children in the Colored Orphan Asylum for five months, her daughter, Nora, received unauthorized medical treatment. The girl had acquired the family trait of bow-leggedness that had never hampered her movement. When a doctor from the orphanage requested permission to have the girl's legs straightened, Frida immediately refused. Nevertheless, administrators at the orphanage sent Nora to a local hospital for surgery. The failure of the procedure to eliminate the bone curvature forced the girl to permanently wear a heavy metal cast on her right leg.[20]

Charity workers in New York, concerned more with black people achieving self-sufficiency than stable families, routinely induced the separation of black parents from their children. Case studies from the Community Service Society (CSS) and the Society for the Prevention of Cruelty to Children (SPCC) reveal that white reformers resolutely pressured black parents to place their children in orphanages. Though many parents initially resisted these recommendations, persistent poverty led some to ultimately capitulate. When Henry Gardner's wife died in 1901, his sister, Louisa, took the three children in exchange for his promise of financial support. He worked as a longshoreman and provided his sister with two dollars each week for more than a year. But

December 1902 found Louisa and the children in dire straights, having not heard from Henry in some time. Though the CSS pressured her to place the children in an institution in order to improve her financial circumstances, Louisa refused to "consider [the idea] at all, as she felt it her duty to take care of them." The New York Colored Mission took over the case, supplying Louisa with food and clothing for the children through the end of 1903. Early in 1904, the woman again applied to the CSS for relief. They determined that if she "insisted upon keeping the children . . . she must take the responsibility of their entire care and support." Louisa responded angrily, determined that as "she could not part with the children . . . she would strive in some way to get on." Despite her insistence on the importance of family, however, within two months Louisa had relented. The illness of the children, her own exhaustion, and her inability to afford a decent apartment all contributed to Louisa's decision in March to commit her nieces and nephew to the Colored Orphan Asylum.[21]

The pain of separation made removal of the children from an institution a top priority for many families, but such action demanded tremendous sacrifice and effort. Mary Henry, whose husband had deserted her, left her four children in her mother's care in Richmond, Virginia. When the grandmother could no longer provide for them, she sent the children back to New York City to be with their mother. Financially unprepared for the sole responsibility of caring for so many mouths to feed, Mary left all but the youngest at the orphanage while she made arrangements to rent a larger apartment. Though the Riverdale administration had approved a two months' stay for the children at the asylum, within thirty days Mary removed them from the institution and took them with her to a San Juan Hill tenement. By taking in washing rather than leaving home to work, Mary succeeded in keeping all of her children together. But Mary's success represented only a portion of the cases; Riverdale and Howard Orphanage records are replete with stories of children left by their parents through the duration of their childhoods.[22]

Responding to concerns about growing numbers of very young black children being forced into orphanages or living without proper care at home, a white woman, Mrs. E. E. Greene, began making efforts in 1901 to open a day nursery that would serve the black community. She offered her own ministration, suggesting that black caregivers "possibly not intentionally" neglected their charges. Despite her appeal to "concerned citizens," a half-year later no nursery had yet been established. In 1902, however, a group of black women succeeded in creating the Hope Day Nursery, "where mothers, who are compelled to go from their homes to labor during the day, may leave their little ones to be properly cared for." Until 1913, when the Department of Health granted permission to increase enrollment to forty, the nursery cared for twenty-five children each day. The New York Colored Mission opened a second nursery in 1912, and forty-seven "hard working, sorely tired mothers" regularly took advantage of the services provided while they went out by day to work. In 1915, however, there were still only four day nurseries in Manhattan and Brooklyn that provided care for black children, nowhere near adequate for the number of black children requiring daytime care. And these institutions could not meet the need for overnight care when mothers held live-in servant jobs.[23]

For children, the tenements could be frightening, unfriendly places without parental protection. Frederick Johnson, left under the supervision of his older sister while his parents worked, could not escape the girl's short temper. Angry that the boy wouldn't leave her alone, she had set Frederick upon the hot stove causing a severe burn to his thigh. Over his distraught parent's protests, the SPCC removed the boy from the home and placed him at Riverdale, leaving strict instructions not to permit family visitation. As in so many other cases, the organization failed to address the reasons why black children spent so much time without adult care, further hampering black parents' efforts to maintain and provide for their families.[24]

In the anonymity of the tenements, few neighbors either noticed or prevented child abuse. Four-year-old Willie Mitchell suffered abuse by the husband of the woman hired to care for him. Willie's parents both went out to work each day. The boy's incessant screams finally compelled the building's other tenants to call the police, but by then his body was covered with evidence of his suffering. Sexual predators found easy prey in the darkness of apartment hallways. Percy Jones repeatedly sodomized black boys living in his building. Though he served a six-month jail sentence for his actions, at the end of his term Jones was back in the neighborhood. Harry Boykin threatened Frank Maltanado with physical violence if the boy told anyone that Harry had attacked him in the basement of their building. Similarly, Richard Schermerhorn raped five-year-old Lena Schneider, taking advantage of an opportunity provided by the absence of her working mother. These counted among the rare cases successfully prosecuted. Most attacks undoubtedly went unreported by frightened children or their parents, who viewed municipal authorities with mistrust and who feared that instead of removing the culprit of the abuse, police would take away their children.[25]

Children left to fend for themselves had to find their own strategies for enduring loneliness, fear, and poverty. Edward, a young boy found at home alone one morning by a visiting nurse, shared his creative techniques with her. Eating the lunch of hominy and dry bread that his mother had left for him, he asked the nurse if she would like a piece of chicken. At her negative reply, he offered her some pie. Again she said no and insisted that he explain his prevarication, knowing full well that he had none to offer. "Didn't you ever make believe?" he asked the woman. Eagerly, he explained the game: "Sometimes when my mother goes to work I stay here all alone until she comes. If she's late and it gets dark, I climb into my bed and shut my eyes and go to the country, and there I chase the cows – and the pigs – and the chickens; and then I pick the flowers and the fruit and I have a lovely time. It's great fun!" Though the nurse marveled at the boy's ability to remain optimistic, the story poignantly reveals the toll exacted on black children as they suffered chronic loneliness, fear, and hunger.[26]

The streets offered powerful attractions to older children left without parental supervision. Unlike black adults, black children had few recreational options in New York. At the turn of the twentieth century, reformers concerned about children in the city clamored for the construction of playgrounds as a salutary influence in crowded districts. While white neighborhoods, including those substantially comprised of immigrants, might receive the attention of reformers encouraging the development of playgrounds, black neighborhoods rarely enjoyed such largesse. In fact, when playground advocate Mary Simkovich fought in 1913 to have the city create play space for the working-class children of Greenwich Village, she specifically suggested that the buildings on Minetta Street and Minetta Lane be razed for that purpose. The vast majority of the stalwart black holdouts still living in Greenwich Village resided on these blocks, almost the only places in the neighborhood where black people might successfully rent an apartment. Simkovich's plan would have virtually eliminated the remaining black presence in the area, simultaneously ensuring that black children would not reap the benefits of a new playground. Black neighborhoods in general boasted no parks or playground space, even as other areas in the city began enjoying publicly funded park development. Harlem did not receive its first playground until 1914, and that proved to be little more than the addition of simple playground apparatus to some vacant lots.[27]

Children therefore took to the streets for recreation, exposing them to new dangers. Black children in Harlem found themselves relegated to the occasional empty lot, which not only offered few activities of interest but also exposed them to "questionable practices" that often transpired in the unsupervised areas. Without dedicated play areas, black children competed with cars for open spaces. In 1913, the year before the playground campaign in Harlem, an automobile ran over a young boy skating on West 135th Street. Though the boy survived, one of his friends mordantly noted, "he can't skate half as fast as he could before." Despite admonitions to be careful, other boys continued the practice

Figure 10. Street children playing at the site of a demolished building, circa 1902. Mary Rankin Cranston, "The Housing of the Negro in New York City," *Southern Workman* 31, no. 6 (June 1902): 329.

just days after the accident. "I want to skate and I've got to skate somewhere," one of the boys insisted to a concerned adult. In the absence of organized recreational activities, children also developed informal games and social practices. One observer noted that black children, more than any other tenement population, enjoyed simple visiting among friends after school and made-up games such as taffy-pulls. However, many children could not enjoy even this, being admonished by their parents not to open the apartment door to any outsider in the parents' absence. Lacking designated and safe recreation sites, children sought alternative ways to entertain themselves, often defying explicit instructions from their parents.[28]

As they escaped the cramped, dark quarters of the tenements, black children might be enticed by a variety of temptations and deleterious influences. Florence Wallace pleaded with Mayor Mitchell to intervene on behalf of her son who had been convicted of juvenile delinquency. She and her husband both worked in order to keep their seven children in school. "My aim is to give my family an education my daughter is now in her second year and attends Washington Irving High School to be a teacher," she assured the mayor. "My boy is not a bad boy but was easily led. . . . I need this boy and he has every chance before him and trust some day he will be a good citizen." The court's removal of the boy from the home left the family with one fewer wage earner and without a guardian for the younger children. It also virtually ensured the end of this boy's education. Despite the Wallaces' efforts to make a better life for their children, their sacrifice came at a heavy cost. The absence of the parents left children to their own, sometimes destructive, devices.[29]

The challenge to parental authority marked one of the most painful costs of black New Yorkers' economic struggles. Free of many parental restraints, children could become outright incorrigible. The New York House of Refuge housed many black children at the request of desperate parents who could no longer control their offspring. One girl admitted that although she loved her foster mother, the two had become estranged. The girl explained that her foster mother "refused to allow her any pleasures, had misunderstood her, and kept her closely at home." She left for a boardinghouse. There she met a sailor who left her when she became pregnant. The foster mother complained that the girl had been rebellious and dishonest despite the many sacrifices the family had made to provide for her upbringing and education. Unable to cope any longer, they committed the girl to the House of Refuge. Mary White Ovington described the "terrific struggle" made by black parents to teach and raise their children. But left alone, these children could quickly ignore parental dictums. When a group of black girls behaved rudely to Ovington, she wondered aloud whether they perhaps did not know any better. In a revealing moment of deep filial loyalty, one ten-year-old turned "almost fiercely" on Ovington, insisting, "It's our fault; we know better. Our mothers learn us. It's we that's bold."[30]

Hoping to mitigate the impact of regular and prolonged separations, black parents made extraordinary efforts to protect and provide for their offspring. Lillian Wald, active in the settlement house movement, noted that "[c]olored women are often conspicuously good and tender mothers, and when I have watched large groups of them . . . exhibiting their babies with justifiable pride, I have felt a wave of unhappiness because of the consciousness of the enormous handicap with which these little ones must face the future." Fathers also proved attentive with their children. Mary White Ovington recognized that many black men, far from being the loafers that so many white people believed them to be, in fact worked at night. Though difficult in many ways, this schedule permitted them to dote on their children, often lavishly, during the daytime.[31]

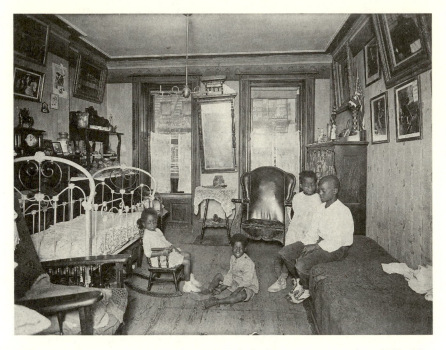

Figure 11. The interior of a well-appointed Harlem apartment, circa 1910–15.
Brown Bros.

Unavailable to demonstrate their affection on a daily basis, parents
tried to surround their children with physical symbols of love. Black
mothers and wives took special pride in maintaining a clean and cheerful apartment. Commentators regularly noted the "pleasant and home-
like rooms" found within the squalor of the city's most dilapidated
tenements. "We may have been, wife and I, a little extravagant in . . .
furnishing our house," explained a black man, "but the house in which
we were born had none of these things, and we are trying to make up to
our children what we missed when we were little." For people who boasted few luxuries, keeping a bright and clean home could offer a ray of
joy in an often bleak world. "We didn't have an expensive home,"
Naomi Washington explained, "but he had a clean home." Mary White
Ovington observed that many black families "love the neat bed with its
spotless white or patchwork counterpane, the shelf of bright china, and
the gay pictures on the walls." Others noted similar conditions. "[T]hey
will oft paper and adorn their apartments so as to give them an aesthetic
appearance," remarked Columbia University sociologist Robert Johnstone of the black families he studied.[32]

Food and clothing became important emblems of the nurturing that parents lavished upon their children. Naomi Washington recalled that her father and his colleague shared a friendly competition over their respective children's sizes. He and the deacon at the Metropolitan Baptist Church would compare their children's weight in a constant battle to boast the heavier offspring. "[T]hey'd be so proud of their [plump] children," she remembered. Setting an elaborate and full table for meals became a regular ritual in black New York. One woman declared to a researcher, "a good table is tantamount to good thoughts." Despite the cost and effort, many women served multicourse meals. An investigator happened upon a Thanksgiving feast, replete with "over bountiful supplies of chicken, turkey, and such loads of good things [that] would be a matter of envy to most white families getting the same income as these negroes." Even ordinary meals seemed excessively lavish to him, with "two or three vegetables . . . , also tea or coffee, cream or milk, bread, butter, pickles, and condiments and desert of puddings, pies or cake." Women typically served the meals on formal dinnerware. "When breakfast or dinner comes you will almost always find the table set. . . . [I]n the most modest homes . . . the meal carried with it the air of a social function; the mother would use many dishes though she must take the time from her laundry work to wash them." Women working as live-in domestic servants often made special meals for their families on days off.[33]

Whenever possible, parents dressed their children well, particularly on Sundays. "We weren't raggedy by a long shot," explained one girl. "I had a Sunday dress, although all my life I wanted to have more than one." Good clothing became a symbol of respectability and status in the face of white outsiders' homogenization of the black population. Though some whites criticized the "fantastic and garish" clothing, black people enjoyed bright and cheerful outfits. "As one watches the boys and girls walking quietly up the street of a Sunday afternoon to their Sunday school, neatly and cleanly dressed," noted a sympathetic observer, "one appreciates the anxious, maternal care that strives as best it knows how, to rear honest and God-fearing men and women."[34]

Madam C. J. Walker's hair-straightening technique offered black parents a new method of asserting pride in their children's appearance. "My God!" writer Richard Nugent exclaimed, "to be like white people you had to do something with that hair. That's how Madame Walker made all that money." Naomi Washington remembered her first experience with the hot combs. "I was a little girl when Madame Walker's product came out. Everybody had it done. . . . I was very tender-headed and afraid, because she had these hot combs. I was crying. She wasn't hurting me, but I was just afraid she would." Washington liked the outcome. "When she was done, Papa said I looked like his grandmother, who was an Indian. I liked the way it looked, but I didn't like those hot combs." Hair straightening became very popular, though women would leave the back of their hair, known as the kitchen, untreated. Doll Thomas recounted a long-standing joke:

Child, your hair certainly looks good.
Oh, yeah? Madame Walker just came over.
Yeah, but she forgot to walk through your kitchen.[35]

Just as they provided material comfort to their children, many black parents, painfully aware of their own educational and occupational limitations, struggled to offer their children a better future. "Mothers keenly alive to the advantages of education [that was] denied to themselves keep their children steadily at school," reported the New York Colored Mission in 1892.[36] But parents faced numerous challenges in trying to provide a decent education for their children. Even the simple walk from home to school could prove difficult. A young kindergarten student, walking with her class to Central Park, encountered a group of angry Irish boys who began taunting and harassing the members of the procession. At the shouts of "nigger," one of the girls began to hang back. "Don't notice them," admonished the small leader. "Walk straight ahead." From a very young age, black children learned to endure hostility all around them. San Juan Hill, notorious for its interracial pitched battles, staged daily conflicts among children. Black mothers regularly complained that their children could not travel unmolested to and from school. They often returned home bloody. "Oh, my father," cried one boy, "I don't want to go to school. The white children will beat me up." When parents were away at work, some black children avoided harassment by shunning school altogether.[37]

The prejudice that prevailed within the school walls further undermined black youths' desire for an education. Black students complained about white teachers referring to them as "niggers," to no avail. Teachers' contempt for black students mirrored the stereotypes held by the white population generally. In a 1915 investigation, a group of teachers denounced black men for being "idle" and "supported by their wives." They based their beliefs on the presence of many black fathers at meetings with teachers and the absence of black mothers. Though the teachers later learned that black men attended school functions because most worked at night as elevator operators, their scorn was slow to fade. Teachers who viewed their students with such disdain had little incentive to effectively educate their pupils.[38]

Once in school, black students found themselves almost exclusively surrounded by other black children. Though school segregation legally ended in New York City in 1884, investigators repeatedly reported the unwillingness of public schools to admit black children. "[N]one of the public school principals," declared a 1915 report, "welcomed colored children." Almost as soon as segregation became illegal, certain schools in the city came to be known unofficially as "colored schools." But in the late nineteenth century, even those schools designated for black students had a relatively diverse population. Grammar School 48, for example, widely recognized to be a "colored school," had a student body in 1896 comprised of black, German, Irish, and Italian students. By the early twentieth century, segregation had grown more rigid, marking an unofficial return to the days preceding the passage of civil rights legislation. The NAACP found in 1913 that fewer than two hundred black students in the city attended racially mixed high schools.[39]

The influx of black migrants and immigrants had a profound impact on the schools serving the black population. The Henrietta Industrial School in San Juan Hill, founded in 1892, experienced a dramatic change in its student population as black residents flooded into this neighborhood. Formerly a nearly all-white institution, by the first years of the twentieth century Henrietta was serving an overwhelmingly black student body. Most were newcomers to the North, having come from either the Caribbean or the South. At times, teachers had to broker ethnic tensions that created strife between U.S.-born and immigrant black students. The greatest challenge, however, came in addressing the varied educational backgrounds of the children. The principal disparaged the black pupils, "especially those who have not been North very long," complaining that they "have no idea of discipline" and that teachers had a difficult time "instruct[ing] these children [so] that they will become good citizens." To be sure, many southern migrants had received little education in the South. An investigator found that many of these newcomers had acquired so little training "that it necessitated practically a fresh start in the lowest grades." Immigrants from non-English-speaking Caribbean islands had the added burden of learning the language.[40]

School authorities reported high black truancy rates that they attributed to the lack of supervision at home. "The children, coming home to solitary lunches, succumbed to the temptation not to return to school after lunch; or, in cases where mothers left home in the early morning before the children were awake, leaving no one to waken and hurry them off to school, they preferred on finding that they were late not to go to school at all." Despite the perception that black pupils had a disproportionate tendency to be absent from school, the first extensive study of black schoolchildren, conducted in 1915, found that their percentages were little higher than those of other groups in the city. None-theless, the belief in disinterested black parents and uneducable children combined to persuade administrators not to expend much energy on teaching black youths.[41]

The tremendous mobility of black families undermined efforts to keep black children in school. "Scholarship is greatly affected by the instability of the school life of the colored children because of the fre-quent shifting of occupation and residence of their parents," observed Frances Blascoer in her seminal 1915 study of black schoolchildren in New York City. "Colored men and women who go to Florida, the West Indies, Bermuda, etc., for hotel service during the tourist season, take their children out of public school and either take them with them or place them in a boarding school. The children then return to school in the spring, or perhaps not until the fall term of the next year." The eco-nomic conditions for blacks in New York contributed to the vicious cycle that prevented black youths from receiving an adequate education and rationalized whites' continued exclusion of blacks from industrial and professional opportunities.[42]

Black students who attended New York City's schools received an infe-rior education and fewer resources than white pupils did. In 1915, the white principal of a nearly all black school in Harlem fought against aug-menting the arithmetic courses available to his students. He preferred expanding offerings in "physical exercise, music, singing, or manual training." Arithmetic, he argued, "would be giving the pupils a double dose of something they did not like." Vocational training became virtu-ally the only educational opportunity available to black high school stu-dents in New York by the turn of the twentieth century. Many white reformers, concerned about black male unemployment, black women's overwhelming presence in the work force, and high black poverty rates, attributed these conditions to blacks' lack of skills. "[T]here is beyond question too large a number of unemployed colored persons in New York," declared the Committee for Improving the Industrial Condition of the Negro in New York. "[I]f employed, [they are] employed in voca-tions more or less menial, and entirely apart from that skill of hand which they acquired in the South or West Indies. City boys and girls can be taught elementary subjects to a certain point, but after that there is little to hold them in school." These critics, along with proponents of Booker T. Washington's manual training philosophy, began to encour-age the formation of industrial public schools for black pupils.[43]

Dr. William L. Bulkley, the only black principal in New York City's public school system, initiated the push for industrial schools in an effort to improve the job opportunities available to the city's black popu-lation. In 1905 he opened an evening manual training program at Public School 40. Its popularity among youths and young adults inspired an expansion of industrial training opportunities. Within two years, three industrial schools had opened in Manhattan and Brooklyn. Though they helped to teach black youths manual skills, these schools could do little to force industries to accept black workers. At the same time, the limitations placed on black children's education contributed to the persistent perceptions that blacks belonged in manual occupations but had little capacity for intellectual pursuits.[44]

Though many parents tried to ensure that their children received a good education, poverty often interfered with those efforts. Thirteen-year-old Fred Walters had been out of school for some time because his parents could not afford proper shoes or clothing. His mother "had tried in every way to get clothes by begging from different friends who had boys but none had clothing to spare." The cost of shoes kept many children barefoot and precluded them from attending classes.[45] A parent's illness, not uncommon in black New York, could force children to stay out of school in order to maintain the household. "[I] am verry sorry that i cannot spare my Boy i am not able to keep him home but i am oblige to Because i am not able one half the time to go out myselfe," Agnes Jones wrote to the COS, explaining why her son was not in school. But the need for more wage earners contributing to a family's income represented the most common reason for pulling children out of school. The Federation of Churches reported in 1897 that two black children worked for every one of any other group. Some girls helped their mothers with laundry work at home when school was out. But most young black women who worked found full-time jobs, shortening their education, forcing them to live away from home, and weakening parental authority. In 1910, 75 percent of unmarried black women who worked for wages either lived with their employers or boarded; only one-fourth who worked still lived at home.[46] Boys were more likely to live at home, working odd jobs that could help the family. Irving Glasgow earned five dollars per month, which he gave to his widowed mother. Another boy washed dishes after school and on Saturdays, earning money to supplement his mother's income from her janitorial and laundry work. The boy's father was unemployed. Like the girls, however, many boys quit school altogether in order to find full-time jobs.[47]

William L. Bulkley recounted a conversation he had with one of his most promising students. The young man approached Bulkley to request working papers. The student had been employed at odd jobs in the afternoons and on weekends while his mother washed laundry in their two-bedroom apartment. Their combined wages could not pay the expenses, however, so he decided to quit school and seek full-time employment. The principal tried to encourage him to stay and finish his studies, but the boy steadfastly defended his decision. "I am old enough now to help mother; she needs me," he told the older man. "And, again, there is nothing better for a colored boy to do if he finishes the course." A dejected Bulkley furnished the youth with his working papers and determined to challenge the prejudice plaguing black job seekers. He helped to organize the Committee for Improving the Industrial Conditions of Negroes which later became part of the National League on Urban Conditions among Negroes.[48]

Conflict with unsympathetic school authorities could challenge parental decisions about their children's education and their family's needs. Mary Frederick, a single mother, found a domestic position for her sixteen-year-old daughter, Laura. Despite the girl's age (she was legally permitted to work at sixteen), a truant officer insisted that she return to school, eliminating both the additional income and the supervision that came with the job. Left to her own devices every day, Laura spiraled out of control. Her mother complained that she "remains away from home until 12 o-clock at night and spends her time on the streets with a disorderly gang of young men." Mary saw her child slipping away; unable to work and lacking the self-motivation to attend school, Laura wound up committed to an institution.[49] Experiences like the one between Mary Frederick and the school officials exacerbated the already difficult circumstances endured by black parents fighting to maintain economic solvency and familial control.

The poverty that kept some children from school impacted black families more than any other group of New Yorkers. Parents at times had to sacrifice their own and their children's food in order to pay the rent. A reform agency reported numerous cases of babies dying "for want of nourishment." In periods of particular penury, black people could be found literally starving to death. During the bitter winter of 1893 to 1894, a particularly harsh one because of both the unusually inclement weather and the economic strife facing the nation, a caseworker from the New York Colored Mission discovered a desperate black woman warming coffee grounds in order to feed her baby. She had not found food for days. In a second dramatic example of material want, caseworkers from the mission found an elderly couple stealing bones from a dog.[50]

The unrelenting struggle to maintain a family as the threat of destitution hovered took a heavy emotional toll on many black men and women. The strain manifested itself in countless ways, perhaps most commonly in a prevailing feeling of hopelessness. "You cannot imagine how deeply humiliated I feel because circumstances compel me to continually appeal for assistance," Ernest L. Williams wrote dejectedly to his former employer, Charles Bennett. "Sometimes, I get so thoroughly down hearted, so completely discouraged, that I feel like giving up the struggle." Williams had taught himself to read and write and had become a fairly successful notary public despite recurrent illnesses. But changes in New York's licensing of notary publics in 1904 left him unable to afford the twenty-five-dollar fee and struggling to obtain the two required affidavits attesting to his character. In his "battle for life & bread," Williams sought nothing more than "to be a man among men." Although he garnered sympathy and respect from white charity workers, both his health and personal solvency remained tenuous for another decade.[51]

The New York Colored Mission reported that during the harsh winter months, some black men, unable to afford food or coal, literally begged for the chance to chop wood. The especially harsh depression that devastated the nation in 1893–94 forced the city's most vulnerable people into desperate straits. The Colored Mission recounted various instances in which black men committed suicide rather than watch their wives and children starve.[52] Benjamin Jones, a salesman from St. Christopher who moved his family to New York City "hoping to improve their condition in this country," experienced the despair and hopelessness that white men would only begin to encounter during the economic upheaval of the Great Depression. Distraught by the unexpected difficulty he endured trying to find a steady and well-paying job in the United States, Jones worked during the summers on the Fall River boats and hoped to save enough to return with his family to the West Indies. During the winter when he regularly faced unemployment, his wife, Ida, found work as a day laborer. In 1901, Ida pleaded with the COS for help with Benjamin. She had begun to "fear for his mind, as he would sit and brood by the hour about their destitute condition and his inability to secure work." A month later a charity worker visited the family and found Benjamin caring for the children and "doing the family washing." The family was experiencing both an emotional and an economic struggle. "Lord knows how we want to fight our own battles and get along," Ida asserted, but Benjamin's continued unemployment left him feeling "wretched." By remaining at home "while his wife goes out to work almost every day," Benjamin considered himself a failure as a husband and father. After three years in New York City, the bulk of which he spent without a job, Benjamin's mental and physiological health had deteriorated dramatically. On March 25, 1903, he died at St. Luke's hospital.[53]

Because of the economic hardships black men in New York encountered, many experienced the loss of their patriarchal authority. Benjamin Jones's wife, for example, as the steady breadwinner for the household, considered major family decisions to be her prerogative. When Benjamin informed a charity worker about the waywardness of their daughter, Ida scolded him publicly and ceased consulting him about family affairs.[54] Like Benjamin, black men who could not fulfill their responsibility as their family's sole—or even primary— breadwinner found themselves deprived of an essential symbol of manhood. Traditional authority relationships within white families, between husbands and wives and between parents and children, did not exist in the same way for black families in New York City. Where white men were typically secure in the knowledge of their families' dependence on them, black men often found themselves economically reliant upon the women in their lives. Samuel Singleton, uncomfortable with his wife's independent income, attempted to shut down her grocery store in San Juan Hill. When she applied for a small loan during a slow period, he intervened, refusing the ten dollars that was offered and questioning "if the shop is an especially good thing for his wife to be engaged in," despite the significant contribution the store made to the family's income.[55]

Black men found their parental authority especially difficult to assert and maintain. Theodore Marsh's complaint about his son's disrespectful behavior represented some of the challenges waged against black male authority in the urban environment. Marsh claimed that his son brandished a knife in the house, threatening to "cut" and "kill" his father. Court, reformatory, and orphan asylum records suggest that some black men in New York City had difficulty disciplining their children. Decades later, the Great Depression would cause similar hardships for white families as white men lost patriarchal status when they ceased to be the chief breadwinner. For black families, however, the ramifications of black men's inability to find adequately paying jobs began with the initial thrust of urban migration in the 1880s. No other group, even those new to the city and country, faced such dramatic assaults on traditional gender relationships.[56]

Black women also felt the strain of the constant struggle for economic and familial survival. Often enduring the stresses without a partner, women shouldered the burden of earning an income, putting food on the table, scraping together the rent every two weeks, and raising the children. In 1913, Agnes Littleton wrote to the COS pleading for financial assistance. "I'm struggling under a heavy burden," she explained in her letter. "I am left in the world with five small children and scarely [sic] bread and some without shoes," Agnes elaborated. "Please help if you can." When the COS sent a worker to investigate, the nurse found Agnes to be seriously ill, "being subject to fits of crying when she allows herself to think of her troubles, and sometimes being unable to sleep."

Her health had deteriorated in recent days; she had developed "most unpleasant sensations in the head." Upon review by a doctor, the malady was identified as "anxiety of keeping the home together, especially anxiety about money." He determined "that her present condition is nothing abnormal" in light of her overwhelming responsibilities. Most days "she gets up at four a.m. and gets five children off to school before going to work. . . . [F]or a woman naturally fragile and with a strong sense of responsibility, such a situation could not but tell on her nerves." The doctor recommended "rest and freedom from worry," two unlikely prospects for a black woman in New York City.[57]

Weary of the unceasing struggle and concomitant feelings of failure, some black parents relinquished their responsibilities altogether. Abandoned black children were periodically found wandering on city streets. Though rare, these episodes left reform agencies scrambling to deal with a population rarely served by these institutions. They typically sought ways of sending orphaned black children out of the city. In 1902 a porter found a bundle at a train station, discovering an infant inside. The baby's mother was never found. The agency in charge of the infant found a black family in upstate New York willing to adopt the child. Emiline Lee, an eleven-year-old girl, recounted a story of parental abandonment to police officers. Her mother had left home some years earlier never to be heard from again. Emiline's father disappeared not long after his wife. The girl survived in the "undesirable surroundings" of Minetta Lane until the SPCC sent her to Boston to live with her paternal grandmother. James Waller was forced to commit two of his children to the Riverdale Orphan Asylum in 1904 after his wife deserted the family and he found himself unable to care for his dependents.[58]

The stresses of poverty, overcrowding, and single parenthood also contributed to episodes of physical violence within black families. Spousal abuse occurred between partners of all classes, races, and circumstances. But as the black domestic economy changed in the industrializing North, excluding black men from productive endeavors while encouraging black women's participation in the work force, black men at times became violent in order to subdue a woman's independent spirit or assert a male prerogative. In an effort to demonstrate his authority in the household, Edward Brown became abusive toward his wife and live-in niece. Angry that the woman permitted the girl to drain their limited resources, he demanded that the child be returned to her family in Trinidad. His persistent outbursts and physical intimidation finally won him a victory in his household. Gertrude Johnson Ayer recalled that her father badly mistreated and manipulated her mother, often threatening to leave her for another woman. The fear of being left alone with small children forced Ayer's mother to comply with his demands, despite his abuse. "I can still feel how miserable she must have been," Ayer wrote bitterly many years later.[59]

Some black women, however, fought back against their abusers, demonstrating a degree of assertiveness and independence less common among other New York women. As breadwinners themselves, sometimes the primary earner in a family, black women might be less frightened of being left alone than women without any income would be. Mary Vails testified in court that her partner, Robert Allen, struck her "several times." She had him arrested for assault, although she later withdrew the charge. After spending two years with Allen, she finally left him "because of his bad treatment of her." When Walter Halliburton punched his common-law wife, Maggie Hunt, he felt her wrath in the form of a manicure knife to the arm and chest.[60]

Like Mary Vails, some black women developed a degree of independence that allowed them to leave—or threaten to leave—their husbands rather than endure an untenable relationship. Daisy Siegel Garey, a wife and mother of three, fled her home after her husband struck her during an argument. Her resentment toward Charles had been building; she was angry that he spent too much time with his brother concocting business schemes while ignoring his family. When she left, she took the children, thirteen dollars in rent money that was in the house, and another fifteen dollars that she withdrew from his savings account. Only one dollar remained in the bank, forcing him to borrow from friends in order to pay the rent that month. She admitted that she had a quick temper but claimed he did as well, calling him "quarrelsome and abusive." The two argued frequently, even over small matters, making life unbearable for her. Daisy refused to return to her husband and vowed he would never take their children from her. Two months later, however, Charles convinced his wife that he would curb his temper and she returned home. He remained true to his word for the next six months until Daisy developed acute appendicitis and died after an emergency operation.[61]

While adults could fight back, children had no recourse of escaping their tormentors, and the SPCC prosecuted a number of cases of black children being abused by parents or other family members. An agent of the SPCC found a scarred and disfigured Nellie Gardner in a Tenderloin tenement building. The girl spent her days with her aunt while her mother worked steadily as a laundress. According to court testimony, the woman beat the girl with a hot iron stove poker as a means of punishment. The judge sentenced the woman to a year imprisonment. The judge also removed Nellie from the home and placed her in the New York Juvenile Asylum, leaving a devastated mother whose efforts on behalf of her daughter had come to naught. A similar case emerged from Minetta Lane where Evaline Scott, who took over her father's household upon her mother's death, repeatedly punished her little sister with a "red-hot" stove poker, "burning the child's face and hands." The young woman received a two-and-a-half year prison sentence while the little girl was removed permanently from her father's household and placed in the care of the Colored Orphan Asylum.[62]

Though the SPCC aided in removing children from abusive homes, white elites' conception of mistreatment often differed from that of black parents. With her aunt away at work, thirteen-year-old Josephine Gardner had the daily responsibility of attending to the morning fires and putting out the lights after dark in the apartment building her adoptive family managed. Louisa Gardner had taken in her brother's three children after their mother died. Her deep commitment to the family caused her to resist placing the children in an asylum, despite her own poverty and ill health. Instead, Josephine helped with the chores in order to allow Louisa to work during the day. A white caseworker from the COS was concerned about Josephine's workload, noting that the girl also washed the family's laundry. Discounting the importance of keeping the family together, the COS agent recommended that the girl "be removed from her aunt's home."[63]

Prevailing stereotypes about black female immorality left black families vulnerable to the critical scrutiny of unsympathetic white reformers. An anonymous complaint about the activities of Annie Hall, a black woman living on West Thirty-second Street, led to the removal of her twelve-year-old child from the home. The investigating officer arrested Annie for exposing the girl to "pernicious influences." When the police court judge imposed an insurmountable bail of $700, Annie was forced to remain incarcerated while she awaited trial. On spurious evidence, the judge convicted Annie of prostitution and "endangering the morals of a child." Unable to pay the $250 fine for her conviction, Annie served an extended jail term while Alice became a parentless child in the New York Juvenile Asylum.[64]

The tension between black parents and white authorities left black people in a vicious and nearly inescapable cycle of recriminations. Black parents' economic endeavors on behalf of their families, a prerequisite for any assistance from white organizations, opened the door to criticism from outside observers for being irresponsible parents. By overriding parental authority, demanding the institutionalization of children, and forcibly removing children from their parents' home, white people did as much to undermine the black family structure as poverty itself did. Though black families overwhelmingly withstood the pressure, some succumbed to the persistent and pernicious assaults waged by normative whites and the poverty exacerbated by racial stereotypes.

Not surprisingly, given the structural conditions endured by New York

City's black population and the pressure imposed by white reformers, sociologists found that more often than any other ethnic group in New York, blacks lived in disrupted or broken homes. The transience of the population encouraged informal, nontraditional marriages to proliferate. Columbia University sociologist William Ogburn found numerous instances of common-law marriages in San Juan Hill, "easily made and easily broken," with "no interferences on the part of the law, church, or society." Still, the overwhelming majority of black families remained intact despite frequent separations, and in 1905, over 80 percent of black families claimed a male head. One-tenth of adult black women headed their households, though most of those women were more than forty years old by the time they became the primary adult figure in their families. Aside from widows, almost no black women under the age of thirty with more than one child lived without a husband.[65]

But the frequent—albeit temporary—separations of black families allowed outsiders to cultivate an image of weak familial bonds among blacks. John Clyde, in his study of black New York in 1898, believed that blacks' "looseness about sexual relations, frequent swapping of wives, desertion of family, and general lack of feeling of responsibility in the home, are all sources of great social weakness. There is little family love. The children grow up with out restraint but are furiously beaten at times." Another sociologist noted that "the economic situation of the New York Negro does not lead to a strengthening of the home life and of the marriage tie." Many blamed the instability on black women's presence in the work force. "Home life can mean very little to a people whose mothers are wage earners," Clyde argued.[66] In an era when middle-class values eschewed paid labor for women, black women's economic activities created a rationale for denouncing the black population as a breeding ground for a variety of social ills:

The economic independence of the woman and the frequent absence from home of the man lead to desertions and separations. The attractive woman who is able to care for herself may grow to resent the presence of a husband whose support she does not need, and the lazy man may find another woman than his wife to support him. . . . That there are many separated families among the poorer class of colored people all charitable workers know, and the woman's economic independence coupled with the man's inability to earn a good wage does something to promote such a condition.[67]

White reformers witnessed and judged black people's behaviors without acknowledging the unique economic challenges facing New York's black population, leading to increased tensions between the two groups. Most significantly, white people in positions of power and authority, and with the capability of mitigating some of the challenges facing the black population, held little sympathy for the plight of blacks.

The disdain foisted upon black men and their difficulty in fulfilling expected and traditional masculine roles within the family contributed to the emergence of a culture of black male dependency among a small cohort of young black men in late nineteenth-century New York City. The subversion of traditional patriarchal functions resulted from the economic hardships and demographic imbalances experienced by black New Yorkers at the turn of the twentieth century. Black women's relative success in finding urban employment caused more black women than men to migrate to northern cities. The disproportionate number of gainfully employed, young and single black women in the city combined with the shortage of eligible black men promulgated an environment in which some black men bargained for lucrative relationships rather than face the humiliating prospect of unsuccessfully searching for work. Instead, they chose to be "kept" by their wives and girlfriends. "The lounger at the street corner, the dandy in the parlor thrumming on his banjo, means a Malindy of the hour at the kitchen washboard," noted one critic. Young black women could do little to change their husbands' behavior. "[I]t don't do fer me ter complain," explained one black woman about her role as the family's breadwinner, "else [my husband] gits 'high' an' goes off fer good." When Jennie O'Neil accused her partner, Charles Graves, of "wasting the money she had earned," he stabbed her to death.[68]

The "sweet men" or "pimps" who appropriated women's wages proudly and publicly displayed their status. "Colored men in New York command their 'mark,' and girls are found who keep them in polished boots, fashionable coats, and well-creased trousers," wrote Mary White Ovington. White and black elites both criticized the "showiness of dress" exhibited by men with little money to spare. The bold, flashy uniform of the pimps proclaimed the wearer's repudiation of his economic subordination by subverting the physical portrayal of the black body as an "instrument of menial labor." By openly renouncing unattainable middle-class ideals, these men cultivated a sense of dignity in a world that rejected their claims to self-respect.[69]

Naomi Washington recalled seeing a particular black man across the street from her San Juan Hill apartment when she was a little girl. His appearance and especially his clothing struck her. He was "dressed to kill," she remembered. She asked her father why he only dressed that way on Sundays. "Today I worked hard," he told her. "I can't afford to go to work dressed like that. . . . I work every day to feed you, and I come home and bring my money to your mother. That man dresses up every day and takes his wife's money. He don't give her anything." Black men who chose to wear fancy clothing in a public display of their economic dependency on women subverted traditional gender roles. Rejecting society's contempt for their failure to act as "proper" men, they instead appropriated women's money and wore the results as physical symbols of their power and prestige.[70]

Many white observers took this cadre of men as representative of standard black male behavior. They perceived all black men as indolent and unwilling workers, contentedly relying on women for their material comfort. Social commentators blamed "lazy" black men for the high proportion of working wives. One condemned male loafers who "stand on the street corner while their wives go out to wash and scrub." The *Tribune* noted also in 1895 that most Negro men "do nothing but lounge about street corners," whereas women slaved over washtubs "making their apartments perpetual 'steam rooms.'" These observers fostered the perception that black men could not function effectively in an industrial environment. Though some black men willingly eschewed work, many either held nighttime jobs or found themselves unwillingly shut out of the labor force altogether. But the subversion of traditional gender roles permitted critics to perpetuate stereotypes about threatening and inappropriate black male behavior.[71]

White people in New York developed a broad critique of black morality, grounded also in the conditions in which black people lived. Manhattan's black people encountered higher rents than any other group in the city, obligating many to share their living spaces with strangers. As New York City became more crowded with immigrants and migrants living in the apartments of non-kin members, reformers increasingly condemned the threat that they imagined lodging posed to chastity and morality. The incorporation of strangers into a household, warned a government report, destroyed "all privacy, and the lodger or boarder becomes practically a member of the family. . . . [S]uch conditions . . . cannot help but blunt a girl's sense of proper relations with the other sex and foster standards which are not acceptable." The fear expressed in this report—that the nation's rapid urbanization was causing the disintegration of traditional families—was compounded when applied to blacks, a group already believed to have deficient moral standards. "Family life is conceded to be the Negroes' gravest weakness," wrote white reformer Mary Rankin Cranston in 1902, "and by taking strangers into the privacy of their homes and permitting the consequent intimate association with their growing children, domestic life is destroyed and demoralization ensues."[72]

The system of values held by white elites and with which they judged the black population did not reflect black peoples' realities—either economic or social. As a result, even when a handful of white reformers turned their attention to the needs of impoverished black children and families near the end of the nineteenth century, prejudice and the reformers' failure to understand the special needs of the black population inhibited their success. Their efforts covered a broad array of strategies; during this period city groups such as the Association for the Improvement of the Condition of the Poor (AICP) pioneered "fresh air work," sending "ocean parties" to Coney Island and city children to rural homes in upstate New York for the summer months. But reformers' prejudices diminished their success in reaching the city's black population. Lilian Brandt, a white reformer witnessing one of the "colored parties" on a fresh air outing, mocked the excitement felt by those escaping the city heat for an afternoon. She mimicked their accents, laughing at the simple joy with which they partook of the "scursion" and "festible." The absence of a sizable black middle class also hampered reformers' efforts. The COS found that they could not find sufficient families outside of the city that would accept black children for a week during the summer. When, in 1906, the Association of Neighborhood Workers at last found space for black children to spend two weeks in rural homes, reform workers encountered new obstacles. Black parents could not always spare their children: some of them provided critical aid around the house, others worked for much-needed wages, and still others were so poor that they did not have proper clothing.[73]

The ways in which organizations addressed the issue of black poverty directly resulted from white reformers' internalization of stereotypes about degenerate and irredeemable urban black men and women. Their methods of assistance often undermined black peoples' struggles to maintain their families, assert their dignity, and establish a degree of independence under conditions that impaired their efforts at every turn. The AICP, for example, began providing relief to indigent black families after the turn of the twentieth century. Between 1911 and 1912, it placed a family named Butcher, comprised of a West Indian immigrant, his wife, and their four young children, on its relief roster. The father worked at various low-paying jobs, earning a small salary and experiencing periodic episodes of unemployment. The family applied for assistance in 1911, and over the ensuing twelve-month period they received approximately one hundred dollars in monetary and material aid. At the end of the year an investigator assigned to review the case disagreed with the relief expenditures. In his report, he questioned "whether a crisis in the family would not have been desirable," obligating the man to find a steady job or pushing the woman into the work force. The presumption that the man chose to remain unemployed belied the economic constraints placed on black men in New York City. Even had he found steady work, few black men earned enough to sup-

port their families without the assistance of additional family wage earners. And the reformers' willingness to drive a black mother out of the
home revealed their assumption that black women were more suited to
work than white women.[74]

Even when reformers chose to provide help to indigent black people
in the city, they insisted on a set of normative behaviors that rarely
reflected blacks' economic challenges. In 1881, the New York SPCC
committed William Gear, a thirteen-year-old boy, to the New York Juvenile Asylum when they found the child "miserably clad." His father was
an unemployed waiter and his mother peddled corn on the street.
Rather than grant financial relief to the family, they removed the child
from his parents' care. Similarly, the COS refused to support the Joynes
family when Florence, the head of the household, did not behave as the
case workers demanded. Her partner, Edward, often left the family for
extended absences, during which time the family frequently found itself
in dire economic straights. This situation pushed Florence to plead with
the COS for assistance. The organization rejected her petition for relief
because she insisted "on taking [Edward] back when he turns up." Case
workers demanded that she renounce any connection with a man whom
they determined had failed to fulfill his familial duties. They instead recommended that Florence accept a live-in service position, keeping her
youngest child with her, and place William, her elder son, "who is also
reaching the age where it is increasingly difficult for his mother to look
properly after him when she has to go out for work," at an orphanage.
In 1905, the SPCC went to court to place Rachel Hawthorne at the Riverdale Orphan Asylum and insisted that her mother, perceived to be
engaging in immoral activities, not be permitted to visit. "Should the
mother reform in the future," the SPCC's secretary informed the
administrator at Riverdale, "of course the Society will cause an investigation to be made, and, if proper, recommend the child's discharge to
her." These encounters with white charity organizations that often
imposed untenable normative expectations left black people feeling
friendless in their struggles. Experiencing both prejudice and poverty,
black New Yorkers learned to find their own strategies for enduring the
hardships that the city inflicted upon them.[75]

One August morning in 1908, a twelve-year-old black girl, Annabel,
urgently brought white reformer Mary White Ovington to her San Juan
Hill home on West Sixty-second Street. They mounted four steep flights
of stairs and entered a dark apartment, sparsely furnished with only a
bare mattress and two chairs. Annabel's infirm mother had just sold the
remainder of the family's belongings for ten dollars. On the way home
from the pawnbroker's shop, the money had been stolen. "It's the end,"

the woman said quietly to Ovington, "there's nothing left for us." Without the rent money they were to be dispossessed the following morning.

Annabel's mother recounted her story to the reformer. She had spent years working as a domestic servant and periodically taking in laundry as well. Despite the physical strain, the family had remained solvent. But the summer exodus of her employers from the city meant enforced idleness. "There's not a penny but what goes for rent," the woman explained. "Annabel don't have enough to eat, and look at her shoes." Despite her pleas to charity organizations in the city, they refused to help her. "[T]hat woman is too softhearted," a case worker explained to Ovington. "She has a hulking son of eighteen who never keeps a job, and who has been living on his mother ever since I have known about them. As long as she has a cent she shares it with him." Despite the criticism, Ovington offered the woman some money.[76]

Later that evening, Ovington returned to Annabel's apartment. Looking in she found the "hulking boy" eating dinner. Though embarrassed, the mother looked at Ovington "almost with a challenge," as though to say, "Shall I eat and deny food to my son?" As Ovington left the apartment for a summer stroll with Annabel, she probed the girl about her future plans. "What are you going to do when you grow up?" she questioned the child. "I'm going to be a dancer!" came the quick reply. A shocked Ovington pushed the girl to explain why she would so readily choose a socially opprobrious occupation. Annabel provided a pragmatic answer. "I'm going to make *money.* Look at my mother, she works and works and she hasn't got a thing. They took her best chair and my bed."[77]

Annabel and her mother's experiences paralleled those of many black people in turn-of-the-century New York. The poverty, the inhospitable living conditions and cycle of indebtedness, and their struggles with unyielding reformers illustrate some of the hardships in the city. Without kin in the city and few friends, Annabel's mother had no support network to help her. But the close bond between mother and son, the optimism revealed in Annabel's aspirations for the future, and even the girl's desire to participate in the thriving black bohemia centered close to her Sixty-second Street apartment also shed light on some of the ways in which blacks not only survived but even delighted in New York. Despite poverty, the constant shifting and changing of the black population, and the judgments of unsympathetic whites, black New Yorkers developed strong ties to their churches, societies, and organizations, creating small social enclaves in an otherwise harsh and anonymous world. And in the face of the multiple obstacles uniquely confronting black people, the family proved to be a bedrock of support and sustenance.

Chapter 6
Negro Metropolis

In the face of pressing poverty and deteriorating race relations, black New Yorkers nevertheless found ways to create community within overcrowded tenements and to assert their claim to the city. Despite tremendous mobility even after arrival in the metropolis, black people established roots in the form of fraternal organizations, churches, and benevolent associations. The vanguard of migrants from the South and immigrants from the Caribbean encountered a city that bore little resemblance to their imagination and did a great deal to make their foray into the urban North a failure. But in their common refusal to concede defeat, black people transformed their portion of the city into a dynamic and vibrant blending of myriad cultures. Even as they struggled for mere survival in the harsh urban environment, black people also carved out time to revel in the opportunities unique to city life. They danced, sang, worshipped, forged friendships, and collectively made New York City into the country's most dynamic Negro metropolis.

Central to the vitality of New York City's black population was its diversity. Contrary to the simplistic assumptions made by white observers, the black population housed discrete, heterogeneous groupings that represented various ethnic, linguistic, class, and religious distinctions. Migration and immigration made the diversity more pronounced as newcomers clung to familiar customs and fiercely refused to succumb to whites' homogenizing stereotypes. A sociologist described the cosmopolitan nature of a black neighborhood. "[O]ne finds a newly arrived family from the West Indies eagerly and perilously hanging out of fourth story windows to view the strange street life of their adopted city. . . . [A]nother few steps discloses a front stoop alive with children and a bandanaed 'Auntie' fresh from the South. Sandwiched among these is the New York Negro family, thoroughly and typically American in its mode of life and ideals."[1] Within this dynamic but geographically limited environment, even a stranger to the city might find someone who hailed from the same region or whose own experiences promoted empathy with the newcomer's plight.

Upon arriving in New York City, early migrants and immigrants alike faced the immediate and pressing challenge of re-creating the support networks that had sustained them back home. In the rural communities of the South and the Caribbean, black people turned to one another for everything from economic assistance to child care to providing an evening of conversation. Family members often lived in close proximity, promoting mutual reliance. As newcomers to New York, few black people in the initial migration years enjoyed the security of arriving with connections already established. For an impoverished population receiving little support from white charity organizations and with minimal capital for the creation of their own welfare programs, social isolation might translate into outright failure in the urban experiment. Ernest Williams encountered that harsh reality when he first came to New York City in 1887, friendless and penniless. Unable to find work or a place to stay, he was forced to sleep in the parks at night while he sought a job during the day. He contracted rheumatism that permanently damaged his health, had no money for medical care, and finally begged his way home to North Carolina. For many new black New Yorkers, the timely formation of social connections became imperative simply to survive.[2]

Responding to this pressing need, many migrants quickly sought out the companionship of others hailing from the same geographic region. A blues song captures this urgency:

I'm a poor boy and I'm a stranger blowed in your town
I'm goin' where a friend can be found.

Aletha Dowridge sought comfort in a strange land by surrounding herself with compatriots from Barbados. Even after her marriage, she lived for a time with her husband at 246 Adams Street in Brooklyn, a boardinghouse run by her aunt, Constance Payne. Many family members and friends from the Caribbean island used the Adams Street address as the starting point for their lives in the United States and viewed it as a place of refuge. When Fred Challenor found himself out of work and struggling to establish a secure economic future for his family, he returned to "Aunt Con's" boardinghouse where he felt buffered by the people he knew. Violet Murrell, arriving from Barbados in 1915, went directly to the house upon her release from Ellis Island.[3]

Mary White Ovington, studying the black population of New York in 1911, discovered that the tendency for southern and Caribbean newcomers, like "any other strangers," to "make their home among familiar faces," helped create a welcoming environment within the morass of the city's population by establishing discrete ethnic enclaves. "The housewife who timidly hangs her clothes on the roof her first Monday morning in New York is pleased to find the next line swinging with the laundry of a Richmond acquaintance, who instructs her in the perplex-ing housekeeping devices of her flat. No chattering foreigner could do that. And while to be welcome in a white church is inspiring, to find the girl you knew at home, in the pew next to you, is still more delightful when you have arrived, tired and homesick, at the great city of New York."[4] In this way, lonely and friendless newcomers with no emotional ties in the city began to reconstruct a sense of home and belonging, the first step in calling New York City their own.

But movement did not cease once black migrants and immigrants landed at New York's shores, posing an ongoing impediment to building social ties. The unremitting search for decent and affordable housing led to almost constant movement as families relocated numerous times a year either to avoid paying rent or to seek accommodations that better met their budgets and needs. Charles and Annie Graves, for example, migrants to New York from the South, moved at least three times during their first year in the city. They lived on Minetta Lane for the first half of 1901, but they fell into debt with the coal dealer, to whom they owed twenty-six cents, and with the butcher shop, where they owed another twenty-four cents. After falling into arrears on the rent as well, the Graves fled the neighborhood, moving to a lodging house on Third Street, where they spent a lonely three months in a place with no friends. The landlady later admitted that so many tenants came and went that she could not remember anyone by the name of Graves. They moved again, this time to the Tenderloin, where they resided for only three weeks on West Twenty-sixth Street. In the next few years, the cou-ple lived at numerous other addresses, moving frequently in order to stay ahead of the eviction notice. The poorest among the population, those most in need of the help that might come by establishing friend-ships with neighbors, were the most likely to relocate often, sometimes while still owing many months' rent. Their perpetual movement made this group the most challenged in forging lasting social ties.[5]

The fluidity of New York's black residents marked a significant change from black people's experiences elsewhere. Black southerners and West Indians were accustomed to living in fairly stable communities. Share-cropper contracts in the South obligated black people to remain in one place for at least a year; pervasive debt peonage and vagrancy laws often extended the year almost indefinitely. The relative permanence of the population permitted the development and preservation of communal ties. In New York City, however, where black people regularly changed apartments and newcomers continued to transform the population, people might not know their neighbors. Investigators found that the widespread vice and crime in black neighborhoods caused many black tenement dwellers to look upon others with suspicion, often refusing to open the door to a stranger. Many, like John Telby, had learned from painful experience to be cautious. When Telby, a migrant from Savannah, heard a noise outside his San Juan Hill apartment door, he opened it only to discover Louis Jackson attempting to break the lock with a file. Jackson threatened to kill Telby and proceeded to burglarize the apartment. Some people never grew accustomed to the anonymity of New York's tenements. A middle-aged woman from Richmond who had achieved a degree of financial success in New York by running a small restaurant and who acknowledged that the city offered greater recreational opportunities than she had enjoyed back home, nevertheless aspired to go back to Virginia to "the stability and intimacy of the place where most of her friends are." Even after numerous years in New York, she admitted that she did not "mingle . . . with people" as she had done in Richmond.[6]

The prevalence of lodging among the black population also impeded the establishment of lasting social networks. Exorbitant rents and low wages conspired to force as many as 40 percent of black families to take lodgers into their homes, only half of whom claimed a blood tie to their landlords. Many renters used their apartments like boardinghouses, subleasing portions of their living space to people whose poverty precluded them from securing a place of their own or whose jobs kept them away from the city for extended periods of time, making it inexpedient to maintain a permanent household. These circumstances encouraged a climate of anonymity. George Levane used his apartment as a means of augmenting his meager earnings from irregular employment. He rented rooms by the week, posting a sign outside his door announcing the availability of space to passersby. Because his tenants typically did not remain for long, coming and going with the shifting of their fortunes, Levane often did not even know the names of those who lived with him.[7]

Concern about safety and a general sense of anonymity could inhibit the creation of social ties with strangers. When William Fielding Ogburn endeavored to conduct field research for his master's degree in sociology from Columbia University, he discovered to his surprise that black residents of San Juan Hill demonstrated marked reluctance to open the door to a stranger's knock. "The tendency among some to have few friends," he concluded, "is increased by the negro's suspicion of his environment." A series of sociological studies conducted by Columbia University graduate students early in the twentieth century confirmed the notable decline in the number of social contacts made by black migrants to New York as compared with their home experiences. While "visiting" was a traditional custom in the South and the Caribbean, creating and strengthening community bonds, the practice was far less common in the city. Longer workdays than many had experienced at home, a correspondingly small amount of leisure time, and a limited number of acquaintances all contributed to the decline. One migrant from Virginia who claimed few friends in New York had little opportunity to forge more social ties. Her work as a laundress often left her exhausted, so she spent her small amounts of leisure time in resting or attending church. Consequently, a woman who had been "active socially" prior to migrating encountered a far more isolating urban experience. This situation held true for many. Of twenty-four Caribbean immigrants surveyed, all but two admitted to making fewer social visits in the United States than they had been accustomed to making at home. When they did spend time with acquaintances, the majority acknowledged that they principally socialized with other West Indians, preserving their ethnic insularity.[8]

As discrete ethnic clusters developed in black New York, many of these communities sought to reestablish customs and traditions from home. The replication of culinary practices became an important way for black people in New York City to maintain their cultural identities and ease the transition to urban life. Harriet Dowridge sent packages with jams, peas, cassava cakes, and homemade jelly to her daughter, Aletha, in New York City. Aletha's aunt sent "barbadoes biskits" for Christmas. "[Y]ou all must have a rail west india breakfuss," Harriet insisted. Virtually impossible to find in local stores, these foods helped foreigners maintain a tangible connection to their culture and family members. Aletha Dowridge always looked forward to receiving packages from her mother. For mother and daughter, the food represented an emotional bond that distance did not easily sever.[9]

Like Caribbean immigrants, southerners maintained their culinary habits as well. Naomi Washington, whose parents had migrated to New York from the South, recalled that as a child she ate grits, pancakes, biscuits, eggs, bacon, greens, chitlins, and hog maws (pig feet). Anna Murphy remembered the rabbits her grandmother would cook in southern fashion. She "would skin 'im, and soak it overnight in brine and cook it. . . . I hated to see it, but I loved to eat it." Booker T. Washington arranged to have a package of chitterlings sent to Charles Anderson living in New York. Soon entrepreneurs tapped into the growing demands of a diverse clientele. The Hotel Maceo, one of the few serving black people in the city, occasionally offered an "old-fashioned Southern dinner." In February 1907, the hotel provided "roast possum, pigstails and cabbage, Virginia ham, cutlings, conepone, sweet potato pie," and other southern delicacies. And with blacks' move to Harlem and the concentration of a growing southern black population, specialized eateries began to appear. The Southern Restaurant prominently advertised "Home-Made Rolls Served Hot" and promised "Real Home Cooking."[10]

While adapting to life in New York City, many black people chose at the same time to maintain vibrant ties to their distinctive cultures by continuing practices learned from home.

Despite the many challenges to the creation of community, as the time of residence in New York City increased, so too did the number of social ties formed. The very fact of poverty in some ways fostered the development of connections between strangers, as people were forced to seek out help from others, forging a community grounded in mutual dependence and the common experiences of hardship. "My friend is one Mrs. Howell," Sarah Larsen Armstrong, herself an immigrant, explained to a charity worker. "When she first came on to this country I was kind to her and she remembers it." After the death of one of Sarah's daughters, the other child moved in with a friend on Sixty-seventh Street while Sarah and her son stayed with Mrs. Howell on Fifty-ninth Street. When charity workers came to the apartment to investigate the veracity of Sarah's claims of indigence, Mrs. Howell protected her lodger's interests, refusing to speak to the nurse about Sarah's health or her decision to remain in New York rather than return to the West Indies, as the charity organization recommended. After a month, Sarah and her son had saved enough money to move to their own apartment. However, their friendship with Mrs. Howell convinced them to stay close; they rented an apartment in the building next door.[11]

Tenuous connections premised on geographic origin or proximity in overcrowded tenements became the basis for deeper bonds of friendship and mutual support. Sarah Larsen Armstrong's decision to remain near Mrs. Howell suggested both the depth of the emotional bond between the two women and Sarah's unwillingness to relinquish an important source of support. A good friendship became a treasured commodity, and its preservation across time or distance could mean the difference between success and failure in the inhospitable urban setting. William Green encountered the helplessness of isolation after his wife's death in 1900. Without family in the city or friends willing to help, William was forced to commit his three children to the orphan asylum in order to keep his job. Conversely, Frances Fischer discovered that her friendship with a fellow New Yorker meant the difference between freedom and incarceration. Even after completing her six-month prison term for the possession and attempted sale of cocaine, Fischer found herself still stranded in jail because of her inability to pay the five hundred dollar fine included with her sentence. The prison chaplain interceded on her behalf, insisting that her good behavior merited a suspension of the hefty fine. More importantly, Frances's friend, Mrs. Grenin, agreed to take the woman into her home and guarantee her good behavior. "Don't you worry," she assured Frances, "I will do all

that I can for you, my home will be open to you as soon as you are free."
Mrs. Grenin offered to help Frances find work, placing her trust in the
woman despite the drug conviction. "I . . . still believe that you are not
guilty of breaking any law, we must trust in god, the good will receive
their reward." Frances had become despondent about ever regaining
her freedom, but her close friendship with Mrs. Grenin offered her
much-needed hope that her ordeal might not ruin the rest of her life.[12]

In New York's tenements, where overcrowding made privacy nearly
impossible, neighbors quickly learned about each other's problems and
often came to each other's aid. The willingness of black New Yorkers to
ease one another's suffering helped to replicate the kin networks reminiscent of their rural experiences. When recent migrants Walter and
Josephine Clinkens found themselves on the brink of destitution, sympathetic neighbors, though relative strangers to the newcomers, ensured
that the family had at least some food each day. A visiting nurse discovered that Josephine had received cabbage and potatoes that she shared
with her young son. Walter's death some months later aggravated the
Clinkenses' poverty and forced Josephine out of her small apartment.
But by that time the woman had formed relationships with her neighbors, and a friend, Mrs. Johnson, agreed to take the woman into her
home for a time while Josephine found work and achieved a degree of
financial independence. Persistent difficulties finally convinced Josephine's mother to move to Harlem in 1914 in order to help care for her
grandchildren, further expanding the family's support network. But the
Clinkenses' perseverance in New York during the critical early years
resulted not from kin but from the kindness of people who had once
been strangers.[13]

The common experiences of loneliness and financial hardship led to
some creative forms of cooperation within black New York, especially
among women who often struggled to raise and feed their children in
the absence of a partner. Sarah Larsen Armstrong, who emigrated with
her husband and three children from St. Croix in the 1890s, became a
widow five years after her arrival in the city. She roomed with friends for
a time, but soon felt beholden to them and sought other avenues for
mitigating her family's suffering. "I am in peoples way," Sarah complained, "and I promest never to be any more trouble again." Finally,
in 1903 she befriended a neighbor, Mrs. Rodette, who lived in the same
building. The two women, one a widow and the other often alone
because her husband worked as a chef onboard a ship, decided to secure
a four-room flat together and divide the expenses. Pooling their
resources, they shared food and rent costs, and Mrs. Rodette acquired a
deep fondness for Sarah's children, offering to take the youngest Larsen
son with her when she visited her sick father down South. These women,

both without family in the city, turned to each other like sisters. They developed a mutual affection that helped to fulfill pragmatic financial needs and allowed each to feel less socially isolated in the anonymity of the city. Even after Sarah moved out, she continued to depend on friends made since coming to New York. Some provided small monetary loans of twenty-five to fifty cents or outright gifts of food during her frequent episodes of penury. As her poverty deepened, Sarah lived with a series of friends until eventually some acquaintances and family members from home immigrated to New York City, providing a more permanent source of support to Sarah and her children.[14]

Conflict over the expectations and demands of different relationships, however, could interfere with women's responses to the daily pressures of caring for their children, making ends meet, and creating a supportive and interdependent community. The presence of strangers impinged on family life; the loss of intimacy might eventually threaten marital stability. Men who sought a sanctuary from the outside world might not welcome others into their homes. Mrs. Rodette's husband complained about the loss of privacy when he returned from his stints on the ships, and his wife eventually felt compelled to ask Sarah and her children to leave. Another woman, Mrs. Schuster, took the Larsens into her apartment after they left the Rodettes', but she too had to evict the woman and her two children. She explained that her husband was "growing somewhat irritated at having so many strangers in his home," despite the fact that Sarah was no stranger to Mrs. Schuster. Tensions arose when men and women held divergent views about the proper uses of domestic space and sought different types of succor when spending time there. On the one hand, women who faced long periods without adult companionship and who bore the responsibility of caring for children and meeting daily expenses, the physical setting of the home might offer a place for the development of camaraderie and mutual support from other women. The company of another adult could mitigate the loneliness of always being surrounded by children or white folks.[15]

On the other hand, men who spent much of their time away from their loved ones might begrudge sharing their hard-earned wages with people who were not part of the immediate family. Valeria Brown's husband, Edward, warned his wife that he would leave her if she insisted on permitting their niece to continue lodging with them. He had been forced to borrow sixty-one dollars from friends to pay for the girl's passage from Trinidad. Edward's resentment toward the girl caused "a great deal of trouble" between the couple, not only because of the extra mouth to feed but also because he keenly felt his loss of authority in dictating the rules of the household. For some black men, the assertion of patriarchal authority in the home served as an antidote to the frustrations and emasculation of low-paying service jobs. When women controlled not only the expenditures of the household but its inhabitants as well, men might feel powerless and superfluous when they returned from a period away. These conflicting expectations of home life could hamper women's efforts to establish methods of cooperation and friendships in the tenements. Nevertheless, the prevalence of interdependency among non-kin black New Yorkers suggests that while some men might interfere with these connections, women nevertheless forged a community in the tenements through the creation of a system of mutuality to sustain each other through their travails.[16]

The support networks that emerged in black New York functioned only when participants recognized customary limits on generosity and abided by the expectations of reciprocity. Afraid to overtax the bonds of friendship, most black people made the choice to ask for assistance very cautiously and only once all other avenues had been pursued. When Sarah Larsen finally gave up her apartment and began rooming with friends, she admitted that she considered herself a burden on others. She made the decision in desperation only after she had sold all of her belongings in an effort to make ends meet. "I am in deadly want this day," she wrote to her late husband's former employer beseeching him for financial assistance. "I am ashame to say I have pawn all my things to rais money to pay my rent and buy food." In another instance, during the middle of a frigid January, Sarah sent her daughter, Mildred, to the pawnbroker with Sarah's shoes in order to raise cash for food. She had already sold everything else in her possession. "I never like to beg but what can I do just now," she explained. When all other possibilities had been exhausted, including prevailing on numerous white elites and white charity organizations, Sarah finally turned to neighbors for relief.[17]

The choice to request assistance from white people offered a strategy—albeit at times a problematic one—for avoiding an imposition on friends who suffered similar financial straits. During a five-month period, Louisa Singleton wrote to at least four different white individuals requesting pecuniary support. By receiving small donations from a variety of sources, Louisa managed to cobble together the rent money and groceries for her family. Armonia Williams had less success in her appeals to a well-known white philanthropist. She sent at least a half-dozen letters to Mrs. Russell Sage in 1906, trying to convince the "Dear Lady and Friend" (though the two had never met) to share some of her abundant wealth with a "black old Aunty." Armonia hoped that her fulfillment of a comforting racial stereotype would tug at Mrs. Sage's sympathies. "I knew that the Lady was a child of God by your kind acts. . . . God will bless you that helps the poor and I will pray for it." When she received no reply, Armonia wrote again. "It seems that the Lady did not receive my appeal." This time she implored Mrs. Sage to "not throw this in the waste basket without noticeing it." Having failed to achieve her goals through an entreaty to Mrs. Sage's tenderness, Armonia tried for her vanity. "I will have it publish whatever the Lady does for me." Mrs. Sage forwarded the woman's letters to the COS. They recommended that Armonia seek hospital care and closed the case, forcing Armonia at last to turn to neighbors and friends. Sarah Johnson permitted Armonia to share her apartment for a month while others ensured that she had some food each day.[18]

The complex relations within the tenements cultivated a sense of connectivity among black New Yorkers and forged the foundation for their perception of each other as members of a shared community. Though many newcomers had fewer friends than at home, informal social visiting and more formal gatherings within the tenements nevertheless comprised an important component of black New Yorkers' social life. Friends might get together as often as two or three evenings each week, playing cards, drinking beer, telling jokes, and talking. Even with all of the recreational opportunities in New York, this remained, for many, the preferred social activity. In addition, as with the Armstrongs and Clinkins, over time, chain migrations began forming from this vanguard as extended families started following pioneers to New York City. Emily Thornton Higgins and her three children moved to New York while her husband worked in various parts of the country. Struggling with ill health, raising young children alone, and experiencing severe difficulty finding work, she moved in with her husband's sister, Mrs. Smith, for a time while she became financially independent. Her mother also lived with them for a while to help care for the children. Similarly, Annie Graves's mother moved to New York from Virginia upon learning of her daughter's illness. Though she had intended to stay in the city only briefly while her daughter convalesced, the woman ultimately decided to remain permanently. Through this process, New York's black population and community continued to grow. Isolation diminished as extended families reunited in the North, transplanting families, communities, networks, and cultures.[19]

Outside of the tenements, black New Yorkers forged ties with each other and demarcated ethnic and religious communities through institutions and organizations that offered sustenance, support, and a sense of identity within the city's cold and anonymous environment. Though the black church did not have the hold on New York's black population that it did in the South, it nevertheless remained the center of black life. The last decades of the nineteenth century saw a marked rise in the number of churches serving New York's black population. By 1900, large and small churches together numbered nearly forty, with seven or eight primary institutions. Black newcomers to the city increasingly found religious services that catered to their customs and traditions from home. The Union Baptist Church, for example, located in a storefront and led by the Reverend Dr. George H. Sims of Virginia, gathered the "very recent residents of this new, disturbing city" and made Christianity come "alive Sunday morning." Ministering to a mostly Virginian congregation, Reverend Sims ensured that the worshippers felt comfortable in their new church. In addition to offering a "southern style" of services, Union Baptist also provided regular and special events such as fairs, suppers, and lectures that resembled the church activities back home. Union Baptist held annual revival meetings that attracted as many as one hundred new converts and performed baptisms every second week. It became known within the black population as a "shouting church."[20]

Immigrants from the Caribbean and migrants from the South prayed separately from each other and from black Knickerbockers in the myriad churches serving the needs of specific ethnic, class, and geographic groups within black population. Caribbean-born blacks, for example, overwhelmingly preserved their affiliation with the Episcopal Church, having a strong heritage of this denomination in the British islands. St. Cyprian's Chapel, an Episcopal church built in the early twentieth century and located in San Juan Hill, served an almost exclusively Caribbean population. The "predominance of mulatto" members considered themselves among the "aristocracy of the negro." They attended "formal" services during which the pastor delivered sermons "without . . . emotional strain." Consistent with their desire to demonstrate an elite status, the congregants arrived "excellently dressed" each Sunday. "Display, pride, and intellect" characterized St. Cyprian's. The city's other principal black Episcopal church, the venerable St. Philip's, its roots dating back to the eighteenth century, also catered to a privileged membership. St. Philip's boasted a congregation of bluebloods—descendants of elite free blacks from the slave era who sought to distinguish themselves from those with less estimable heritages.[21]

Storefront and established churches periodically offered ministrations and events specifically targeting former residents of individual southern states. On "South Carolina Day" at Bethel, the church brought in a speaker from Charleston to preach a sermon on southern race relations. Bethel used the opportunity to attract ten South Carolinian migrants into church affiliation. Many others accepted communion on that day in 1906. As early at 1897, the Society of the Sons of Virginia sponsored an annual lecture at Bethany Baptist Church in Brooklyn. At

Figure 12. Office workers at St. Philip's Guild House, circa 1896–98. Museum of the City of New York, The Byron Collection, 93.1.1.2556.

the tenth anniversary event, the membership listened to a sermon that "waded out into the deep things which concern both the spiritual and temporal." These programs benefited New York's black churches—by reaching out to specific elements of the city's diversifying black population, many successfully and substantially increased their membership and the money in their coffers. The membership of the Society of the Sons of Virginia chose to make a monetary donation to Bethany at the culmination of their 1907 festivities. The targeted programs also reflected the dramatic demographic and cultural changes occurring in New York. The increasing commitment demonstrated by the various churches to serving the particular needs and wishes of newcomers revealed the growing importance of that portion of the population. Not only were newcomers numerically significant (comprising a majority of the black population by the turn of the twentieth century), they were gaining power as culture brokers, influencing the behavior of longtime New Yorkers and forcing the creation of new institutions that served their interests.[22]

Southerners brought their particular style of preaching and music to

New York City and introduced gospel to the North. This method of praying made its way into established Protestant churches and newer storefront churches founded largely by the migrants. The gospel churches
stressed vocal expressions of spirituality; when Reverend Martin R.
Franklin, Zion African Methodist Episcopal (A. M. E.; "Mother Zion")
Church's leader in the late nineteenth century, ministered from the pulpit, he expected to hear a traditional "call and response" from his flock.
Silence from the congregation would precipitate action from the minister, asking them if they loved their Jesus and prompting a resounding
"Yes, Lord!" or "Amen!" Ejaculations of "Hallelujah," "Praise Be," and
"Glory to God" might follow. The exchanges continued until many
parishioners would collapse, exhausted, with tears streaming down their
cheeks. Many longtime black New Yorkers initially rejected the new
sound as sensual and overly emotional, making the church one more
site of contestation between newcomers and established residents of
black New York. The Reverend T. H. Gilbert, pastor of the Mount Olivet
Baptist Church, became one victim of the conflict when he introduced
an "intellectual manner" to the services. Gilbert's congregation found
his method of preaching "distasteful," preferring the previous pastor's
"emotional" style. His tenure at the church lasted only briefly. After just
a short appointment, Gilbert resigned under pressure and left New York
City, much to the dismay of T. Thomas Fortune, the editor of the *New
York Age*, who welcomed Gilbert's introduction of a more orderly and
cerebral manner to Sunday services.[23]

Informal churches also began proliferating, responding to the growth
and diversity of the black migrant population. Unable to purchase permanent buildings, these storefront churches met the spiritual needs of
those unfamiliar with the formality of New York's black churches.
According to one observer, every block in the heart of Harlem housed
between two and five of these organizations, allowing the "Danish West
Indian [to have] his chapel, as has also the West Indian from Barbadoes
[*sic*]," and so forth. To attract the wayward back into the fold, some
churches offered "open air" preaching. Naomi Washington remembered her parents "testifying" on street corners. "There were quite a
few people doing that. If there was one on 135th Street and Lenox Avenue, there might be another one on 134th and Seventh. They were
called street meetings. They would sing. . . . Large crowds would come
around and listen, and they would take up a collection."[24]

Churches provided critical services to the black population. They
hosted social events and religious revivals, campaigned to clean up vice
in black neighborhoods, and offered aid to the needy. A number of the
larger churches organized annual summer excursions for their members, leasing a ferry to transport the crowd up the Hudson River to enjoy

a day of food, sports, and relaxation. In 1904, six hundred affiliates of the Union Baptist Church left the pier at West Fiftieth Street onboard the "Walter Sands," bound for River View Grove just north of Yonkers for a day of festivities. The Metropolitan Brass Band set a tone of excitement as they sent the barge on its way with rousing music. The Bethel A. M. E. Church sponsored similar outings every year. In 1913, fifteen hundred members of the church enjoyed the annual event. Throughout the hot July day, they played baseball and other games and then enjoyed an elaborate picnic prepared by the church women. Though only held once a year, the outings gave to the members of Bethel A. M. E. a special occasion to anticipate during the monotony of daily life. Opportunities to participate in planning committees and meetings built the excitement until the church community enjoyed the shared vacation each summer.[25]

Bethel had regular events as well, offering "wholesome amusements" every night of the week in an effort to mitigate "the evils of city life." Monday was concert night, and Tuesday and Wednesday evenings were dedicated to club and class meetings. On Thursday nights members could attend entertainments consisting of "literary activities, reciting, and singing." Friday was reserved for prayer meetings, with choir rehearsal on Saturdays. Though not all churches provided as many activities as Bethel, the larger ones typically developed a regular schedule of events. Even fund-raisers served to promote a sense of community among parishioners. One or two evenings a week were usually devoted to entertainment, "social or sacred," and while intended to help raise money for the church, these events gave expression to the demand for social functions. They characteristically consisted of music, singing, recitations, and refreshments.[26]

Church services themselves became venues for socializing and an escape from the drudgery of everyday life. Observers often noted the elaborate dress on display every Sunday when black people walked to and from church. "White gloves and fine raiment" prevailed, despite the economic hardship caused by the purchase of such apparel. Church-going members of the black community scrimped and saved in order to purchase Sunday finery. For men, that typically meant a dark suit, "black derbies, black or dark brown or dark grey overcoats, and in many cases . . . canes." Black women brought color to services with bright dresses and elaborate hats. The Sunday spectacle became an important psychological moment in the lives of New York's black people. Long before "black is beautiful" slogans, they reveled in the opportunity to look fine, both to themselves and to others. Women especially gained social stature through their ability to "outdress" one another. On Sundays, black men and women took advantage of the excuse to exchange the degradation and homogeneity of servants' uniforms in favor of finery and implicit assertions of beauty and self-worth.[27]

Pastors worked hard to support individual members of their congregations, often using their influence to mitigate confrontations with the white community. When Nelson Browne faced criminal charges for the illegal possession of a firearm, the Reverend Edward Wainwright served as a character witness on the man's behalf. Wainwright testified that the accused not only worked hard and steadily as a driver for a moving company, but that for the last seven years he had regularly attended church services and other church functions in Harlem. The pastor of Samuel Booth's church wrote a similarly supportive reference to the judge presiding over a first-degree assault charge against Booth. Reverend Sims of the Union Baptist Church intervened more deeply in the lives of the Singleton family, regular members of his congregation. Unable to assist them through tough financial times (too many poor parishioners had tapped the church's resources), Sims urged the COS to provide financial assistance to the family. In 1913, he permitted Mrs. Singleton to have use of the church in order to hold a concert; she raised twenty dollars from the sale of tickets.[28]

Ministers also led the movement for racial uplift, instructing their pastorate in proper behavior. From the pulpit, religious leaders warned their flock against the dangers of dancing (though some black people affiliated with the Episcopal churches because of their more liberal views toward amusements such as dancing), gambling, drinking, and the theater. They cautioned against outlandish dress or provocative comportment that might reflect immorality or undermine fragile race relations. "Woe to the wicked," admonished Reverend Henderson, pastor of Bethel Church in the early twentieth century. "If our young men continue to frequent dens of evil and get into trouble," he counseled, "we must leave them to pay the penalty for so doing." The Reverend J. Francis Blair offered blunt advice. "[S]top spending . . . hard earnings in theatres and swell restaurants," he commanded, "making the white man rich and sinking [your]selves into poverty." On the streets, pastors waged fierce battles against vice in black neighborhoods. Because black people could not separate themselves into distinct residential areas, and with widespread police neglect and corruption, many pastors led the crusade against criminal activities. The ministers of St. Cyprian's Episcopal Church and the Union Baptist Church, both in San Juan Hill, significantly contributed to the reduction in the number of "dens and clubs" nearby, as did the Reverend Adam Clayton Powell of Abyssinia in the Tenderloin.[29]

Religious organizations were often at the forefront of social protest movements in New York, as they sought to improve racial justice in the city. A number of ministers joined in the creation of the Committee for Improving the Industrial Condition of the Negro in New York, later to become one of the organizations forming the National League on Urban Conditions. They used their pulpits to disseminate the organization's message of industrial training and promote the fight for occupational opportunities. When Thomas Dixon's viciously racist novel *The Clansman* was performed on stage at Manhattan's Grand Opera House in 1906, six of the city's black pastors signed an open letter to the chief of police demanding an injunction against the production. The play, they argued, threatened the fragile peace that existed between the races in New York. "Indeed, there are certain sections where it might truthfully be said the races maintain an armed truce," the ministers noted. Mentioning the numerous prior episodes of "almost irrepressible outburst[s] of race hatred," they urged that the play be banned in the interest of public welfare. Nine years later, when *The Clansman* became the basis for the venomous and wildly popular movie, "Birth of a Nation," church leaders again led the (unsuccessful) assault on its presentation in New York.[30]

But a disproportionate amount of the churches' efforts went into the construction or purchase of buildings, due in part to the growth of the congregations, but also as the result of an effort to impress. Either way, the expenditures limited the amount of money and energy available for charitable endeavors or programs of social uplift. St. Mark's Methodist Episcopal Church, founded in 1871, quickly outgrew its cramped quarters as migrants more than doubled church membership in the late 1880s. The congregation helped pay the ten thousand dollar difference between the earnings from the sale of the original building and the purchase of a larger one on West Forty-eighth Street. Within two decades they had moved again; a membership of more than fifteen hundred and the migration uptown convinced St. Mark's to purchase a building on West 53rd Street.[31]

Observing the many social services such as hospital visitations offered by New York's white churches for their constituents, Gertrude Chrystal wrote a scathing editorial for the *Crisis* magazine in 1914. "What on earth are the colored churches of New York doing?" she demanded. Many were erecting and refurbishing buildings. The restoration of Mother Zion Church (A. M. E.) in 1890 cost five thousand dollars, all of which was raised by the members. In 1902, the Abyssinia Baptist Church decided to follow its congregation uptown and sold its building on Waverly Place. It moved to the Tenderloin, purchasing a $65,000 building that severely taxed the community's financial resources. Each church member pledged up to ten dollars to support the new edifice. Among the poor, this was a substantial sum of money. The *Age* reproached church leaders for considering "church building and money raising as the principal business of a preacher, the primary question of saving the wayward from bad associations and making a good reputation for himself and his people in his community being subordinated." James Weldon Johnson echoed the criticism, charging, "And for what purposes is the money gathered? Does it go to feed the hungry? to clothe the naked? to care for the widow and the orphan? To some extent yes; but the great bulk of it goes to maintain costly temples." Johnson admonished the churches to create a "new baptism of Christ-like simplicity."[32]

Despite the criticisms, church membership continued to grow before World War I. The myriad religious organizations offered a wealth of spiritual and social opportunities; nevertheless many young newcomers sought a different form of succor in the city. Overwhelmingly, young people expressed their preference for the city's exciting nightlife over religious ministrations or formal organizations. Migrants and immigrants both admitted that they attended church less frequently in the city than they had at home. In place of worship or church-related activities, most conceded that they spent more time at dances, theaters, and clubs than they had previously enjoyed. Indeed, New York's alluring nightlife had enticed many to the city in the first place. One migrant acknowledged that she arrived in New York City planning for a brief sojourn, but the attraction of the city's "amusements" persuaded her to stay. "I didn't have a job for some little time," she recalled, but the variety of activities available compared so favorably to the "prayer meetings and little parties held very infrequently [in the South,] the same thing over and over again," that she never returned home. Seeking to alleviate the monotony of daily life and escape the dreariness caused by poverty and service positions, many sought out "pleasure and revelry after dark."[33]

New York furnished many opportunities for entertainment. Dozens of poolrooms and bars sprang up in black neighborhoods, affording respite from cramped tenements and daily travails. Pleasure-seekers could find gambling clubs and poker clubs, professional clubs and sporting clubs. Most working-class blacks, however, frequented the dark rathskellers in tenement house basements that offered inexpensive alcohol, usually a pool table, and sometimes music that ranged from "a wheezy old accordion" to pianos and drums. "[S]ailors, laborers, thieves, shoestring gamblers, and . . . wretches" could be found "whirling . . . around the floor," engaging in flirtations, and socializing until dawn. Some women plied their wares to men interested in engaging their services. The rathskellers became thriving social centers where black people felt a sense of belonging and release. For those seeking a complete escape, some rathskellers became known for the sale of cocaine and opium.[34]

Many of the patrons of rathskellers frequented the basement rooms in order to enjoy illicit games of chance. Policy playing was one of the most popular forms of gambling in black New York. Linked to numbers drawn in legal state lotteries such as Kentucky's or Louisiana, policy players made private wagers on the result of a lottery outcome. While scores of numbers vendors sold chances by visiting the tenements directly, many people instead chose to transact their business in designated policy shops. In that way, gambling became a social activity as much as an opportunity to make or lose money. A policy industry thrived, with a variety of superstitions helping to dictate numbers choices. The sale of lottery "dream books" flourished, and "lucky" individuals at times garnered a substantial profit. However, while the basement clubs offered a much needed social outlet, they also drained already meager incomes. Some men and women drank and gambled away their wages. "My Husband is a hard working man," implored a "poor woman who needs her husbands earnings" to the mayor in 1910. She sought help in extracting her husband from the saloons and pool rooms. "[H]e have got into the habit of going to these clubs and gambling away all or a greate portion of his weeks earnings and dont have enough left to support me and my little children."[35] The poorest of the black population, who desperately sought an escape from mind-numbing and exhausting work or the psychological toll of poverty, also suffered the most from their expenditures on social entertainments.

A racier crowd enjoyed the "black and tans," clubs with a mixed clientele that provided the opportunity for interracial dalliances. While loudly denounced by many whites in New York, in the South this transgressive behavior might well result in far more dire consequences for a black person. In the less restrictive northern environment, some black enthusiasts certainly chose to frequent black and tans as a means of flaunting social conventions, especially the ones that circumscribed blacks' activities. Perhaps because of the presence of whites, the black and tans tended to provide a more formal milieu than the rathskellers. A typical club, the New Belmont in Harlem, offered a spacious room on the first floor of a building. A bar in the front served drinks while intimate clusters of chairs and tables ringed the dance floor. Three black singers entertained the patrons. Though damned by white critics, blacks and whites danced together "until the perspiration rolls in streams down their faces." A wide spectrum of whites—"sailors, young clerks, countrymen"—frequented these clubs to "indulge in sensuality" in the libertine setting. In the bawdier clubs, "the women amuse their male friends by the can-can dance," during which they "kicked high above each other's heads," exposing "their person." "There is a contest among them to see which can kick the highest, and they take their skirts in their hands, and amid the applause of the spectators kick a cigar from the lips of one of the men."[36]

A cadre of clubs catering to the black elite (and often whites) flourished in New York as well. The city's growing black population sustained a vital artistic core that had made the trek from the Tenderloin to San Juan Hill along with the bulk of the community, and later moved on to Harlem, forming the nucleus of the group forging the Harlem Renaissance in the 1920s. The Marshall Hotel at 129 West Fifty-third Street offered a high-class restaurant and club for the aristocracy and celebrities of the city's black population. With its location in the heart of black bohemia, the Marshall became the center for the black artistic crowd. A "good grade" of black performers entertained mixed-race audiences. Though the Committee of Fourteen reported that the Marshall was "patronized largely by white women and colored men" who engaged in "questionable orgies and revels . . . nightly," they admitted that the club would be difficult to close because of its tremendous popularity. Diverse members of black bohemia, including poet Paul Laurence Dunbar, jockey Isaac Murphy, composer James Reese Europe, and vaudevillians Bert Williams and George Walker—among many others—frequented the Marshall and made it black bohemia's most popular club.[37] James Weldon Johnson, himself a member of the black bohemia before branching off as a political and social activist, joined his brother Rosamond in rooming at the Marshall during their summer sojourns to Manhattan. By "dwell[ing] in the sunshine of greatness" at the "headquarters of Negro talent" rather than a regular rooming house, the two hoped to establish themselves as legitimate members of the artistic circle. Along with Bob Cole (whom they met at the hotel), the brothers aspired to produce an opera. During their first summer at the fashionable stomping ground, James and Rosamond met Will Marion Cook, Ernest Hogan, Bert Williams, George Walker, Harry Burleigh, and other members of the black theatrical crowd. Johnson recalled an especially thrilling moment while still a relative unknown, when Paul Laurence Dunbar walked into a rehearsal that Johnson was attending.[38]

In addition to guest quarters, the Marshall had two public rooms with a distinct ambiance in each. In one, musicians played piano and other instruments; singers regularly entertained as well. Couples could dance or simply enjoy the music. James Weldon Johnson claimed that the Marshall hosted the first modern jazz band to play in Manhattan. Called the Memphis Students, the orchestra used a combination of banjos, saxophones, clarinets, and tap drums to forge the new sound. The Marshall's west dining room offered a quiet atmosphere for conversation and discrete rendezvous, periodically between black men and white women. On a typically busy Wednesday evening in the spring of 1910, James Europe supped with a white female friend, Helen Russell, and another interracial couple. After ordering champagne, the women began to dance, much to the enjoyment of the men who eventually stood up to accompany them. They stayed until the early hours of the morning. A place like the Marshall offered to black New Yorkers the opportunity for upscale entertainment like those available to the white population. Though not entirely unmolested—the Committee of Fourteen worked assiduously to close places like the Marshall – still, the elite could find in the Marshall one of the only places in the city in which they could receive genteel accommodation.[39]

The popular Baron Wilkins' Place, in the Old Tenderloin, had a reputation for being the "swellest club in town." A "higher class of sporting people" frequented Wilkins' at 253 West Thirty-fifth Street, enjoying the hired entertainers, the ragtime dancing, and the all-night hours. The club boasted an entrance direct from the street to the basement where the rathskeller was located. A separate doorway for "ladies" permitted circumspection, especially for interracial trysts. Wilkins' was noted for its fine furnishings, the large dance floor, and a large painting of a nude woman in the rear of the hallway. Even critics admitted that the club was tastefully decorated. An evening's entertainment might consist of a three-piece orchestra and "nice looking brown-skinned girls, neatly dressed," who "sing popular and suggestive songs." The women sometimes danced as well. Like Marshall's, Wilkins' Place offered first-class facilities to an interracial group of patrons. In the back room, "white women and colored men can meet and be protected from the public rathskeller in the basement."[40]

But as the favorite haunt of Jack Johnson, the Negro heavyweight boxing champion, Baron Wilkins' Place came under mortal attack in 1910. Widespread white fury at Johnson's convincing Fourth of July victory over Jim Jeffries, the nation's "white hope," precipitated not only a spontaneous wave of violent assaults against black people in New York and nationwide but also the immediate initiation of proceedings against Baron Wilkins' Café, where Johnson lived with his white wife. Only days after Johnson's pugilistic success, the Committee of Fourteen began a campaign to rescind Wilkins's liquor license with the excuse that the club served as a meeting place for white women and black men. The limited number of adequate accommodations available to black New Yorkers meant that many organizations held their large meetings at Wilkins' Place, including the National Association of Colored Physicians and Surgeons, a number of fraternal organizations such as the Odd Fellows and Knights of Pythias, and the National Negro Business League.

When a judge learned that Booker T. Washington presided over the latter organization and had visited Wilkins' Place, he issued a temporary stay on the closure of the "Negro resort." Nevertheless, the Committee of Fourteen finally prevailed; in December of that year, Baron Wilkins lost his liquor license.[41]

Ike Hine's Club opened in 1900, competing with the Marshall by attracting "the best elements from the various circles of Bohemia." In his 1912 novel, *The Autobiography of an Ex-Colored Man*, James Weldon Johnson described Ike Hine's as "a center of colored Bohemians and sports. Here the great prizefighters were wont to come, the famous jockeys, the noted minstrels, whose names and faces were familiar on every bill-board in the country." Avoiding any possible legal action by the city or conflict with reformers, Ike Hine's club held no liquor license and permitted no gambling. According to Johnson, "the conduct of the place was surprisingly orderly." Instead, patrons enjoyed quiet conversations in carpeted and tastefully decorated rooms with lace curtains adorning the windows. In the piano room, chairs and tables ringed the bare dance floor, leaving it vacant for "singers, dancers and others who entertained." Reflecting racial pride, the owner lined the walls with "photographs or lithographs of every colored man in America who had ever 'done anything.'" Ike Hine's became a preferred haunt for white New Yorkers clandestinely seeking forbidden pleasures with illicit cross-racial flirtations, an escape from restrictive moral coda, or merely exposure to new dance and music forms. Johnson noted that "[t]here was at the place almost every night one or two parties of white people, men and women, who were out sightseeing, or slumming.[42]

The sexually charged atmosphere between whites and blacks made places like the Marshall and Ike Hine's targets of reformers' wrath. Most of the artists and athletes who comprised New York's black bohemia, however, remained relatively unmolested, and many even enjoyed popularity among whites, as long as they eschewed Jack Johnson's predilection for white women and conformed to racial stereotypes. As New York's black population grew, it supported a rising number of aspiring actors who began to enjoy greater success among both white and black audiences. Like James and Rosamond Johnson, who sought to make their artistic mark by moving to New York, others recognized that the city provided the greatest opportunities for fame. Though forced to comply with vaudevillian caricatures, some black performers such as Bert Williams and George Walker achieved tremendous popularity and financial success on stage. The pair, popularizers of the "cakewalk" dance, became renowned as comedians and soon developed full-length theatrical productions, including "Sons of Ham" in 1900; their highly successful "In Dahomey" in 1902, which brought them national attention and onto the Broadway stage; and finally "Bandana Land" in 1907. Their comedic representations of black life, though often psychologically problematic for the performers, made the pair rich. In a six-week period during 1906 the two reportedly earned nearly $35,000. George Walker's failing health forced Williams to continue alone after 1907. As a mark of his popularity in white circles, Williams was invited to join Ziegfeld's Follies on Broadway in 1914.[43]

The success and fame of people like Williams and Walker held out the hope of a life better than the one offered in service work. The tantalizing prospect of riches and glory attracted young people to the club scene, where they sought a breakthrough opportunity to dance or sing for white audiences. In his grim, cautionary antimigration novel *Sport of the Gods*, Paul Laurence Dunbar described the remarkable impact of the theater on black "provincials" newly arrived from the South. Having only recently come to New York, rural southerner Kitty Hamilton "was enchanted" when she witnessed her first live performance. The women on stage "seemed to her like creatures from fairy-land." Kit's brother, Joe, reacted even more dramatically. He "was lost, transfixed" by the performance. "His soul was floating on a sea of sense. He had eyes and ears and thoughts only for the stage. His nerves tingled and his hands twitched." Joe immediately aspired to join "the swaggering, sporty young negroes" who, for him, represented the city's glamorous nightlife. Kitty felt drawn to the club scene as well. A meeting with one of the regular singers at the fictitious Banner Club lands her a spot in the chorus line, which she accepts over her mother's objections. Kitty insists that the well-paying job will carry the family through hard financial times, though for this family, Kit's decision proves disastrous. Like Kit, many young black women in New York aspired to a life in the theater. The *Age* regularly carried advertisements for actors. One sought a "good looking" actress with "natural dramatic talent . . . , not too conceited." The sharp rise in the number of black artists and theatrical productions convinced the paper to devote an entire page of each edition to news of "Music and the Stage," further enticing black New Yorkers to participate in the city's nightlife either as performers or as members of the audience.[44]

While many black New Yorkers availed themselves of the city's night scene, much of their socializing reflected distinct ethnic identities. New York City offered far more numerous and diverse recreational activities than most black people had encountered previously, and many newcomers eagerly imbibed the excitements offered. But they often chose to do so in the comfortable and safe presence of their compatriots and could in that way maintain connections to the life they had left behind. In dances held especially for former southerners, for example, migrants used music to "invoke tradition." The pianist James P. Johnson recalled that at these gatherings the participants would sometimes call out "Let's go home." Johnson understood that they were asking for a more southern style of music. For those few hours, homesick migrants "re[-]created the South right in the middle of Manhattan." Similarly, Caribbean immigrants organized cricket teams and tennis clubs while southerners participated actively in baseball.[45] In the company of others with similar backgrounds, black New Yorkers reproduced entertainments reminiscent of home; in so doing, they perpetuated the geographic and ethnic distinctions that were defining the black population of the city.

Perhaps most important to the preservation of distinct identities was the formation of mutual aid societies and social organizations based on geography and nationality. In 1884, partly as a response to the growing southern population in the city and to guard against the encroachment of their status as elites, the "cream" of the black population formed the Society of the Sons of New York. They established a women's auxiliary two years later. Though they periodically admitted members of impeccable character not born in New York, such as T. Thomas Fortune of Florida, Adam Clayton Powell of Virginia, and Alexander Walters from Kentucky, these "honorary" New Yorkers could not participate in the deliberations of the group. This society, the first to privilege geographic origin as the basis for creating status and community, laid the groundwork for the formation of a variety of organizations representing numerous southern states and Caribbean islands.[46]

In quick succession, southern migrants established the Sons and Daughters of South Carolina, Sons of North Carolina, Sons of Virginia, Sons of the South, and the Southern Beneficial League. Forty individuals hailing from Bermuda organized the Bermuda Benevolent Association in 1897, while Cuban immigrants created the Cubans' Society of Thirty and the Cuban Fraternity. The Montserrat Progressive Society formed in 1914 to "assist in uplifting [the members] socially, morally and intellectually, to care for its sick, and those in distress, and to bury its dead." The following year a group of Virgin Island women created the Danish West Indian Ladies Aid Society to address the specific mutual aid needs of immigrant women. All of these organizations, designed to provide mutual assistance in times of sickness and death, also served the important function of highlighting distinctions among a people seen by white outsiders as a homogeneous group. Each society restricted membership to those born—or who could claim a minimum residence—in a specific geographic locale. This requirement helped to bring together people of similar cultural and ethnic backgrounds, "keeping alive the feeling of love for the native land and of respect for the homely virtues they learned there." At the same time, these organizations exaggerated

Figure 13. Toussaint L'Overture Club, Sons of New York Club Building, Thirtieth Street, 1880. Photographs and Prints Division, Schomburg Center for Research in Black Culture, The New York Public Library, Astor, Lenox and Tilden Foundations.

the differences between northerners, southerners, and Caribbean-born blacks, exacerbating tensions between the groups. When a native of North Carolina was appointed in 1910 as assistant district attorney of New York County, his compatriots responded "in the fullness of North Carolinian pride" by throwing a celebration. This expression of geographic unity reflected many migrants' continued sense of identity with their place of birth as they confronted the many challenges of life in New York City.[47]

The impediment to unity against white discrimination, however, led some black New Yorkers to denounce the divisiveness fostered by an emphasis on ethnic divisions. In 1886, only two years after the formation of the first geography-based organization, William E. H. Chase wondered about any "advantage gained in the discrimination practiced by the colored people of the city in the organization of [geographically restrictive] societies." The response made by the editor of the *New York Freeman* stressed the human desire to seek out others with similar backgrounds and interests. The advantage, he argued, "is such as would come to persons who know each other most intimately and are therefore prepared to work most harmoniously" toward common goals. "Every man has a right to select his associates, you know," the editor continued in an unconscious mimicry of arguments made in support of racial segregation, "and we have no right to complain if he refuses for any reason to select us as such."[48] This attitude only grew over time as black people from different parts of the country and the world sought to privilege their own status, often at the expense of others.

Divisions within and prejudice from outside made the urban experience for black New Yorkers a tremendously challenging one. The alluring images of the city rarely matched the reality, as whites repeatedly clamped down on virtually everything that offered the prospect of a brighter future. Though granted freedoms in the North that they could not enjoy in the South, the early black migrant and immigrants still found New York City to be an inhospitable environment. During the 1920s, as Harlem burgeoned into the artistic and cultural capital of black America, Langston Hughes expressed the frustration suffered by a population witnessing the city progress all around them, yet not be welcomed as participants in its prosperity. In his poem "Afraid," Hughes captured the essence of the black experience in industrializing New York. As the city enjoyed spectacular growth, inspiring onlookers with its fantastic promise, New York's black population could claim to be little more than bystanders to its advancement.

We cry among the skyscrapers
As our ancestors
Cried among the palms in Africa
Because we are alone,
It is night,
And we're afraid.[49]

The many changes occurring in black New York from the late nineteenth century until World War I helped to create a more segregated world than had existed at any previous time in the city. Black migrants, viewed by white and black alike with disdain, banded together for mutual support. While black Knickerbockers resented the sense that newcomers were creating a color line where one had not fully existed before, their diminishing voice and influence held little sway with either the migrants or the larger white community. Growing residential and occupational restrictions, many of which came as the result of changing perceptions of black people among white Yankees, pushed blacks further outside the white world. With the move to Harlem and the reduction even of service jobs, the Negro metropolis became an increasingly

isolated one over time. Like New York City itself for many black southerners, the white world became little more than a notion "vague and far
away" that "seemed to them the center of all the glory, all the wealth,
and all the freedom of the world." Physical geography and racial prejudice led New York's black people to form "a world among themselves,"
in which they seldom came into contact with the outside.[50]

Yet black New Yorkers always pushed back against the discrimination
and stereotyping that they faced. Their resistance to the strictures
placed upon them came to visible fruition in 1917. Responding to the
tragic violence of race riots that had killed scores of black people and
damaged hundreds of thousands of dollars worth of property in the city
of East St. Louis, New York City's black religious and civic leaders organized a massive march down Fifth Avenue. The Silent Protest Parade of
July 28, boasting as many as fifteen thousand participants, highlighted a
community coming of age after decades of development. "For once,"
the black press triumphantly noted, "the American Negro, [British]
West Indian Negro and Haitian worked in unison as black men." The
newspaper might have added that southern- and northern-born black
Americans also overcame their differences as a wide array of institutions
and individuals joined together to organize and sponsor the antilynching event. The Bermuda Benevolent Association, the American
West Indian Ladies Aid Society, the Danish West Indian Benevolent Society, the Montserrat Benevolent Association, the St. Vincent Cricket
Club, and the Caribbean American Publishing Company united with a
range of American-based societies in a show of unity and pride. For that
moment in 1917, black New Yorkers identified their common bond as
victims of racism and presented a cohesive front to white America.[51]

By taking to the streets of New York City, particularly the metropolis'
most famous thoroughfare, black New Yorkers simultaneously asserted
their claim to a city being stolen from them. Though organizers called
for the procession in response to events transpiring outside of New York,
the city's black residents seized the opportunity to symbolically challenge the racism that increasingly limited their freedoms at home.
Harassment by whites worked to ensnare black people in Harlem, but
the physical reclamation of Manhattan's major artery demonstrated
blacks' unwillingness to concede defeat. As black men, women, and children marched in disciplined order to the muted sound of muffled
drumbeats, wearing their Sunday finery and holding aloft a banner that
quoted from the Declaration of Independence, they commanded their
rightful place within the American republic generally and the city specifically. The patriarchal arrangement of the parade also defied the stereotypes that branded black people as subversive of gender norms. A
line of black male leaders headed the procession, followed by the mass

of black marchers in specific order: the children walked first, followed
by women, with men bringing up the rear. Women and children were
bounded by male guardians, and members of the boy scouts distributed
circulars that explained, in part, "We march because we want our children to live in a better land."[52] The emphasis on the protection of children, both in the physical procession and in the explicit written
messages, deliberately presented to white New Yorkers an image of con-
formity to normative moral expectations.

The quiet defiance of the Silent Protest Parade, with black people
striking back against geographic restrictions in New York City, against
the perception of black people as un-American, and against the stereotypes that they failed as proper men and women, heralded the emergence of a new activism forming in black New York. Black New Yorkers
struggled every day to survive in the city's inhospitable environment. But
as they established organizations and social connections, they slowly
developed the infrastructure that permitted attention to wider concerns.
And the ethnic diversity of the population, though at times an impediment to unification, nevertheless helped to spark the creative ingenuity
that eventually became the Harlem Renaissance. By the 1920s, Harlem
had become both a tragedy and a triumph—undeniably a ghetto replete
with problems of poverty, overcrowding, and crime, but also a refuge
and a haven, a physical place whose very name evoked heaven. "Oh, to
be in Harlem," effused Jamaican-born writer Claude McKay in his 1928
novel *Home to Harlem*. "The deep-dyed color, the thickness, the closeness
of it. The noises of Harlem. The sugared laughter. The honey-talk on its
streets. . . . Oh, the contagious fever of Harlem. Burning everywhere in
dark-eyed Harlem."[53] Though scorned and rejected by whites, black
people consistently took their share of New York City and made it, indu-
bitably, their own.

Notes

Columbia University   CU
New York Municipal Archives   NYMA
New York Public Library   NYPL
New York State Archives, Manuscripts, and Special Collections   NYSAMSC
Schomburg Library for Research in Black Culture   SLRBC

Introduction

1. James Weldon Johnson, *Along This Way: The Autobiography of James Weldon Johnson* (New York, 1933), pp. 47–48.
2. Johnson, *Along This Way*, p. 50; Gilbert Osofsky, *Harlem: The Making of a Ghetto: Negro New York, 1890–1930*, 2nd ed. (New York, 1971), pp. 71, 105, 130.
3. United States Census, *Tenth Census, 1880, Population* (Washington, D.C., 1883), vol. 1, pp. 417–22.
4. Johnson, *Along This Way*, p. 48.
5. Edwin G. Burrows and Mike Wallace, *Gotham: A History of New York City to 1898* (New York, 1999), pp. 1050–52; Donald Martin Reynolds, *The Architecture of New York City: Histories and Views of Important Structures, Sites, and Symbols* (New York, 1984), p. 149; Henry Hugh Proctor, *Between Black and White: Autobiographical Sketches* (1925; repr., Freeport, N.Y., 1971), p. 134; Margaret Clapp, "The Social and Cultural Scene," in Allan Nevins and John A. Krout, eds., *The Greater City: New York, 1898–1948* (New York, 1948), pp. 187–88.
6. Henry Collins Brown, *In the Golden Nineties* (Hastings-on-Hudson, N.Y., 1928), passim.
7. Johnson, *Along This Way*, pp. 150–52.
8. Ibid., pp. 170–90.
9. Osofsky *Harlem*, pp. 3, 8.
10. Ibid., p. 151.
11. *New York Times*, June 16, 1895, p. 16; Seth M. Scheiner, *Negro Mecca: A History of the Negro in New York City, 1865–1920* (New York, 1965), p. 177; Osofsky, *Harlem*, p. 36; *New York Freeman*, July 16, 1887.
12. Kelly Miller, "The Industrial Condition of the Negro in the North," *The Annals of the American Academy of Political and Social Science* 27 (May 1906): 543.
13. See, for example, *New York Times*, October 10, 1911, p. 16.
14. Robert Wilson Jr., "Is the Prevalence of Tuberculosis among Negroes Due to Race Tendency?" *Southern Workman* 37 (December 1908): 649; Osofsky, *Harlem*, pp. 8, 13, 55.
15. Junius Henri Browne, *The Great Metropolis: A Mirror of New York* (Hartford, Conn., 1869), p. 275.

16. Scheiner, *Negro Mecca,* pp. 15–19; Osofsky, *Harlem,* pp. 12–13; Mary White Ovington, *The Walls Came Tumbling Down* (New York, 1947), p. 37.

17. Mary White Ovington, *Black and White Sat Down Together: The Reminiscences of an NAACP Founder,* ed. Ralph E. Luker (New York, 1995), p. 26.

18. Scheiner, *Negro Mecca,* pp. 87–94; Osofsky, *Harlem,* p. 15; Silas Xavier Floyd, *Life of Charles T. Walker, D.D.* (Nashville, 1902), pp. 108–9.

19. Jervis Anderson, *This Was Harlem: A Cultural Portrait, 1900–1950* (New York, 1981), p. 3.

20. Ovington, *Black and White Sat Down Together,* p. 10.

21. See, for example, Allan H. Spear, *Black Chicago: The Making of a Negro Ghetto, 1890–1920* (Chicago, 1967); Kenneth L. Kusmer, *A Ghetto Takes Shape: Black Cleveland, 1870–1930* (Urbana, Ill., 1978); David M. Katzman, *Before the Ghetto: Black Detroit in the Nineteenth Century* (Urbana, Ill., 1973); Frank F. Furstenberg, Theodore Hershberg, and John Modell, "The Origins of the Female-Headed Black Family: The Impact of the Urban Experience," in Theodore Hershberg, ed., *Philadelphia: Work, Space, Family, and Group Experience in the 19th Century* (New York, 1981), pp. 435–54.

Chapter 1

1. William Cohen, *At Freedom's Edge: Black Mobility and the Southern White Quest for Racial Control, 1861–1915* (Baton Rouge, La., 1991), pp. 105–6; Thomas Jesse Jones, "The Negroes of the Southern States and the U.S. Census of 1910," *Southern Workman* 41, no. 8 (August 1912): 460; Richard R. Wright Jr., "The Migration of Negroes to the North," *The Annals of the American Academy of Political and Social Science* 27 (May 1906): 98–99.

2. David A. Gerber, *Black Ohio and the Color Line, 1860–1915* (Urbana, Ill., 1970), p. 278; Osofsky, *Harlem,* p. 24; Kusmer, *Ghetto Takes Shape,* p. 40.

3. Howard N. Rabinowitz, *Race Relations in the Urban South, 1865–1890* (New York, 1978), pp. 334–38.

4. Osofsky, *Harlem,* p. 25; Philip A. Bruce, *The Plantation Negro as a Freeman: Observations on his Character, Condition, and Prospects in Virginia* (New York, 1889), pp. 7–9.

5. W. E. B. DuBois, *The Philadelphia Negro: A Social Study* (Philadelphia, 1899), p. 44; Wright, " Migration of Negroes," pp. 102–3; Clyde Vernon Kiser, *From Sea Island to City: A Study of St. Helena Islanders in Harlem and Other Urban Centers* (New York, 1932), pp. 131, 137; Helen A. Tucker, "Negro Craftsmen in New York. I: Purpose and Method of the Investigation," *Southern Workman* 36 (October 1907): 550.

6. Benjamin E. Mays, *Born to Rebel: An Autobiography* (Athens, Ga., 1971), p. 25.

7. *Alexander's Magazine,* 1 (November 1905): 7.

8. Darlene Clark Hine, "Rape and the Inner Lives of Black Women in the Middle West: Preliminary Thoughts on the Culture of Dissemblance," *Signs* 14 (summer 1989): 914; Wright, "Migration of Negroes," pp. 104, 109; Richard Wright, *Black Boy,* restored ed. (1944; repr., New York, 1993), pp. 233–34.

9. Antilynching crusader Ida B. Wells demonstrated that, during the 1880s, rape was alleged—much less proved—in only one-third of the country's lynchings. Neil R. McMillan, *Dark Journey: Black Mississippians in the Age of Jim Crow* (Urbana, Ill., 1990), p. 235.

10. McMillan, *Dark Journey*, pp. 233–35.

11. Mays, *Born to Rebel*, p. 35.

12. Mary White Ovington, *Half a Man: The Status of the Negro in New York* (1911; repr., New York, 1969), p. 1; Ray Stannard Baker, *Following the Color Line: American Negro Citizenship in the Progressive Era* (New York, 1908), p. 133.

13. "The Scarcity of Farm Labor," *The Voice* 3 (September 1906): 620–21; Archibald Grimke, "Berean Manual Training and Industrial School," *Alexander's Magazine* 4 (October 1907): 313; W. E. B. DuBois, "The Black North," *New York Times*, November 17, 1901, p. 10; Wilmington *Messenger*, quoted in David G. Neilson, *Black Ethos: Northern Urban Negro Life and Thought, 1890–1930* (Westport, Conn., 1977), p. 63; "The Aftermath of the Atlanta Riots," *The Voice*, 4 (January and February 1907), p. 18.

14. *Colored American Magazine* 1 (August 1900): 151; Adam Clayton Powell, *Against the Tide: An Autobiography* (New York, 1938), p. 14; Ida B. Wells, *Crusade for Justice: The Autobiography of Ida B. Wells*, ed. Alfreda M. Duster (Chicago, 1970), pp. 61–62; Johnson, *Along This Way*, pp. 149–89.

15. Cohen, *At Freedom's Edge*, p. 105.

16. Osofsky, *Harlem*, p. 30; Thomas Roy Peyton, *Quest for Dignity: An Autobiography of a Negro Doctor* (Los Angeles, 1963), p. 3.

17. Mays, *Born to Rebel*, pp. 8–9; Theodore Rosengarten, *All God's Dangers: The Life of Nate Shaw* (New York, 1974), p. 27.

18. Kiser, *Sea Island to City*, pp. 125–26.

19. W. C. Handy, *Father of the Blues: An Autobiography* (New York, 1941), pp. 21, 29.

20. Kiser, *Sea Island to City*, pp. 133, 164.

21. John C. Dancy, *Sand against the Wind: The Memoirs of John C. Dancy* (Detroit, 1966), p. 68.

22. Mrs. V. E. Matthews, "Some of the Dangers Confronting Southern Girls in the North," *Hampton Negro Conference, July 1898* 2 (Hampton, Va., 1898): 63; Tucker, "Negro Craftsmen in New York," p. 550; Kiser, *Sea Island to City*, p. 122.

23. Kiser, *Sea Island to City*, pp. 122, 132.

24. George E. Haynes, "The Movement of Negroes from the Country to the City," *Southern Workman* 42, no. 4 (April 1913): 234–35; *Industrial Relations: Final Report and Testimony Submitted to Congress by the Commission on Industrial Relations*, 64th Cong., 1st sess., Senate Doc., 11 vols. (Washington, D.C., 1916), 10: "Pullman Employees," pp. 9552–53; *Colored American Magazine* 3 (July 1901): n.p.

25. Frances A. Kellor, "Assisted Emigration from the South: The Women," *Charities* 15 (October 7, 1905): 12–13; Carl Kelsey, "Some Causes of Negro Emigration: The Men," *Charities* 15 (October 7, 1905): 16–17; Osofsky, *Harlem*, p. 29.

26. "The Exodus from Mississippi," *The Voice of the Negro* 1 (June 1904): 259; William H. Harris, *The Harder We Run: Black Workers since the Civil War* (New York, 1982), pp. 52–53.

27. Frances Richardson Kellor, *An American Crusade: The Life of Charles Waddell Chesnutt* (Provo, Utah, 1978), p. 84; Richard R. Wright Jr., "The Negro in Chicago," *Southern Workman* 35 (October 1906): 557–58; Abraham Epstein, *The Negro Migrant in Pittsburgh* (New York, 1918), pp. 19–20; Haynes, "Movement of Negroes," pp. 233–34; Louis R. Harlan, ed., *The Booker T. Washington Papers*, 14 vols. (Chicago, 1982), 2:472.

28. Mamie Garvin Fields, *Lemon Swamp and Other Places* (New York, 1983), pp. 141–52; *Final Report and Testimony . . . by the Commission on Industrial Relations*, p.

9552; S. F. Collins, "How Colored Youths Get through School," *The Voice of the Negro* 2 (July 1905): 488; Mays, *Born to Rebel*, pp. 38–39.

29. Tucker, "Negro Craftsmen in New York," p. 550; Kiser, *Sea Island to City*, pp. 137, 251.

30. Kiser, *Sea Island to City*, pp. 99–100; "The Reminiscences of Samuel J. Battle," p. 9, Columbia University Oral History Research Office.

31. George Edmund Haynes, *The Negro at Work in New York City* (1912; repr., New York, 1968), pp. 26–31.

32. Osofsky, *Harlem*, p. 25; Wright, "Migration of Negroes," pp. 102–3; Haynes, *Negro at Work*, p. 17; Benjamin H. Locke, "The Community Life of a Harlem Group of Negroes" (M.A. thesis, Columbia University, 1913), passim; Kiser, *Sea Island to City*, p. 163.

33. Calvin B. Holder, "The Causes and Composition of West Indian Immigration to New York City, 1900–1952," *Afro-Americans in New York Life and History* (January 1987): 23; Ira De A. Reid, *The Negro Immigrant: His Background, Characteristics and Social Adjustment, 1899–1937* (1939; repr., New York, 1969), p. 240; Irma Watkins-Owens, *Blood Relations: Caribbean Immigrants and the Harlem Community, 1900–1930* (Bloomington, Ind., 1996), p. 18.

34. Watkins-Owens, *Blood Relations*, p. 4; Gardner Jones, "Pilgrimage to Freedom," *Writers' Program: Negroes of New York* (New York, n.d.), p. 25, SLRBC.

35. "West Indian Migration to New York," *Charities* 15 (October 7, 1905): 2; Philip Kasinitz, *Caribbean New York: Black Immigrants and the Politics of Race* (Ithaca, N.Y., 1992), p. 21; Holder, "West Indian Immigration to New York City," p. 10; Peter D. Fraser, "Nineteenth-Century West Indian Migration to Britain," in Ransford W. Palmer, ed., *In Search of a Better Life: Perspectives on Migration from the Caribbean* (New York, 1990), pp. 19–20.

36. Jeff Kisseloff, ed., *You Must Remember This: An Oral History of Manhattan from the 1890s to World War II* (San Diego, 1989), p. 270; R. B. Moore Papers, box 1, folder 1, SLRBC.

37. James S. Watson Papers, box 3, folder 1, SLRBC; Samuel B. Jones, "The British West Indian Negro: Fifth Paper: The West Indian Immigrant," *Southern Workman* 41 (March 1912): 174.

38. Holder, "West Indian Immigration to New York City," p. 10; Watkins-Owens, *Blood Relations*, p. 21.

39. Ransford W. Palmer, *Pilgrims from the Sun: West Indian Migration to America* (New York, 1995), p. 6; Bonham C. Richardson, *Caribbean Migrants: Environment and Human Survival on St. Kitts and Nevis* (Knoxville, Tenn., 1983), p. 131; Holder, "West Indian Immigration to New York City," pp. 8–9; Kisseloff, *You Must Remember This*, p. 190.

40. Jones, "Pilgrimage to Freedom," pp. 28–29; Dean W. Morse, ed., *Pride against Prejudice: Work in the Lives of Older Blacks and Young Puerto Ricans* (Montclair, N.J., 1980), p. 49; Watkins-Owens, *Blood Relations*, p. 17.

41. Watkins-Owens, *Blood Relations*, pp. 23–24; Richardson, *Caribbean Migrants*, p. 131.

42. Richardson, *Caribbean Migrants*, p.132.

43. Dowridge-Challenor Correspondence, May 4, 23, 1910, SLRBC.

44. R. B. Moore Papers, box 1, folder 1; Dowridge-Challenor Letters; Watkins-Owens, *Blood Relations*, pp. 19, 21.

45. Richardson, *Caribbean Migrants*, p. 133; Kasinitz, *Caribbean New York*, p. 25; De A. Reid, *Negro Immigrant*, p. 244.

46. Burrows and Wallace, *Gotham*, p. 1156.

47. Baker, *Following the Color Line*, p. 130; "Negroes Leaving the South," *New York Times*, March 18, 1901, p. 2; "Negroes Leave the South," *New York Times*, November 24, 1892, p. 1.

48. Frances A. Kellor, "The Problem of the Young Negro Girl from the South," *New York Times*, March 19, 1905, sec. 4, p. 8; Frances A. Kellor, "Southern Colored Girls in the North," *Charities* 13 (March 18, 1905): 585; Matthews, "Some of the Dangers Confronting Southern Girls in the North," pp. 63–67.

49. Kellor, "Problem of the Young Negro Girl," p. 8; Frances A. Kellor, "Associations for Protection of Colored Women," *Colored American Magazine* 9 (December 1905): 695–99; Kellor, "Southern Colored Girls in the North," pp. 584–85; Kellor, "Assisted Emigration from the South," pp. 11–14.

50. Ovington, *Half a Man*, p. 81; Mary White Ovington, "Vacation Days in San Juan Hill: A New York Negro Colony," *Southern Workman* 38 (November 1909): 633.

51. E. M. Rhodes, "The Protection of Girls Who Travel: A National Movement," *Colored American Magazine* 13 (August 1907): 114–15; National League for the Protection of Colored Women, *Annual Report, 1910* (New York, 1910), pp. 3–7; National League on Urban Conditions Among Negroes, *Annual Report, 1910–1911* (New York, 1912), p. 23; *New York Times*, January 30, 1910, p. 8; W. E. B. DuBois, ed., *The Negro American Family* (Atlanta, 1908), p. 36.

52. Paul Laurence Dunbar, *The Sport of the Gods* (New York, 1902), p. 213; Osofsky, *Harlem*, p. 43; DuBois, *Black North in 1901*, p. 45; "Shoots into Ferry Crowd," *New York Age*, June 13, 1907, p. 6.

53. Quoted in Gerber, *Black Ohio and the Color Line*, p. 419.

54. "Movement of the Afro-American Population," *New York Age*, January 10, 1907, pp. 4–5; "The Problem of Living in the North and the South, *New York Age*, April 25, 1907, p. 4; Kelly Miller, "The City Negro: The Inter-Relation of the Country and City Negro," *Southern Workman* 32 (April 1903): 238; "The Negro in New York," *Southern Workman* 31 (June 1902): 308; Osofsky, *Harlem*, pp. 41–42.

55. "West Indians in New York," *New York Age*, September 5, 1891, p. 2.

56. Cohen, *At Freedom's Edge*, pp. 105–6; Wright, "Migration of Negroes," pp. 98–99.

57. Leslie M. Harris, *In the Shadow of Slavery: African Americans in New York City, 1626–1863*, (Chicago, 2003), p. 267.

58. "Wealthy Negro Citizens," *New York Times*, July 14, 1895, p. 17; Ovington, *Half a Man*, p. 94; DuBois, *Black North in 1901*, p. 12; Craig Steven Wilder, *A Covenant with Color: Race and Social Power in Brooklyn* (New York, 2000), p. 114; *New York Age*, August 31, 1905.

59. Kisseloff, *You Must Remember This*, p. 272; William Fielding Ogburn, "The Richmond Negro in New York City: His Social Mind as Seen in His Pleasures" (M.A. thesis, Columbia University, 1909), pp. 50–51.

60. Robert Zachariah Johnstone, "The Negro in New York: His Social Attainments and Prospects" (M.A. thesis, Columbia University, 1911), pp. 58–59.

61. Kisseloff, *You Must Remember This*, pp. 270–71.

62. Watkins-Owens, *Blood Relations*, p. 200, n31.

63. Johnson, *Along This Way*, p. 65; Roi Ottley and William J. Weatherby, eds., *The Negro in New York: An Informal Social History* (New York, 1967), p. 148; Watkins-Owens, *Blood Relations*, p. 5.

64. Quoted in Watkins-Owens, *Blood Relations*, p. 5.

65. Johnstone, "The Negro in New York," pp. 56–57; Paule Marshall, "Black Immigrant Women in *Brown Girl, Brownstones*," in Roy Bryce-Laporte, ed., *Female*

Immigrants to the United States: Caribbean, Latin American and African Experiences (Washington, D.C., 1981), p. 7.

66. Johnstone, "Negro in New York," p. 59; Ovington, *Walls Came Tumbling Down*, p. 6; "Mulattoes Not *Negroes*," *Brooklyn Eagle*, December 5, 1902, p. 18.

67. Johnstone, "Negro in New York," p. 59; Osofsky, *Harlem*, pp. 134–35; James S. Watson Papers, box 12, folder 1.

68. "Thinks New York the Negro's Hope," *New York Times*, October 1, 1911, p. 16.

69. Richardson, *Caribbean Migrants*, p. 134; Carrie Ward Moore, "A Study of a Group of West Indian Negroes in New York City" (M.A. thesis, Columbia University, 1913), p. 30; Watkins-Owens, *Blood Relations*, pp. 28–29; Jones, "Pilgrimage to Freedom."

70. Proctor, *Between Black and White*, pp. 133–34.

71. Alexander Walters, *My Life and Work* (New York, 1917), p. 53.

72. Johnson, *Along This Way*, pp. 8, 46–47; James Weldon Johnson, *The Autobiography of an Ex-Coloured Man* (1912; repr., New York, 1960), p. 90.

73. Proctor, *Between Black and White*, pp. 133–34.

74. Kisseloff, *You Must Remember This*, pp. 276–77.

75. De A. Reid, *Negro Immigrant*, p. 235; Richardson, *Caribbean Migrants*, p. 132; Peyton, *Quest for Dignity*, pp. 3–4.

76. Handy, *Father of the Blues*, p. 29.

77. Hoke Family Papers, box 1, folder 5, March 8, August 4, 1904; box 1, folder 3, December 9, 1894, November 25, 1903, NYSAMSC.

78. DuBois, *Negro American Family*, p. 36.

79. John P. Clyde, "The Negro in New York City" (M.A. thesis, Columbia University, 1898), p. 17; Louise Bolard More, *Wage-Earners' Budgets: A Study of Standards and Cost of Living in New York City* (New York, 1907), pp. 71–72; New York Colored Mission, *Annual Report, 1888* (New York, 1889), p. 16; Hoke Family Papers, box 1, folder 5, August 4, 1904.

80. Scheiner, *Negro Mecca*, p. 31; Jacob Riis, "The Black Half," *Crisis* 5 (April 1913): 299; *New York Times*, December 16, 1915, sec. 7, p. 1.

81. Federation of Churches and Christian Workers in New York City, *Sociological Canvass No. 2* (New York, 1896), p. 26; Herbert G. Gutman, *The Black Family in Slavery and Freedom, 1750–1925* (New York, 1976), p. 509; Elizabeth H. Pleck, "A Mother's Wages: Income Earning among Married Italian and Black Women, 1896–1911," in Michael Gordon, ed., *The American Family in Social-Historical Perspective* (New York, 1978), p. 496; Haynes *Negro at Work*, pp. 62–63; *New York Times*, December 16, 1915, sec. 7, p. 1.

82. National League on Urban Conditions among Negroes, *A Study of Negro Employees of Apartment Houses in New York City* (New York, 1916), p. 22; Ogburn, "Richmond Negro," pp. 63–64.

83. Hoke Family Papers, box 1, folder 5, Aug. 4, 1904, March 8, 1904; Dowridge-Challenor Correspondence, April 19 [no year].

84. Thomas Gilroy Papers, box 14, folder "Police Dept. of 1893," July 17, 1893, NYMA.

85. Richardson, *Caribbean Migrants*, p. 134; Dowridge-Challenor Correspondence, February 22, 1907; Watkins-Owens, *Blood Relations*, p. 19.

86. Dowridge-Challenor Correspondence; Watkins-Owens, *Blood Relations*, p. 20.

87. Dowridge-Challenor Correspondence; Watkins-Owens, *Blood Relations*, p. 11; Hoke Family Papers, box 1, folder 5, March 8, 1904.

88. Green Family Letters, Januray 2, 1900, SLRBC.

89. Claude McKay, *My Green Hills of Jamaica*, ed., Mervyn Morris (Kingston, Jamaica, 1979), pp. 86–87.

90. Dunbar, *Sport of the Gods*, pp. 77–78.

91. Johnson, *Autobiography of an Ex-Coloured Man*, p. 89.

Chapter 2

1. Osofsky, *Harlem*, pp. 46–47.

2. *New York Times*, August 17, 1900, p. 2; Osofsky, *Harlem*, p. 47.

3. Citizens' Protective League, *Persecution of Negroes* (New York, 1900), p. 2.

4. Robert Van Wyck Papers, box 9, folder 24, NYMA; *New York Times*, August 16, 1900, p. 1; Osofsky, *Harlem*, pp. 47–48.

5. Citizens' Protective League, *Persecution*, p. 6; Johnson *Along This Way*, p. 158; *New York Times*, August 17, 1900, p. 2.

6. *New York Times*, August 17, 1900, p. 2; August 18, 1900, p. 2; Osofsky, *Harlem*, p. 49.

7. Robert Van Wyck Papers, box 9, folder 24; *Report of the Police Department of the City of New York, 1900* (New York, 1901), p. 10; *New York Times*, December 9, 1900, p. 14.

8. *New York Times*, August 18, 1900, p. 2; August 27, 1900, p. 1; September 4, 1900, pp. 1–2; Osofsky, *Harlem*, pp. 50–51.

9. Citizens' Protective League, *Persecution*, p. 3; *New York Times*, August 25, 1900, p. 1; September 20, 1900, p. 12.

10. *New York Times*, June 16, 1895, p. 16.

11. Johnson, *Along This Way*, p. 158.

12. David W. Blight, "Quarrel Forgotten or a Revolution Remembered? Reunion and Race in the Memory of the Civil War, 1875–1913," in David W. Blight and Brooks D. Simpson, eds. *Union and Emancipation: Essays on Politics and Race in the Civil War Era* (Kent, Ohio, 1997), pp. 151–53. See also David W. Blight, *Race and Reunion: The Civil War in American Memory* (Cambridge, Mass., 2001).

13. Rayford W. Logan, *The Betrayal of the Negro: From Rutherford B. Hayes to Woodrow Wilson* (London, 1969), p. 169; Rollin G. Osterweis, *The Myth of the Lost Cause, 1865–1900* (Hamden, Conn., 1973), p. 102.

14. Osterweis, *Myth of the Lost Cause*, p. 105.

15. Alexander Saxton, *The Rise and Fall of the White Republic: Class Politics and Mass Culture in Nineteenth-Century America* (London, 1990), p. 176; Robert Toll, *Blacking Up: The Minstrel Show in Nineteenth-Century America* (New York, 1975), p. 88.

16. *New York Times*, March 1, 1881, p. 2; Henry Collins Brown, *Brownstone Fronts and Saratoga Trunks* (New York, 1935), p. 183.

17. *Valentine's Manual* 6 (1922): 30; "Hampton Entertainments in the North," *Southern Workman* 30 (April 1901): 188.

18. Osofsky, *Harlem*, pp. 41–43.

19. William Gaynor Papers, box 15, folder 2, "1910"; box 72, folder 4, "1913"; box 10, folder 6, "1904" NYMA; William Gaynor Papers, box 72, folder 4, "1913."

20. Kisseloff, *You Must Remember This*, p. 273; George McClellan Papers, box 71, folder 2, "1912," NYMA.

21. Brown, *Brownstone Fronts and Saratoga Trunks*, p. 361; Charles W. Gardner,

The Doctor and the Devil, or Midnight Adventures of Dr. Parkhurst (New York, 1931), p. 57; Frank Moss, *The American Metropolis*, volume 3 (New York, 1897), p. 287.

22. "Race Question in New York," *New York Times*, June 15, 1904, p. 6.

23. Nina Silber, *The Romance of Reunion: Northerners and the South, 1865–1900* (Chapel Hill, N.C., 1993), p. 124. For antebellum stereotypes see, for example, David R. Roediger, *The Wages of Whiteness* (London, 1991), especially chaps. 5 and 6; and Jean H. Baker, *Affairs of Party: The Political Culture of Northern Democrats in the Mid-Nineteenth Century* (Ithaca, N.Y., 1983), chap. 6.

24. Johnson, *Along This Way*, pp. 52–53; Tom Fletcher, *100 Years of the Negro in Show Business* (New York, 1984), p. 139; Richard M. Sudhalter, "Don't Give the Name a Bad Place: Types and Stereotypes in American Musical Theater, 1870–1900," Compact Disc Insert (New York, 1978), pp. 6–7.

25. James D. McCabe, *Lights and Shadows of New York Life; or, the Sights and Sensations of the Great City* (Philadelphia, 1872), pp. 485–86; for the transformation of cultural behavior, see, for example, Lawrence W. Levine, *Highbrow Lowbrow: The Emergence of Cultural Hierarchy in America* (Cambridge, Mass., 1988), pp. 171–242, passim.

26. Lewis A. Erenberg, *Steppin' Out: New York Nightlife and the Transformation of American Culture, 1890–1930* (Westport, Conn., 1981), p. 73; Sam Dennison, *Scandalize My Name: Black Imagery in American Popular Music* (New York, 1982), p. 357; Baker, *Affairs of Party*, p. 218; Toll, *Blacking Up*, p. 71.

27. North, quoted in Ralph E. Luker *The Social Gospel in Black and White: American Racial Reform, 1885–1912* (Chapel Hill, N.C., 1991), p. 160.

28. Dennison, *Scandalize My Name*, p. 368; *New York Journal and Advertiser*, December 11, 1898, Musical Supplement, Minstrel Song Collection, NYSAMSC.

29. *New York World*, September 17, 1899, Musical Supplement, Minstrel Song Collection, NYSAMSC.

30. *New York World*, September 17, 1899, Musical Supplement, Minstrel Song Collection. NYSAMSC.

31. *New York Sunday Press*, November 11, 1900, Musical Supplement, Minstrel Song Collection, NYSAMSC.

32. *New York Journal and Advertiser*, January 23, 1898, Musical Supplement, Minstrel Song Collection, NYSAMSC. For more on the struggle to create and maintain relationships, please see Chapter 5.

33. Brown, *In the Golden Nineties*, pp. 173–74; Elliott J. Gorn, *The Manly Art: Bare-Knuckle Prize Fighting in America* (Ithaca, N.Y., 1986), pp. 192–93; Minstrel Song Collection, NYSAMSC.

34. Carroll Smith-Rosenberg, *Disorderly Conduct: Visions of Gender in Victorian America* (New York, 1985), pp. 167–81 passim.

35. James H. Dorman, "Shaping the Popular Image of Post-Reconstruction American Blacks: The 'Coon Song' Phenomenon of the Gilded Age," *American Quarterly* 40 (December 1988): 455.

36. *New York World*, February 18, 1900, Musical Supplement, Minstrel Song Collection, NYSAMSC.

37. *New York Journal*, June 3, 1900, Musical Supplement, Minstrel Song Collection, NYSAMSC.

38. John Graziano, "Music in William Randolph Hearst's *New York Journal*," *Notes: Quarterly Journal of the Music Library Association* 48 (December 1991): 394.

39. Kenneth W. Goings, *Mammy and Uncle Mose: Black Collectibles and American Stereotyping* (Bloomington, Ind., 1994), pp. 1–14; Henry Louis Gates Jr., "The Trope of the New Negro and the Reconstruction of the Image of the Black," *Representations* (fall 1988): 149–50.

40. Brown, *In the Golden Nineties*, p. 294; Currier and Ives' "Darktown Comics" Collection (Albion College Archives); Logan, *Betrayal of the Negro*, p. 170; Brown, *Brownstone Fronts and Saratoga Trunks*, pp. 269–70.

41. Art collections of Currier and Ives prints published prior to the 1950s make prominent mention of the Darktown Series; only recently have any historical examinations been made of these prints. See, for example, Bryan F. LeBeau, "African Americans in Currier and Ives's America: The *Darktown* Series," *Journal of American and Comparative Cultures* 23 (2000): 71–83; Bryan F. LeBeau, *Currier & Ives: America Imagined* (Washington, D.C., 2001), especially chap. 7; Brown, *In the Golden Nineties*, p. 294; Brown, *Brownstone Fronts and Saratoga Trunks*, pp. 269–70.

42. Kevin K. Gaines, *Uplifting the Race: Black Leadership, Politics, and Culture in the Twentieth Century* (Chapel Hill, N. C., 1996), pp. 68, 70.

43. Ibid., p. 70.

44. Mary Frances Berry and John W. Blassingame, *Long Memory: The Black Experience in America* (New York, 1982), pp. 350–51; J. Stanley Lemons, "Black Stereotypes as Reflected in Popular Culture, 1880–1920," *American Quarterly* 24, no. 1 (spring 1977): 104.

45. Ogburn, "Richmond Negro"; Johnstone, "Negro in New York"; Ernest Jasper Hopper, "A Northern Negro Group" (M.A. thesis, Columbia University, 1912); Seymour Paul, "A Group of Virginia Negroes in New York City" (M.A. thesis, Columbia University, 1912); Carrie Ward Moore, "A Study of a Group of West Indian Negroes in New York City" (M.A. thesis, Columbia University, 1913); Benjamin H. Locke, "The Community Life of a Harlem Group of Negroes" (M.A. thesis, Columbia University, 1913).

46. Clyde, "Negro in New York City," p. 15.

47. Gaines, *Uplifting the Race*, p. 68.

48. August Meier, *Negro Thought in America, 1880–1915* (Ann Arbor, Mich., 1969), pp. 88–89.

49. William Pickens, "The Educational Condition of the Negro in Cities," *The Voice* (October 1906): 427–28.

50. Meier, *Negro Thought in America*, pp. 90–99.

51. Bruce, *Plantation Negro as a Freeman*, pp. 175–76, 180.

52. Timothy J. Gilfoyle, *City of Eros: New York City, Prostitution, and the Commercialization of Sex, 1790–1920* (New York, 1992), pp. 274–75.

53. George Kneeland, *Commercialized Prostitution in New York City* (New York, 1913), pp. 108–10; Committee of Fourteen, *Annual Report, 1915–1916* (New York, 1916), p. 59; Howard B. Woolston, *Prostitution in the United States, vol. 1: Prior to the Entrance of the United States into the World War* (New York, 1921), pp. 15–16.

54. Haynes, *Negro at Work*, p. 81; National League on Urban Conditions among Negroes *Study of Negro Employees of Apartment Houses*, p. 23; Kneeland, *Commercialized Prostitution*, pp. 300–302; Ovington, *Half a Man*, p. 85.

55. New York State Senate [The Lexow Committee], *Investigation of the Police Department of New York* (New York, 1895), pp. 5217–20; Committee of Fourteen, *Annual Report, 1915–1916*, p. 86.

56. Reginald Wright Kauffman, *The House of Bondage* (New York, 1910), passim.; Matthew Hale Smith, *Sunshine and Shadow in New York* (Hartford, Conn., 1869), p. 375; Kneeland, *Commercialized Prostitution*, pp. 6, 21, 108–10, 298; Lexow Committee, *Investigation of the Police Department of New York*, p. 1879; Frances A. Kellor, *Out of Work: A Study of Unemployment* (New York, 1915), p. 231.

57. Kellor, *Out of Work*, pp. 227–28; Woolston, *Prostitution in the United States*, pp. 15–16.

58. John H. Warren Jr., *Thirty Years' Battle with Crime, or the Crying Shame of New York* (Poughkeepsie, N.Y., 1874), pp. 110–11.

59. See, for example, Clifford G. Roe, *The Great War on White Slavery; or Fighting for the Protection of Our Girls* (n.p., 1911), passim.

60. Kellor, *Out of Work*, pp. 229–30; Warren, *Thirty Years' Battle with Crime*, p. 115.

61. Kneeland, *Commercialized Prostitution*, pp. 45, 295–96.

62. George W. Walling, *Recollections of a New York City Police Chief* (New York, 1887), pp. 485, 486–87; H. B. Gibbud, *The Story of Nellie Conroy* (New York, 1887), p. 4; William McAdoo, *Guarding a Great City* (New York, 1906), p. 100; Jimmy Durante and Jack Kofoed, *Night Clubs* (New York, 1931), pp. 15–16.

63. Locke, "Harlem Negroes," p. 32.

64. Gibbud, *Nellie Conroy*, pp. 4–10.

65. See, for example, Committee of Fourteen Papers, box 28, folders 1910, 1910–12, 1912, "Invest. Rep. 1912," NYPL.

66. Committee of Fourteen Papers, box 28, folder 1910–12, NYPL.

67. Kisseloff, *You Must Remember This*, p. 267; Committee of Fourteen Papers, box 28, folder 1910–12, NYPL.

68. Committee of Fourteen Papers, box 28, folder 1910–12, NYPL.

69. Committee of Fourteen, *Annual Report, 1915–1916*, p. 58

70. Committee of Fourteen, *Annual Report, 1912* (New York, 1913), p. 24; *Annual Report, 1913* (New York, 1914), p. 37; *Annual Report, 1914* (New York, 1915), p. 15; *Annual Report, 1915* (New York, 1916), pp. 1, 26, 58; Augustine E. Costello, *Our Police Protectors: History of the New York Police* (New York, 1885), p. 351.

71. *Crisis* 3, no. 6 (April 1912): 243.

72. Dunbar, *Sport of the Gods*, pp. 212–13.

73. *New York Times,* July 14, 1895, p. 17; *New York Globe,* January 20, 1883, p. 2.

74. *New York Age,* July 4, 1907, p. 4.

75. William Gaynor Papers, box 36, folder 3, "1911"; box 55, folder 1, "1912."

76. *Crisis* 4 (June 1912): 61.

77. *New York Age,* November 22, 1890, p. 2; "The White Rose Mission," *New York Age,* March 22, 1906, p. 1; "Victoria Earle Matthews," *New York Age,* March 14, 1907, p. 6; Lassalle Best, "History of the White Rose Mission and Industrial Association," Writer's Program Research Paper (New York, n.d.), pp. 2–3, SLRBC; Mary L. Lewis, "The White Rose Industrial Association," *The Messenger* 7 (April 1925): 158.

78. Matthews, "Some of the Dangers Confronting Southern Girls in the North," p. 67; White Rose Industrial Association, *Annual Report for the Year Ending December 31, 1912* (n.p., n.d.), pp. 4–6, White Rose Home Papers, SLRBC; *Crisis* 3 (December 1911): 51.

79. National League for the Protection of Colored Women, *Report, 1910* (New York, 1911), pp. 3–7; National Urban League, *Report 1910–1911* (New York, 1912), p. 23; Cheryl Hicks, "Confined to Womanhood: Women, Prisons, and Race in the State of New York, 1890–1935" (Ph.D. diss., Princeton University, 1999), pp. 66–68.

80. James Weldon Johnson, *Black Manhattan* (New York, 1930), p. 128; see, for example, *New York Times,* August 17, 1900; *New York Daily Tribune,* August 16, 17, 1900.

81. William Gaynor Papers, box 72, folder 4.

82. Dennison, *Scandalize My Name*, p. 419.

Chapter 3

1. Seth M. Scheiner, "The New York City Negro and the Tenement, 1880–1910," *New York History* 45 (October 1964): 306–7; *New York Times*, April 14, 1889.

2. *New York Times*, April 28, 1889, p. 9.

3. Ibid.

4. Citizens' Association of New York, *Report of the Council of Hygiene and Public Health* (New York, 1866), pp. 24, 67, 89, 132, 148, 240, 341; Lloyd Morris, *Incredible New York: High Life and Low Life of the Last Hundred Years* (New York, 1951), p. 275.

5. Riis, "Black Half," *Crisis* p. 299.

6. Community Service Society, box 260, folder R520 (Case #41599), CU.

7. Cornelius W. Willemse, *A Cop Remembers* (New York, 1933), pp. 132–34.

8. More, *Wage-Earners' Budgets*, p. 11; Gerald W. McFarland, *Inside Greenwich Village: A New York City Neighborhood, 1898–1918* (Amherst, Mass., 2001), pp. 16, 85; William Gaynor Papers, box 71, folder 5, letter dated February 21, 1913.

9. Powell, *Against the Tide*, pp. 49–57, 68.

10. Hugh Grant Papers, box 40, folder 4, NYMA; *New York Tribune*, January 27, 1889.

11. William Gaynor Papers, box 35, folder 3 and Box 77, Folder 3; Kisseloff, *You Must Remember This*, p. 190; Jacob Riis, *The Battle with the Slum* (New York, 1902), pp. 110–11.

12. Thomas Jesse Jones, *The Sociology of a New York City Block* (New York, 1904), pp. 35, 103; *Thirteenth Census, 1910, Population* (Washington, D.C., 1914), 3: 253–58; "Interview with Samuel J. Battle, February 1960," p. 35, SLRBC; Charles Lockwood, *Manhattan Moves Uptown: An Illustrated History* (Boston, 1976), p. 290; Osofsky, *Harlem*, pp. 12–13; Morris, *Incredible New York*, p. 275.

13. Ovington, *Half A Man*, p. 22; Ovington, *Walls Came Tumbling Down*, p. 43.

14. Jessie C. Sleet, "In the Day's Work of a Visiting Nurse," *Charities* 15 (October 7, 1905): 73; Lilian Brandt, "Consumption in the United States. Part III – Race," *Charities* 9 (December 6, 1902): 570.

15. Wilson, "Is the Prevalence of Tuberculosis among Negroes Due to Race Tendency?" p. 649; Ovington, *Half a Man*, pp. 29–30; *New York Age*, February 7, 1907, p. 5; February 14, 1907, p. 8; December 9, 1912, p. 8; "The Prevention of Tuberculosis among Negroes in New York," *Charities* 14 (June 10, 1905): 825.

16. *New York Age*, March 21, 1915, p. 3; Ovington, "Vacation Days in San Juan Hill," pp. 333–34.

17. Kisseloff, *You Must Remember This*, p. 269; *New York Age*, March 21, 1915, p. 3.

18. Community Service Society, box 260, folder R520 (Case #41599.

19. Johnstone, "Negro in New York," pp. 12–13; Department of Probation Records (Brooklyn), box 3, 1911 (Case #924, Frances Fischer), NYMA.

20. Supreme Court Records, box 10546, Charles Albright (1913), NYMA; see also, for example, House of Refuge Papers, Case #27892 (Viola George), May 12, 1900, NYSAMSC; Supreme Court Records, box 10550, Louis Jackson (1913), NYMA.

21. Community Service Society, box 241, folder R59 (Case #10627).

22. J. Gilmer Speed, "The Negro in New York," *Harper's Weekly* 44 (December

22, 1900): 1249–50; *New York Age,* July 30, 1908; Ogburn, "Richmond Negro in New York City," p. 50; Harriet Quimby, "Better Homes for Negroes," *Southern Workman* 34 (November 1905): 596; William Gaynor Papers, box 73, folder 1.

23. Ovington, *The Walls Came Tumbling Down,* p. 35; Scheiner, "Negro and the Tenement," p. 307; Kisseloff, *You Must Remember This,* pp. 190, 268; John P. Mitchel Papers, box 127, folder 9, NYMA.

24. Kisseloff, *You Must Remember This,* p. 190.

25. *New York Times,* July 20, 1905, p. 12; *New York Age,* July 27, 1905, p. 1.

26. *New York Times,* July 20, 1905, p. 12; July 25, 1905, p. 12.

27. Osofsky, *Harlem,* p. 111; New York Colored Mission, *Annual Report, 1912* (New York, 1913), p. 8.

28. DuBois, *Black North in 1901,* p. 12; Community Service Society, box 269, folder R719 (Case #82130); box 254, folder R370 (Case #40756).

29. Osofsky, *Harlem,* p. 96; *New York Age,* March 7, 1907, p. 1.

30. Osofsky, *Harlem,* p. 107; *Crisis* 9 (February 1915): 168; *New York Times,* quoted in Ovington, *Black and White Sat Down Together,* p. 51. The *New York Times* extensively covered the shifting Harlem population and the ensuing tensions in dozens of articles between 1904 and 1912.

31. William Gaynor Papers, box 77, folder 1.

32. Jervis Anderson, *This Was Harlem, 1900–1950* (New York, 1981), p. 59.

33. Noel Ignatiev, *How the Irish Became White* (New York, 1995), frontispiece; Osofsky, *Harlem,* p. 45.

34. McAdoo, *Guarding a Great City,* pp. 93–94, 96–97.

35. Ibid., p. 97.

36. Ibid., pp. 98–99.

37. Willemse, *A Cop Remembers,* p. 127; Abram Hewitt Papers, box 26, folder "Department of Police, 1887," NYMA.

38. Cornelius W. Willemse, *Behind the Green Lights* (New York, 1931), pp. 84–86.

39. Christopher P. Thale, "Civilizing New York City: Police Patrol, 1880–1935" (Ph.D. diss., University of Chicago, 1995), pp. 97–111.

40. *New York Age,* June 7, 1890, p. 1; November 6, 1891, p. 9; November 7, 1891, p. 2.

41. Supreme Court Records, box 10546, "4/25/1913," NYMA.

42. Bureau of Municipal Research, "A Report on the Homes and Family Budgets of 100 Patrolmen, Submitted to the Aldermanic Committee on Police Investigation as of March 31, 1913," in Board of Aldermen, *Police in New York City: An Investigation* (New York, 1971), p. 4507.

43. Willemse, *Behind the Green Lights,* pp. 85, 112, 113; Hopper, "Northern Negro Group," p. 12.

44. James McCabe, *New York by Sunlight and Gaslight* (Philadelphia, 1881), p. 144; Seth Low Papers, box 5, folder 6 (1903), NYMA; William Gaynor Papers, box 56, folder 2 (1912). NYMA; Neil R. McMillen, *Dark Journey: Black Mississippians in the Age of Jim Crow* (Urbana, 1990), p. 24.

45. William Gaynor Papers, box 54, folder 3 (1912).

46. William Gaynor Papers, box 14, folder 1, letter dated February 14, 1910.

47. Bruce, *Plantation Negro as a Freeman,* p. 17.

48. Supreme Court Records, box 10546, 4/25/1913, NYMA.

49. Frances Blascoer, *Colored School Children in New York* (1915; repr., New York, 1970), p. 23.

50. James D. Corrothers, *In Spite of the Handicap: An Autobiography* (New York,

1916), p. 208; Community Service Society, box 269, folder R719 (Case #82130); box 261, folder R533 (Case #37803); Paul, "A Group of Virginia Negroes in New York City," pp. 28–29.

51. Blascoer, *Colored School Children*, p. 24.

52. *New York Times*, December 31, 1904, p. 5; *New York Age*, December 14, 1905, p. 1; *New York Times*, July 20, 1914, p. 3.

53. Richard R. Wright Jr., "Recent Improvement in Housing among Negroes in the North, *Southern Workman* 37 (November 1908): 602; Kusmer, *A Ghetto Takes Shape*, pp. 48–49.

54. Willemse, *A Cop Remembers*, p. 129.

55. George B. McClellan Papers, box 20, folder 4.

56. W. T. Stead, *Satan's Invisible World Displayed, or Despairing Democracy* (New York, 1897), pp. 96–97, 102; Osofsky, *Harlem*, p. 14. In 1905, Schmittberger was accused of using excessive violence in a raid on a gambling house occupied by white and black patrons. When no complainants appeared at the hearings, the matter was dismissed. George B. McClellan Papers, box 20, folder 4.

57. Willemse, *Behind the Green Lights*, pp. 64, 72, 111; Willemse, *A Cop Remembers*, pp. 132, 134–36; William Gaynor Papers, box 16, folder 4; M. R. Werner, *It Happened in New York* (New York, 1957), p. 85; "Report of the Special Committee of the Board of Aldermen," p. 6.

58. Costello, *Our Police Protectors*, p. 267; Brown, *In the Golden Nineties*, pp. 372–77; The Press, *Vices of the Big City: An Exposé of Existing Menaces to Church and Home in New York City* (New York, 1890), pp. 101–2.

59. Edward Winslow Martin [James D. McCabe], *The Secrets of the Great City* (Philadelphia, 1868), p. 517; Robert Van Wyck Papers, box 11, folder 16; William Gaynor Papers, box 55, folder 3.

60. William Gaynor Papers, box 35, folder 4; box 15, folder 1; box 35, folder 3.

61. Werner, *It Happened in New York*, p. 85.

62. Osofsky, *Harlem*, pp. 146–47.

63. E. F. Dyckoff, "A Negro City in New York," *The Outlook* 108 (December 23, 1914): 952.

64. Committee of Fourteen, *Annual Report, 1915–1916*, p. 86; Osofsky, *Harlem*, p. 146.

65. William Gaynor Papers, box 15, folder 5.

66. Thale, "Civilizing New York City," pp. 97–109.

67. *New York Times*, June 20, 1873, p. 4.

68. *New York Times*, June 3, 1886, p. 8; *New York Age*, February 14, 1891, p. 2.

69. "The Reminiscences of Samuel J. Battle," pp. 16–17.

70. Ibid., pp. 17–20, 28–33; *New York Times*, June 29, 1911, p. 6; August 17, 1911, p. 4.

71. "Reminiscences of Samuel J. Battle," pp. 23, 35.

72. William Gaynor Papers, box 15, folder 5.

73. Ogburn, "Richmond Negro in New York City," pp. 51–52; *New York Times*, July 13, 1903, p. 1; *New York Age*, August 1, 1907, p. 4.

74. William Gaynor Papers, box 55, folder 3 (1912). See also Hugh Grant Papers, box 40, folder 4 (1889); William Gaynor Papers, box 36, folder 3 (1911).

75. Department of Probation Records, box 2, 1911 (Case #727, Sydney White); box 2, 1911 (Case #653, John Place), NYMA.

76. Department of Probation Records (Brooklyn), box 1, 1910 (Case #431, Frank Miller), NYMA.

77. Supreme Court Records, box #10546 (Nelson Browne), NYMA; Department of Probation Records (Brooklyn), box 10, 1914 (Case #2934), NYMA.

78. Department of Probation Records (Brooklyn), box 5, 1912 (Case #1716, Walter F. Saunders); box 2, 1911 (Case #653, John Place); box 6, 1912 (Case #1807, Violet Jones); box 3, 1911 (Case #924, Frances Fischer), NYMA.

79. Department of Probation Records (Brooklyn), box 1, 1910 (Case #458, Isaac Glasper); box 2, 1911 (Case #653, John Place); box 3, 1911 (Case #924, Frances Fischer), NYMA.

Chapter 4

1. Dowridge-Challenor Correspondence.

2. *Twelfth Census of the United States: 1900. Special Reports: Occupations* (Washington, D.C., 1904), pp. 634–40; *Thirteenth Census of the United States: 1910. Population, IV* (Washington, D.C., 1914), pp. 571–74.

3. "Will They Supplant Us As Laborers?" *New York Age* January 31, 1891, p. 2.

4. *Twelfth Census of the United States: 1900. Special Reports: Occupations*, pp. 634–40; *Thirteenth Census of the United States: 1910. Population, IV*, pp. 571–74; Osofsky, *Harlem*, pp. 5–6; Brown, *In the Golden Nineties*, p. 84; Kelly Miller, "The Economic Handicap of the Negro in the North," *Annals of the American Academy of Political and Social Science* 27, no. 3 (May 1906): 84; Lorenzo J. Greene and Carter G. Woodson, *The Negro Wage Earner* (Washington, D.C., 1930), pp. 83, 95; Mary White Ovington, "The Negro in the Trades Unions in New York," *Annals of the American Academy of Political and Social Science* 27, no. 3 (May 1906): 95; Morse, *Pride against Prejudice*, p. 50.

5. Burrows and Wallace, *Gotham*, pp. 1116–17.

6. Ibid., p. 1116; Susan A. Glenn, *Daughters of the Shtetl: Life and Labor in the Immigrant Generation* (Ithaca, N.Y., 1990), pp. 64, 73, 90; Eileen Boris, *Home to Work: Motherhood and the Politics of Industrial Homework in the United States* (Cambridge, 1994), p. 192.

7. Ovington, *Half a Man*, pp. 89, 146; Mary Kingsbury Simkhovitch, *Neighborhood: My Story of Greenwich House* (New York, 1938), p. 100.

8. A more detailed breakdown of domestic jobs demonstrates the overwhelming concentration of black males in the least skilled positions. In 1900, for example, of 11,843 black men employed in Manhattan as domestic and service workers, 6,280 (53 percent) worked as servants and waiters. Another 3,719 (31 percent) were employed as common laborers, including elevator tenders, laborers in coal yards, longshoremen, and stevedores. Only 613 (5 percent) worked in more profitable and independent jobs as barbers, hairdressers, nurses, boardinghouse keepers, hotel keepers, restaurant keepers, saloon keepers and bartenders, watchmen, firemen, or policemen.

9. *Twelfth Census: 1900. Special Reports: Occupations*, pp. 638, 640.

10. National League on Urban Conditions among Negroes, *Study of Negro Employees of Apartment Houses*, pp. 9–10.

11. Ibid., p. 17.

12. Ibid., pp. 19–20; Ovington, *Half a Man*, p. 46; Kisseloff, *You Must Remember This*, p. 270; Dowridge-Challenor Correspondence, 12/5/1912.

13. Arnold Rampersad, ed., *The Collected Poems of Langston Hughes* (New York, 1994), p. 85.

14. Charles B. Barnes, *The Longshoremen* (New York, 1915), p. 3; Ovington, *Half a Man*, p. 47.

15. Ovington, *Half a Man*, pp. 88–89; Maude E. Miner, "Reformatory Girls: A Study of Girls Paroled from the New York State Industrial School and the House of Refuge on Randall's Island," *Charities and the Commons* 17 (October 1906-April 1907): 907; Boris, *Home to Work*, pp. 106–8.

16. Fields, *Lemon Swamp and Other Places*, p. 148; David M. Katzman, *Seven Days a Week: Women and Domestic Service in Industrializing America* (Urbana, Ill., 1981), pp. 10, 44, 90.

17. Tera W. Hunter, *To "Joy My Freedom": Southern Black Women's Lives and Labors after the Civil War* (Cambridge, Mass., 1997), pp. 58–59; quote found in Elizabeth Clark-Lewis, *Living In, Living Out: African American Domestics in Washington, D.C., 1910–1940* (Washington, D.C., 1994), p. 14.

18. Katzman, *Seven Days a Week*, pp. 272–73; Ovington, *Half a Man*, pp. 80–81.

19. Ovington, *Half a Man*, p. 83; Katzman, *Seven Days a Week*, p. 112.

20. Katzman, *Seven Days a Week*, pp. 120–22; Dowridge-Challenor Correspondence, 11/4/1910.

21. Lawrence Gellert, "Blues and Other Songs," WPA Research Paper, SLRBC.

22. New York House of Refuge Papers, Case #27725, December 7, 1899, NYSAMSC.

23. Ruth Reed, *Negro Illegitimacy in New York City* (New York, 1926), pp. 60–61.

24. Haynes, *Negro at Work*, p. 85; Ovington, *Half a Man*, p. 83; Katzman, *Seven Days a Week*, pp. 213, 222.

25. Quotes found in Katzman, *Seven Days a Week*, pp. 8, 9.

26. *New York Tribune*, October 13, 1895, in Scheiner, *Negro Mecca*, p. 58.

27. Ovington, *Walls Came Tumbling Down*, p. 31; Sue Ainslie Clark and Edith Wyatt, *Making Both Ends Meet: The Income and Outlay of New York Working Girls* (New York, 1911), pp. 179–211, passim.; Seymour Paul " Group of Virginia Negroes in New York City," pp. 40–41.

28. Hoke Family Papers, 11/15/1903; Blascoer, *Colored School Children in New York*, p. 119.

29. National League on Urban Conditions, *Study of Negro Employees of Apartment Houses*, pp. 20–21.

30. More, *Wage-Earners' Budgets*, pp. 269–70.

31. Haynes, *Negro at Work*, p. 81; National League on Urban Conditions, *Study of Negro Employees of Apartment Houses*, p. 23.

32. Haynes, *Negro at Work*, pp. 78–79; Hopper, "A Northern Negro Group," p. 34; Johnstone, "The Negro in New York," pp. 10–11.

33. National League on Urban Conditions, *Study of Negro Employees of Apartment Houses*, p. 23.

34. *Report of the New York City Commission on Congestion of Population* (New York, 1911), p. 265.

35. National League on Urban Conditions, *Study of Negro Employees of Apartment Houses*, p. 21.

36. Blascoer, *Colored School Children in New York*, p. 119.

37. Ovington, *Half a Man*, pp. 56–57.

38. Pleck, "A Mother's Wages," p. 372.

39. Gutman, *Black Family in Slavery and Freedom*, p. 508.

40. Scheiner, *Negro Mecca*, p. 49; Ovington, *Half a Man*, pp. 59–64, 86; Osofsky, *Harlem*, p. 4.

41. *Thirteenth Census of the United States: 1910. Population, IV*, pp. 571–74.

42. *Twelfth Census of the United States: 1900. Special Reports: Occupations*, pp. 634–40; *Thirteenth Census of the United States: 1910. Population, IV*, pp. 571–74.

43. Ovington, *Half a Man*, p. 49.

44. Samuel Michelson, "Unemployed Negro Teachers in the Last Century," WPA Research Paper, pp. 1–4, SLRBC.

45. Kisseloff, *You Must Remember This*, pp. 285, 268; Paul, "Group of Virginia Negroes," pp. 26–28.

46. Michelson, "Unemployed Negro Teachers," pp. 1–4; *New York Times*, July 3, 1909, p. 16; Ovington, *Half a Man*, p. 18.

47. Helen A. Tucker, "Negro Craftsmen in New York. IV: Study of Two Hundred and Thirty Negro Craftsmen (Concluded)," *Southern Workman* 37, no. 2 (Feb. 1908): 48; *Crisis* 3, no. 3 (Jan. 1912): 96.

48. *New York Call*, July 23, 1911, quoted in Philip S. Foner and Ronald L. Lewis, eds., *The Black Worker: A Documentary History from Colonial Times to the Present, vol. 5, The Black Worker from 1900 to 1919* (Philadelphia, 1980), p. 38.

49. George B. McClellan Papers, box 41, folder 6, "Municipal Civil Service Commission 1907."

50. Helen A. Tucker, "Negro Craftsmen in New York. I: Purpose and Method of the Investigation," *Southern Workman* 36, no. 10 (October 1907): 549; National League on Urban Conditions, *Study of Negro Employees of Apartment Houses*, p. 14; Committee for Improving the Industrial Condition of the Negro in New York (New York, 1905?), p. 7, in J. G. Phelps Stokes Collection, CU.

51. Morse, *Pride Against Prejudice*, pp. 49–50.

52. Ovington, "The Negro in the Trades Unions," pp. 89–91.

53. Alfred T. White, "Shirtwaist Makers' Union," *The Survey* 23 (January 29, 1910): 588.

54. Tucker, "Negro Craftsmen: IV," p. 49.

55. Ovington, *Half a Man*, p. 55.

56. Helen A. Tucker, "Negro Craftsmen in New York. V: The Negro and Organized Labor," *Southern Workman* 37, no. 3 (March 1908): 141; *New York Age*, March 28, 1907, p. 1; October 3, 1907, p. 8; December 19, 1907, p. 1; National League on Urban Conditions among Negroes, *Annual Report, 1912–1913* (New York, 1913), pp. 12–13.

57. *New York Age*, May 17, 1906, p. 1; *New York Age*, July 12, 1906, p. 3; "Negroes in New York," *The Survey* 23 (October 2, 1909): 5; National League on Urban Conditions, *Annual Reports, 1910–1915*, passim.

58. "Colored Janitors Efficient," *New York Times*, March 1, 1914, sec. 2, p. 14.

59. *New York Age*, June 28, 1906, p. 2; July 12, 1906, p. 1; December 20, 1906, p. 5; *Crisis* 3, no. 2 (December 1911): 54.

60. Quoted in Osofsky, *Harlem*, p. 42.

61. Daniel Murray, "The Industrial Problem of the United States and the Negro's Relation to It," *Voice of the Negro* 1 (September 1904): 405.

62. Scheiner, *Negro Mecca*, pp. 68–69.

63. William M. Tuttle Jr., "Labor Conflict and Racial Violence: The Black Worker in Chicago, 1894–1919," *Labor History* 10 (1969): 426; Leslie H. Fishel Jr., "The North and the Negro, 1865–1900: A Study in Race Discrimination" (Ph.D. diss., Harvard University, 1953), p. 464; Charles H. Wesley, *Negro Labor in the United States* (New York, 1927), p. 261; Murray, " Industrial Problem," p. 403; Osofsky, *Harlem*, p. 42.

64. James D. Wallace, "Riots Possible in North, Too," *New York Age*, September 27, 1906, p. 3.

65. Eric Foner, *Reconstruction: America's Unfinished Revolution, 1863–1877* (New

York, 1988), p. 32; Sterling D. Spero and Abram L. Harris, *The Black Worker: A Study of the Negro and the Labor Movement* (New York, 1931), pp. 198–99; Barnes, *Longshoremen*, pp. 8–9; Ovington, "Negro in the Trades Unions," p. 93.

66. Spero and Harris, *Black Worker*, p. 199.

67. *New York Age*, May 30, 1907, p. 4.

68. Spero and Harris, *Black Worker*, p. 199; Barnes, *Longshoremen*, p. 9; Brown, *In the Golden Nineties*, pp. 296–97.

69. *New York Times*, May 31, 1912, p. 1; June 1, 1912, p. 1.

70. *New York Times*, June 1, 1912, pp. 1–2, 10; June 3, 1912, p. 3; June 4, 1912, p. 10.

71. Meredith Tax, *The Rising of the Women: Feminist Solidarity and Class Conflict, 1880–1917* (New York, 1980), pp. 205–6.

72. Ibid., pp. 223–24; Ovington, *Half a Man*, pp. 88–89; Boris, *Home to Work*, p. 192.

73. Tax, *Rising of the Women*, pp. 224–25.

74. Ovington, *Black and White Sat Down Together*, p. 32; "Women's Sphere," *New York Call*, January 4, 1910, quoted in Tax, *Rising of the Women*, p. 225.

75. "Negroes and the Ladies Waist-Makers Union," in Foner and Lewis, *Black Worker*, pp. 108–9.

76. Tax, *Rising of the Women*, p. 226.

77. Tucker, "Negro Craftsmen in New York: I," pp. 549–50.

78. Moore, "West Indian Negroes," p. 25.

79. Baker, *Following the Color Line*, p. 137; C. J. Harrah, quoted in Cohen, *At Freedom's Edge*, pp. 104–5; *Industrial Relations: Final Report and Testimony Submitted to Congress by the Commission on Industrial Relations*, 10: "Pullman Employees," pp. 9552–53.

80. National League on Urban Conditions, *Study of Negro Employees of Apartment Houses*, pp. 12–13.

81. Kisseloff, *You Must Remember This*, p. 271.

82. Dowridge-Challenor Correspondence, February 24, 1910; National League on Urban Conditions, *Study of Negro Employees of Apartment Houses*, pp. 13, 20.

83. Suzanne W. Model, "Work and Family: Blacks and Immigrants from South and East Europe," in Virginia Yans-McLaughlin, ed., *Immigration Reconsidered: History, Sociology, and Politics* (New York, 1990), pp. 133–36.

84. Pleck, "A Mother's Wages," pp. 373, 383; Model, "Work and Family," pp. 139–41; John Bodnar, Roger Simon, and Michael P. Weber, *Lives of Their Own: Blacks, Italians, and Poles in Pittsburgh, 1900–1960* (Urbana, Ill., 1983), pp. 60–61.

85. Glenn, *Daughters of the Shtetl*, p. 135.

86. Ann Douglas, *Terrible Honesty: Mongrel Manhattan in the 1920s* (New York, 1995), p. 311; Bodnar, Simon, and Weber, *Lives of Their Own*, pp. 59, 60.

87. Harris, *The Harder We Run*, frontispiece; W. E. B. DuBois, *Darkwater: Voices from within the Veil* (New York, 1920), p. 110; Osofsky, *Harlem*, p. 4.

88. Baker, *Following the Color Line*, p. 132.

89. DuBois, *Darkwater*, pp. 110–13.

90. NY Colored Mission, *Annual Reports, 1880–1915* (New York, 1881–1916); see, for example, NY Colored Mission, *Annual Report, 1902* (New York, 1903), p. 10; Clyde " Negro in New York City," p. 15.

91. Model, "Work and Family," p. 141.

Chapter 5

1. Hoke Family Papers, box 1, folder 5.
2. New York Colored Mission, *Annual Report, 1898* (New York, 1899), p. 13.
3. Tucker, "Negro Craftsmen in New York: IV," p. 48.
4. Paul, "A Group of Virginia Negroes in New York City," pp. 41–43.
5. Ovington, *Half A Man*, p. 45; Locke, "Harlem Negroes," p. 33; Anonymous, *America and the Americans from a French Point of View*, 8th ed. (New York, 1897), pp. 233–34.
6. Dowridge-Challenor Correspondence, May 13, 1910, June 9, 1910.
7. Community Service Society, box 269, folder R719 (Case # 82130).
8. Community Service Society, box 276, folder R890 (Case #297).
9. Department of Probation Records (Brooklyn), box 3, 1911, Case 888 (Emanuel Travis), NYMA.
10. Dowridge-Challenor Correspondence, January 12, 1912, March 25, 1912, September 17, 1912 September 6, 1910.
11. W. E. B. DuBois, *Some Notes on the Negroes in New York City* (Atlanta, 1903), p. 3; Scheiner *Negro Mecca*, pp. 57–58; Kelly Miller, "Surplus Negro Women," *Southern Workman* 34 (October 1905): 524.
12. Foner, *Reconstruction*, p. 85; Martin Summers, *Manliness and Its Discontents: The Black Middle Class and The Transformation of Masculinity, 1900–1930* (Chapel Hill, N.C., 2004), p. 4.
13. Riis, "Black Half," p. 299.
14. "A Nursery for Colored Children Needed," *Charities* 7 (November 9, 1901): 408.
15. Community Service Society, box 277, folder R921 (Case #2905); New York Colored Mission, *Annual Report, 1898* (New York, 1899), pp. 13–14.
16. Community Service Society, box 281, folder R1056 (Case #159317).
17. Reed, *Negro Illegitimacy in New York City*, pp. 60–61.
18. Riverdale Children's Association Records, box 1, *Admissions 1889–1907*, SLRBC.
19. Howard Orphanage and Industrial School Records, SLRBC; *A Short Sketch of the Work of the Brooklyn Howard Colored Orphan Asylum* (Brooklyn, N.Y., 1911), p. 7; Riverdale Children's Association Records, box 1, *Admissions 1889–1907*.
20. Community Service Society, box 275, folder R877 (Case #215).
21. Community Service Society, box 244, folder R114 (Case #35341).
22. Riverdale Children's Association Records, box 1, *Admissions 1889–1907*.
23. "Nursery for Colored Children Needed," p. 408; Blascoer, *Colored School Children in New York*, 62; *Charities* 8 (June 14, 1902): 551; New York Colored Mission, *Annual Report, 1912* (New York, 1913), pp. 10–11; *Crisis* 8 (May 1914): 9.
24. Riverdale Children's Association Records, box 1: *Admissions, 1899–1907*; Society for the Prevention of Cruelty to Children, *Annual Report, 1893* (New York, 1894), p. 47.
25. Department of Probation Records (Brooklyn), box 12, 1915, Case #3453 (Percy Jones); box 12, 1915, Case #3568 (Harry Boykin); box 12, 1915, Case #3555 (Richard Schermerhorn), NYMA.
26. Sleet, "In the Day's Work of a Visiting Nurse," pp. 73–74.
27. McFarland, *Inside Greenwich Village*, pp. 62–63; Blascoer, *Colored School Children in New York*, p. 25; *New York Times*, June 16, 1914, p. 9.
28. Blascoer, *Colored School Children in New York*, p. 26; *Crisis* 6 (August 1913):165; *Crisis* 8 (October 1914): 267.

29. John P. Mitchel Papers, box 131, folder 2; Blascoer, *Colored School Children in New York*, p. 18.

30. Reed, *Negro Illegitimacy*, p. 77; House of Refuge Papers, cases #26080 (1896), #27434 (1899), #27610 (1899), #27521 (1899), #28083 (1900), NYSAMSC; Ovington, *Black and White Sat Down Together*, p. 31; Ovington, *Half a Man*, pp. 38–39.

31. Lillian D. Wald, *The House on Henry Street* (New York, 1915), pp. 162–63; Ovington, *Half a Man*, p. 39.

32. Robert E. Park, "Negro Home Life and Standards of Living," *The Annals of the American Academy of Political and Social Science* 27 (May 1906): 160; Kisseloff, *You Must Remember This*, p. 269; Ovington, "Vacation Days in San Juan Hill," p. 629; Mary White Ovington, "The Negro Home in New York," *Charities* 15 (October 7, 1905): 28; Johnstone, "Negro in New York," p. 14.

33. Kisseloff, *You Must Remember This*, pp. 269–70; Paul, "A Group of Virginia Negroes in New York City," pp. 36–37; Hopper, "Northern Negro Group," p. 35; Ovington, "Negro Home," p. 28.

34. Paul, "A Group of Virginia Negroes in New York City," pp. 31–33, 50; Kisseloff, *You Must Remember This*, p. 269; Ovington, *Half a Man*, p. 39.

35. Kisseloff, *You Must Remember This*, pp. 299–300.

36. New York Colored Mission, *Annual Report, 1892* (New York, 1893), p. 14.

37. Ovington, *Half a Man*, p. 40; *Charities* 12 (April 30, 1904): 435; Morse, *Pride against Prejudice*, p. 50.

38. *New York Times*, April 30, 1915, p. 9; Blascoer, *Colored School Children*, p. 87.

39. Michelson, "Unemployed Negro Teachers," pp. 1–4; Robert S. Dixon, "The Education of the Negro in the City of New York, 1853 to 1900" (M.A. thesis, College of the City of New York, 1935), p. 61; *Crisis* 5 (February 1913): 185; *New York Times*, April 30, 1915, p. 9.

40. *Fifty-fourth Annual Report of the Children's Aid Society* (New York, 1907), pp. 88–89; *Fifty-sixth Annual Report of the Children's Aid Society* (New York, 1909), p. 76; Blascoer, *Colored School Children in New York*, p. 16; Community Service Society, box 280, folder R1002 (Case #150939).

41. Blascoer, *Colored School Children in New York*, pp. 18, 135.

42. Ibid., p. 16.

43. Wald, *House on Henry Street*, pp. 161–62; "Committee for Improving the Industrial Condition of the Negro in New York" (n.p., 1905?), Phelps Stokes Collection, box 18, folder "Misc. Negro Schools, etc.," CU; "Industrial Education in New York City," *Colored American Magazine* 10 (May 1906): 323–35.

44. "Industrial Education," p. 323; *New York Age*, March 8, 1906, p. 1; August 22, 1907, p. 4.

45. Community Service Society, box 275, folder R877 (Case #215); box 271, folder R776 (Case #102726).

46. Community Service Society, box 241, folder R59 (Case #10627); Federation of Churches and Christian Workers in New York City, *Sociological Canvass No. 2* (New York, 1897), p. 90; Ovington, *Half a Man*, p. 80.

47. Department of Probation Records (Brooklyn), box 1, 1910, Case #488 (Irving Glasgow), NYMA; More, *Wage-Earners' Budgets*, p. 84; Blascoer, *Colored School Children in New York*, p. 120.

48. William L. Bulkley, "The Industrial Condition of the Negro in New York City," *Annals of the American Academy of Political and Social Science* 27, no. 3 (May 1906): 131; Scheiner, *Negro Mecca*, p. 59.

49. Community Service Society, box 244, folder R114 (Case #36341).

50. New York Colored Mission, *Annual Report, 1894* (New York, 1895), pp. 13–14.

51. Community Service Society, box 266, folder R665 (Case #37769).

52. Lizabeth Cohen, *Making a New Deal: Industrial Workers in Chicago, 1919–1939* (Cambridge, 1990), p. 247; New York Colored Mission, *Annual Report, 1894* (New York, 1895), pp. 13–14; *Annual Report, 1898* (New York, 1899), p. 13.

53. Community Service Society, box 260, folder R520 (Case #41599).

54. Ibid.

55. Community Service Society, box 271, folder R776 (Case #102726).

56. Department of Probation Records (Brooklyn), box 12, 1915, Case #3676 (Edwin Marsh), NYMA; Cohen, *Making a New Deal*, p. 247; Peter N. Stearns, *Be a Man!: Males in Modern Society* (New York, 1979), p. 68.

57. Community Service Society, box 271, folder R776 (Case #102726).

58. State Charities Aid Association and the New York Association for Improving the Condition of the Poor, *Fourth Annual Report of the Joint Committee on the Care of Motherless Infants* (New York, 1902), pp. 21–22; Society for the Prevention of Cruelty to Children, *Annual Report, 1896* (New York, 1897), p. 47; Riverdale Children's Association Records, box 1: "Admissions 1889–1907."

59. Leon F. Litwack, *Trouble in Mind: Black Southerners in the Age of Jim Crow* (New York, 1998), p. 350; Community Service Society, box 258, folder R453 (Case #41931); Gertrude Ayer Papers, box 1, folder 2, SLRBC.

60. Department of Probation Records (Brooklyn), box 13, 1915 (Case #3839); box 10, 1914 (Case #2808), NYMA.

61. Community Service Society, box 266, folder R645 (Case #36762).

62. Society for the Prevention of Cruelty to Children, *Annual Report, 1886* (New York, 1887), p. 43; *Annual Report, 1885* (New York, 1886), pp. 22–23.

63. Community Service Society, box 244, folder R114 (Case #36341).

64. Society for the Prevention of Cruelty to Children, *Annual Report, 1886* (New York, 1887), p. 21.

65. Ogburn, "Richmond Negro," pp. 63–64; Gutman, *Black Family in Slavery and Freedom*, p. 452; Osofsky, *Harlem*, p. 4.

66. Clyde, "Negro in New York City," p. 29; Ogburn, "Richmond Negro," pp. 63–64.

67. Ovington, "Negro Home," p. 27.

68. Ovington, *Half a Man*, pp. 45–46, 81–82; Department of Probation Records (Brooklyn), box 9, 1914, (Case #2684), NYMA.

69. Ovington, *Half a Man*, p. 81; National League on Urban Conditions *Study of Negro Employees of Apartment Houses*, p. 23; Shane White and Graham White, *Stylin': African American Expressive Culture from Its Beginnings to the Zoot Suit* (Ithaca, N.Y., 1998), p. 176; Blascoer, *Colored School Children in New York*, p. 59.

70. Kisseloff, *You Must Remember This*, p. 272.

71. Ovington, *Half a Man*, pp. 45, 81; Scheiner, *Negro Mecca*, p. 58.

72. John Modell and Tamara K. Hareven, "Urbanization and the Malleable Household: An Examination of Boarding and Lodging in American Families," in Michael Gordon, ed., *The American Family in Social-Historical Perspective* (New York, 1983), pp. 52–53; U.S. Bureau of Labor, *Report on Conditions of Women and Child Wage-Earners in the United States*, 61st Cong., 2nd sess. Senate Doc. 645 (Washington, D.C., 1910), 5: 62; Mary Rankin Cranston, "The Housing of the Negro in New York City," *Southern Workman* 31 (June 1902): 330.

73. "Fresh Air Outings for Colored Children," *Charities* 7 (October 26, 1901): 340; Lillian Brandt, "What a Day Brought Forth at Sea Breeze," *Charities* 12

(August 6, 1904): 816–17; Association for Improving the Condition of the Poor, *Report, 1892*, box 72, Community Service Society Papers, p. 29, CU; Mary White Ovington, "Fresh Air Work among Colored Children in New York," *Charities and the Commons* 17 (October 1906-April 1907): 115–17.

74. Association for Improving the Industrial Condition of the Poor Papers, Community Service Society Collection, box 19, "Review of Relief Work of New York AICP," Appendix 3, no. 81, CU.

75. Charity Organization Society, box 105, folder "Children's Bureau, NYC, 1914–15 – Cases Referred"; New York Society for Prevention of Cruelty to Children, *Annual Report, 1881* (New York, 1882), p. 38; Riverdale Children's Association Records, "Admissions 1889–1907."

76. Ovington, "Vacation Days in San Juan Hill," pp. 631–32.

77. Ibid., Ovington, *Walls Came Tumbling Down*, pp. 49–50.

Chapter 6

1. Blascoer, *Colored School Children in New York*, p. 75.

2. Community Service Society, box 266, folder R665 (Case #37769).

3. Osofsky, *Harlem*, p. 31; Dowridge-Challenor Correspondence; Watkins-Owens, *Blood Relations*, p. 21.

4. Ovington, *Half a Man*, pp. 26–27.

5. Community Service Society, box 261, folder R533 (Case #37803). For leaving without paying the rent, see, for example, Community Service Society, box 243, folder R99 (Case #79279).

6. Ogburn, "Richmond Negro," p. 61; Supreme Court Records, box 10550 (Louis Jackson), NYMA; Paul, "Group of Virginia Negroes in New York City," pp. 28–29.

7. DuBois, "Black North," p. 12; Supreme Court Records, box 10546 (Samuel Booth), NYMA.

8. Ogburn, "Richmond Negro," p. 61; Paul, "Group of Virginia Negroes in New York City," pp. 36, 40–41, 43; Moore, "West Indian Negroes," p.30; Locke, "Harlem Group of Negroes," pp. 15, 27.

9. Dowridge-Challenor Correspondence, August 3, 1911; April 19, no year; December 1, no year.

10. Kisseloff, *You Must Remember This*, pp. 269–70; *Crisis* 4 (June 1912): 98; Osofsky, *Harlem*, p. 225, n108; Ovington, *Half a Man*, p. 61; *New York Age*, February 28, 1907, p. 7.

11. Community Service Society, box 254, folder R370 (Case #40756).

12. Community Service Society, box 252, folder R292 (Case #37898); Department of Probation Records (Brooklyn), box 3, 1911 (Case #924), NYMA.

13. Community Service Society, box 275, folder R877 (Case #215).

14. Community Service Society, box 254, folder R370 (Case #40756).

15. Community Service Society, box 254, folder R370 (Case #40756).

16. Community Service Society, box 258, folder R453 (Case #41931). The CSS case files are replete with examples of women coming to each other's aid during times of difficulty.

17. Community Service Society, box 254, folder R370 (Case #40756).

18. Community Service Society, box 271, folder R776 (Case #102726); box 243, folder R99 (Case #79279).

19. Johnstone, "Negro in New York," pp. 43–44; Ogburn, "Richmond

Negro," pp. 23–24; Community Service Society, box 276, folder R890 (Case #297); box 261, folder R533 (Case #37803).

20. DuBois, *Black North in 1901*, pp. 16–17; Osofsky, *Harlem*, pp. 13–14; Ogburn, "Richmond Negro," pp. 48–49, 68–70; National League on Urban Conditions, *Study of Negro Employees of Apartment Houses*, p. 16; for a description of a Union Baptist revival, see, for example, *New York Age*, April 5, 1890, p. 3.

21. Moore, "West Indian Negroes," p. 25; Ogburn, "Richmond Negro," pp. 68–70.

22. *New York Age*, May 10, 1906, p. 1; May 30, 1907, p. 6.

23. DuBois, *Black North in 1901*, p. 17; McFarland, *Inside Greenwich Village*, pp. 22–23; Farah Jasmine Griffin, *"Who Set You Flowin'?" The African American Migration Narrative* (New York, 1995), p. 61; *New York Age*, November 14, 1907, p. 1.

24. Scheiner, *Negro Mecca*, p. 90; Blascoer, *Colored School Children in New York*, p. 61; Robert Van Wyck Papers, VWRA-12, folder 9; Kisseloff, *You Must Remember This*, pp. 272–73.

25. *New York Times*, July 20, 1904, p. 5; July 25, 1913.

26. Locke, "Harlem Negroes," p. 24; McFarland, *Inside Greenwich Village*, p. 22; Ogburn, "Richmond Negro," pp. 29, 42.

27. Ogburn, "Richmond Negro," p. 23; McFarland, *Inside Greenwich Village*, p. 22.

28. Supreme Court Records, box #10546 (Nelson Browne); box #10546 (Samuel Booth), NYMA; Community Service Society, box 271, folder R776 (Case #102726).

29. *New York Age*, May 3, 1906, p. 1; May 30, 1907, p. 6; Paul, "Group of Virginia Negroes," p. 15; Locke, "Harlem Negroes," p. 25; Ogburn, "Richmond Negro," pp. 50–51.

30. *New York Age*, May 17, 1906, p. 1; July 12, 1906, p. 3; December 6, 1906, p. 7.

31. *New York Age*, January 25, 1890, p. 4; Hopper, "Northern Negro Group," p. 43.

32. *Crisis* 7 (February 1914): 189; Alexander Walters, *My Life and Work* (New York, 1917), pp. 83–84; Phelps-Stokes Collection, Box 18, Folder "Misc. Negro Schools, etc.," CU; Scheiner, *Negro Mecca*, pp. 90–91; *New York Age*, June 24, 1909.

33. Kiser, *From Sea Island to City*, p. 164; Locke, "Harlem Negroes," pp. 22–25; Moore, "West Indian Negroes," pp. 38–39; "Negro Church Today," pp. 2–3, WPA Research Paper, SLRBC.

34. Simon Williamson, "Sports and Amusements of Negro New York," WPA Research Paper, SLRBC; Johnson *Along This Way*, p. 175; Gardner, *Doctor and the Devil*, pp. 17–18; McCabe *New York by Sunlight and Gaslight*, p. 256; Committee of Fourteen Papers, box 28, folder "Invest. Rep. 1912."

35. Martin, *Secrets of the Great City*, p. 517; Brown, *In the Golden Nineties*, pp. 372–377; The Press, *Vices of the Big City*, pp. 101–102; Costello, *Our Police Protectors*, p. 267; William Gaynor Papers, box 15, folder 1, letter dated May 7, 1910.

36. Committee of Fourteen Papers, box 28, folder "1910–12"; Walling *Recollections of a New York City Police Chief*, pp. 485–87.

37. Committee of 14 Papers, box 28, folder "1910–12"; Johnson *Along This Way*, pp. 175–76; Ottley and Weatherby, *Negro in New York*, pp. 146–167.

38. Johnson, *Along This Way*, pp. 150–52; Ottley and Weatherby, *Negro in New York*, pp. 156–57.

39. Ottley and Weatherby, *Negro in New York*, p. 157; Committee of Fourteen Papers, box 28, folder "1910–12."

40. Committee of Fourteen Papers, box 28, folders "1910" and "1910–12."

41. Ottley and Weatherby, *Negro in New York*, p. 152; *New York Times*, July 17, 1910, p. 4; Committee of Fourteen Papers, box 28, folders "1910" and "1910–12"; *New York Times*, December 22, 1910, p. 7.

42. Johnson *Autobiography of an Ex-Coloured Man*, pp. 103–4.

43. Ottley and Weatherby, *Negro in New York*, pp. 161–64; *New York Age*, November 15, 1906, p. 1; June 27, 1907, p. 6; October 17, 1907, p. 1; *Crisis* 8, no. 3 (July 1914): 112; Eric Ledell Smith, "Early African-American Broadway Performers: Bert Williams and George William Walker in 'In Dahomey,' 1903," *Afro-Americans in New York Life and History* 16, no. 2 (July 1992): 7, 9.

44. Dunbar, *Sport of the Gods*, pp. 58–59, 95; *New York Age*, March 15, 1890, p. 3; April 2, 1908, p. 6.

45. Griffin, "*Who Set You Flowin'?*", p. 55; Locke, "Harlem Negroes," p. 28; Richard B. Moore Papers, box 1, folder 1; *New York Age*, February 28, 1907, p. 7.

46. Scheiner, *Negro Mecca*, p. 94; Watkins-Owens, *Blood Relations*, p. 65.

47. Osofsky, *Harlem*, p. 32; *New York Age*, December 10, 1887, p. 3; Watkins-Owens, *Blood Relations*, pp. 26, 66, 67, 69; Jones, " British West Indian Negro," p. 172.

48. *New York Freeman*, December 11, 1886, p. 2.

49. Rampersad, *Collected Poems of Langston Hughes*, p. 41.

50. DuBois, *Black North in 1901*, pp. 40–41, Dunbar, *Sport of the Gods*, pp. 43–44.

51. Johnson, *Black Manhattan*, p. 236; Craig Steven Wilder, *In the Company of Black Men: The African Influence on African American Culture in New York City* (New York, 2001), p. 194.

52. Johnson, *Black Manhattan*, p. 237.

53. Claude McKay, *Home to Harlem* (1928; repr., Boston, 1987), p. 15.

Index

Abyssinian Baptist Church, 75, 184; sale of, 185

African Americans: attacks by whites on black women, 11; manhood of, 12; Northern attitudes toward, 8; Southern, 4–5; urban life of, 7–8, 18. *See also* African Americans, and employment in New York City; African Americans, and family life in New York City; African Americans, and housing in New York City; African Americans, migration of to the North; New York City, African American communities in; New York City, African American population of

African Americans, and employment in New York City, 107–9, 133–35, 142; and apartment house workers, 112–13; and chauffeurs, 122–23; employment for black women, 111–12, 115, 120–21, 135–37, 142–43, 164; —, as laundresses, 118; —, and nursery work, 143–44; —, and "outwork," 143; civil service reform and the black professional class, 121–22; and "coon" imagery, 133–34; day workers, 118–19; and domestic service, 112, 115–19, 145–46, 210 n.8; —, complaints by whites about domestic help, 116–17; —, sexual assault during, 117; —, and turnover rates, 117–18; —, work hours of, 116; effect on family life, 137–38; and elevator operators, 113–14, 132; employers' manipulation of regional stereotypes, 130–31; exclusion of blacks from labor unions, 124–25, 126–27; —, use of blacks as strikebreakers, 126–30; and geographic origin, 131–32; incursion of white unskilled labor into traditionally black occupations, 109, 111; —, in the textile industry, 111–12; and longshoremen, 114, 127–28; and low wages, 119–20, 134, 167–68; postmen, 121; prospect of high wages, 16–17; and seasonal work in "country hotels," 139; and skilled workers, 121; "sweatshops," 111; and teachers, 122; white employers' complicity in keeping blacks from equal employment, 123–24, 130–32

African Americans, and family life in New York City, 137–38, 168–69; and domestic service, 145–46; and the education of children, 154–58; —, truancy rates, 155–56; effect of the criminal justice system on, 141; and the emotional strain of poverty, 158–61; family separations due to employment opportunities, 141–42; lifestyle of children, 9–10; —, abandoned children, 161; —, abuse of children, 162–63; —, and juvenile delinquency, 150; —, in the streets, 149–51; —, in tenements, 148–49; —, threat of sexual predators, 148; and orphans/orphanages, 145–48; parental relationships with children, 10, 151–54, 160, 177–78; and spousal abuse, 161–62; and transience of the black male population, 138; unfair criticism of, 163–64

African Americans, and housing in New York City, 72–73, 166; close proximity of, 79–80; costs of, 34–35; exploitation of by white landlords, 34–35; in Greenwich Village and the "Minettas," 73–75; in Harlem, 83–85; —, white reaction to, 84–85; health problems as a result of poor housing, 73–74, 77; in the San Juan district, 74, 76–77, 79–80; —, overcrowding in, 77, 82; and the subletting of apartments (the "lodging evil"), 35–36, 78–79, 83, 173; in the Tenderloin district, 74–76, 82; tenement life, 34, 72; —, description of a tenement, 75–76, 77. *See also* New York City Police Department

Acknowledgments

I find it remarkable and humbling to take stock of the many people who have supported me and this project over the years, and I welcome the opportunity to publicly acknowledge them. I owe a deep debt to Nick Salvatore, of Cornell University, who first introduced me to the notion that history could be a professional pursuit, not merely an interest. Nick offered guidance and patience, showed me how to study history, and provided a model for teaching it as well. He exposed me to the joys of research by hiring me as his assistant. Nick has been a mentor to me for years; I am blessed to also call him a friend.

At the University of California at Berkeley, Leon Litwack opened his doors to me, literally. He lent me the use of his office and his extensive library. He taught me the pleasure of writing and the responsibility of giving voice to the too often voiceless. My admiration for him only grows with time. In those formative years of my progress toward becoming an historian, Waldo Martin Jr., the late Barbara Christian, and Paula Fass helped to shape and guide my thinking about the craft of history generally and African American history specifically. At Berkeley, I joined a supportive community that included Karen Leong, Brigitte Koenig, and Michelle Krowl, who offered good dinners and good conversation. And Patrick Rael and Betty Dessants guided and advised with the wisdom of those who had traversed the waters before me.

Since leaving the comforting environs of Dwinelle Hall, I have been fortunate to find support from historians elsewhere. I am especially grateful to Shane White, who has been tremendously generous with his time and energy. James Grossman found time to offer detailed commentary on one of the chapters and persistently nudged me to finish the manuscript. Glenda Gilmore provided valuable feedback, and David Blight has offered moral support and encouragement.

Thanks go to a group of dedicated colleagues at both Hamilton College and Albion College whose pursuit of their own research agendas has inspired me to continue pursuing my own. They have also demonstrated by example that one can aspire to be both a teacher and a scholar. They include Tom Chambers, Geoffrey Cocks, Wes Dick, Andrew Grossman, Chris Hagerman, Maurice Isserman, Deborah

Kanter, William Rose, Yi-Li Wu, and Midori Yoshii. At Albion, I have benefited from the research assistance of Jayne Ptolemy, who promises to soon become an exceptional historian in her own right.

Peter Agree, social sciences editor at the University of Pennsylvania Press, first contacted me about my work when this project was still in its infancy. The confidence he has consistently demonstrated in me and the patience he has unfailingly exhibited have helped me immeasurably. I could not have imagined a more supportive relationship than the one he has offered me. Acquisitions assistant Laura Miller and associate managing editor Erica Ginsburg endured my relentless questions as they guided me through the murky waters of preparing a manuscript for publication.

Numerous librarians have generously provided me with their time and expertise. A late Friday afternoon telephone call to Oberlin College fortuitously put me in touch with Tom Hinders. His efforts on behalf of a total stranger helped me to secure one of the images in the book. Similarly, critical assistance from Jennie Thomas at the Albion College Archives, Linda Gordon at the Brookside Museum, and Ruth Clayman at the New York State Library allowed me to finalize the material for the manuscript.

Generous grants from the New York State Library, the University of California at Berkeley, and the Faculty Development Endowment at Albion College supplied the funding to permit this project to reach fruition.

On a more personal note, Pixie and Sid Markowitz provided extraordinary hospitality over many months of research in New York City. Lynne Sacks read a chapter very early in this process and gave me the confidence to finally share my work in the public sphere. My in-laws, Celia Villegas Montoya and Claudio Zúñiga Leon, granted me the precious gift of time. Year in and year out, they cared for my children over long summer weeks, permitting me the opportunity to research and write without childcare responsibilities. This work could not have been completed without their generosity. My parents, Sharon and Marvin Freedman, have lent their support in many forms over the years. Perhaps most significantly, they have allowed the issues that I study to become a conspicuous part of their lives, as reflected in the steady stream of newspaper articles that have arrived in the mail on issues related to African American history. And my memories of Lionel Sacks have spurred me on to fight for justice since I was a little girl.

My debt to my family cannot be fully measured, nor adequately repaid. Rodolfo Zúñiga Villegas has unwaveringly bestowed on me his love and encouragement. His confidence in me has brought me through times when I felt certain that I would never finish; his willingness to share my life brings me joy that I cannot express. My children, Alejandro and Daniela, have never known me without this project. Without them, I surely would have completed the manuscript far sooner than I did. But without them, it would have had no soul. To those three, I dedicate this book.